Wide Angle

GARY PATHARE

OXFORD
UNIVERSITY PRESS

198 Madison Avenue
New York, NY 10016 USA

Great Clarendon Street, Oxford, OX2 6DP,
United Kingdom

Oxford University Press is a department of the University of Oxford. It furthers the University's objective of excellence in research, scholarship, and education by publishing worldwide. Oxford is a registered trade mark of Oxford University Press in the UK and in certain other countries

First published in 2019
2023 2022 2021 2020 2019
10 9 8 7 6 5 4 3 2 1

ISBN: 978 0 19 452857 3 Wide Angle American 4 SB W/OP Pack
ISBN: 978 0 19 452833 7 Wide Angle American 4
ISBN: 978 0 19 454666 9 Wide Angle American 4 OP

Printed in China

This book is printed on paper from certified and well-managed sources

ACKNOWLEDGEMENTS

Back cover photograph: Oxford University Press building/David Fisher

Illustrations by: A. Richard Allen/Morgan Gaynin Inc pp. 7, 137; John Holcroft/ Lindgren & Smith pp. 52, 145; Shaw Nielsen pp. 13, 25, 37, 49, 61, 73, 85, 97, 109, 121, 133, 145.
Video Stills, Mannic Productions: pp. 12, 24, 36, 48, 60, 72, 84, 96, 108, 120, 132, 144. Oxford University Press: pp. 40.
The Publishers would like to thank the following for their kind permission to reproduce photographs and other copyright material: **123rf:** pp.28 (ice/Galyna Andrushko), 40 (4/byrdyak), 45 (6/Dmitriy Shironosov), 64 (Levi Strauss label/Thodsapol Thongdeekhieo), 65 (shirt/Natallia Khlapushyna), 69 (doctor/racorn), 77 (minimalist living room/skdesign), 88 (VR set/Dinis Tolipov), 91 (movie streaming/ georgejmclittle), (Vinyl record/Giuseppe Porzani), 94 (lecturer /Cathy Yeulet), 106 (Thai fusion dish/Mongkol Aphisuthisarn), 114 (computer code/Yusuke Saito), (hieroglyphics/Fedor Selivanov), 122 (a/Stefano Carocci), 151 (fire alarm/Pisit Khambubpha); **Alamy:** pp. 5 (running up bleachers/Blend Images), 7 (view looking down from Empire State Building/Ryan Deberardinis), 26 (hot air balloon/Johner Images), 28 (underground/Robbie Shone), 30 (Jacques Cousteau/Everett Collection Historical), (Matthew Henson/Granger Historical Picture Archive), 34 (asteroid mining/Stocktrek Images, Inc.), 45 (3/Kerry Elsworth), (5/Lasse Bolstad), 54 (3/tom pfeiffer), 65 (long sleeved/Westend61 GmbH), 68 (tech company interior/Tribune Content Agency LLC), 76 (cluttered room/Noel Yates), 78 (cave paiting/Hemis), (view from plane/Aurora Photos), 81 (bored tourists/Pierre Rochon photography), 91 (movie screen/EditorialByDarrellYoung), 94 (mail carrier/Ian Allenden), 100 (movie award/Mohamed Osama), 103 (Selexyz bookshop/Arcaid Images), 104 (Zagat restaurant guidebook/Patti McConville), 105 (restuarant/Bruce yuanyue Bi), 114 (Voynich manuscript/GL Archive), 116 (ancient manuscript/dpa picture alliance archive), 117 (Loch Ness Monster/Chronicle), (Oak Island Money Pit/gary corbett), 128 (woman watching plane/Anton Unguryanu), 133 (customer and salesperson/ allesalltag), 139 (a/Ink Drop), 150 (Titanic/AF archive); **BLINK:** Cover, Quinn Ryan Mattingly, pp. 3 (young basketball players/Edu Bayer), 11 (Architect and designer Carmela Dacchille/Gianni Cipriano), 15 (Correfoc devils fireworks celebration/ Edu Bayer), 18 (school girls read the paper/Krissiane Johnson), 27 (train passenger/ Gianni Cipriano), 35 (Fucino Space Center/Nadia Shira Cohen), 39 (pottery factory/ Quinn Ryan Mattingly), 47 (shoe designer/Gianni Cipriano), 51 (two woman walking/Krisanne Johnson), 56 (rescuing truck/Edu Bayer), 63 (women Gambia/Edu Bayer), 66 (groom bow tie/Edu Bayer), 75 (man infront of Abbey/Gianni Cipriano), 80 (valley/Quinn Ryan Mattingly), 87 (doctor with x-ray/Quinn Ryan Mattingly), 93 (computers/Edu Bayer), 99 (man In theatre/GIanni Cipriano), 107 (local vegetables on table/GIanni Cipriano), 111 (abandoned boat/Nadia Shira Cohen), 119 (misty road/Gianni Cipriano), 123 (Carneval celebration/Nadia Shira Cohen), 131 (man on computer/Edu Bayer), 135 (mother and child on train/Quinn Ryan Mattingly), 143 (physics lesson/Gianni Cipriano); **Bridgeman:** p. 30 (Amy Johnson/Capstack, John (1881-1967)/Private Collection/Prismatic Pictures), (Gertrude Bell/Pictures from History); **Getty:** pp. 6 (Gary Kasparov playing chess/JOSE JORDAN/Stringer), (Oprah Winfrey/Sunday Times/Contributor), 7 (view looking down from the Abraj Al-Bait Towers/AFP Contributor/Contributor), 19 (photographers/Andrew Hobbs), 21 (journalist/Jeff Greenberg/Contributor), 25 (girl and woman/Ariel Skelley), 30 (Tenzing Norgay/James Burke/Contributor), (Yuri Gagarin/Popperfoto/Contributor), 33 (space/WLADIMIR BULGAR/SCIENCE PHOTO LIBRARY), 45 (4/Tooga), 49 (students/ Westend61), 54 (6/Joe Raedle/Staff), 59 (women talking/Tetra Images), 67 (man with baby/KidStock), 83 (happy tourist/Catherine Delahaye), 88 (driverless car/ NOAH BERGER/Stringer), 90 (VR environment/da-kuk), 94 (futuristic automated workplace/gong hangxu), (trash collector/Blend Images - Don Mason), 101 (cinema/ John Eder), 114 (Braille/Frederic Cirou), 117 (Antikythera Mechanism/LOUISA GOULIAMAKI/Stringer), (DB Cooper sketches/Time Life Pictures/Contributor), 122 (c/ Chicago Tribune/RSVP International Onion Goggles, patented), 124 (family/ Amanda Edwards/Contributor), 127 (man painting/Troy House), 129 (Tim Berners-Lee/Andreas Rentz/Staff), 134 (a/Elena Segatini), (d/Steve Debenport), 136 (books/ maurizio siani), 138 (old man and boy/Camille Tokerud), 139 (c/Credit:Fabrice LEROUGE), 141 (man on tablet/Hero Images), 146 (men drinking juice/Thomas Barwick), 156 (African plain/Vicki Jauron, Babylon and Beyond Photography); **Hugh Pryor:** p. 89 (GPS art/Hugh Pryor); **iStock:** p. xvi, (phone/lvcandy), (tablet/ RekaReka); **OUP:** pp. 26 (snowboarding/Shutterstock/Nurlan Kalchinov), 54 (2/123rf/ federicofoto), (4/Shutterstock/idiz), 88 (drone/Shutterstock/Maria Dryfhout), (GPS/ Shutterstock/Pincasso), 94 (firefighter/Shutterstock/Toa55), 106 (beach/Shutterstock/ Maria Dryfhout), 148 (radio mic/Shutterstock/Planner); **REX:** p. 65 (James Dean/ Warner Bros/Kobal/REX/Shutterstock), 102 (Citizen Kane/Alex Kahle/RKO/Kobal/ REX/Shutterstock); **Shutterstock:** pp. 7 (view looking down from Burj Khalifa/ Stefano Carnevali), (view looking down from Eiffel Tower/Life In Pixels), (view looking down from the Tokyo tower/witaya ratanasirikulchai), 9 (pyramids/Dan Breckwoldt), 10 (woman on laptop/Andrey Bondarets), 16 (cartoon/humphrey), 22 (Burj Khalifa with fireworks/Naufal MQ), 26 (motorcyclist/eZeePics), (parasailing/ Vadim Petrakov), (rock climbing/Vixit), (skydiving/Germanskydiver), 28 (moutains/ Inu), (underwater/fenkieandreas), 29 (artificial intelligence/Lagarto Film), 29 (DNA/Media Whalestock), 29 (human mind /patrice6000), 40 (1/atdr), (2/Kostikova Natalia), (3/MicrostockStudi), 45 (1/Dutourdumonde Photography), (2/Nataliya Hora), 54 (1/Ivano de Santis), (5/anthony heflin), 57 (man/Jack Z Young), (woman/ Monkey Business Images), 65 (cowboy boot /Evgeniya Porechenskaya), 65 (trousers/ Di Studio), 77 (cozy living room/lenisecalleja.photography), 78 (building blending with nature/alionabirukova), 88 (smartphone/leungchopan), (x-ray/create jobs 51), 91 (disc/Early Spring), (music download/Archiwiz), (TV/Hadrian), 94 (office worker/ Pressmaster), 98 (flying car/Peter Albrektsen), 106 (tropical paradise hotel/Vitaly Titov), 112 (mysterious place/Trent Alexander Maxwell), 113 (reading news/Ruslan Guzov), 117 (Easter Island/Anthony Booker), 122 (b/Kullanart), (d/FERNANDO BLANCO CALZADA), 124 (friends café/YAKOBCHUK VIACHESLAV), (man on phone/ WAYHOME studio), (woman and docter/Monkey Business Images), (working hard/ Stokkete), 126 (man with book/Borysevych.com), 134 (b/Subphoto), (c/Lucky Business), (e/David Tadevosian), (f/tharamust), 139 (b/sandsun), (d/Dean Drobot), (post it/Kindlena), 141 (healthy smoothie/LMproduction); **SPL:** p. 34 (space junk/ CHRIS BUTLER).

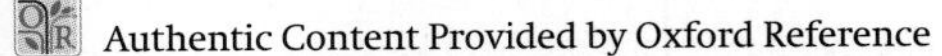

Authentic Content Provided by Oxford Reference

The author and publisher are grateful to those who have given permission to reproduce the following extracts and adaptations or copyright material:

p.16 Laberge, Yves, John A. Lent, William M. Wisser, Char Simons, and Yves Laberge. "Journalism." In *Oxford Encyclopedia of the Modern World*. : Oxford University Press, 2008. http://www.oxfordreference.com/view/10.1093/acref/9780195176322.001.0001/acref-9780195176322-e-837

p.31 Gilmartin, Patricia. "Women Explorers." In *The Oxford Companion to World Exploration*. : Oxford University Press, 2007. http://www.oxfordreference.com/view/10.1093/acref/9780195149227.001.0001/acref-9780195149227-e-0698

p.43 "Film Technology." In *The Oxford Encyclopedia of the History of American Science, Medicine, and Technology*. : Oxford University Press, 2014. http://www.oxfordreference.com/view/10.1093/acref/9780199766666.001.0001/acref-9780199766666-e-163

p.55 Brady, Lisa M., Gregory H. Maddox, and Gregory Clancey. "Natural Disasters." In *Oxford Encyclopedia of the Modern World*. : Oxford University Press, 2008. http://www.oxfordreference.com/view/10.1093/acref/9780195176322.001.0001/acref-9780195176322-e-1093

pp.64 Roth, Marty. "Blue Jeans." In *Oxford Encyclopedia of the Modern World*. : Oxford University Press, 2008. http://www.oxfordreference.com/view/10.1093/acref/9780195176322.001.0001/acref-9780195176322-e-189

p.78 "Environmental Aesthetics." In *Encyclopedia of Aesthetics*. : Oxford University Press, 2014. http://www.oxfordreference.com/view/10.1093/acref/9780199747108.001.0001/acref-9780199747108-e-268

p.88 Littlefield, Melissa M., and Pauline Kusiak. "representation and technology." In *Science, Technology, and Society*. : Oxford University Press, 2005. http://www.oxfordreference.com/view/10.1093/acref/9780195141931.001.0001/acref-9780195141931-e-94

p.104 "Zagat, Tim." In *Savoring Gotham: A Food Lover's Companion to New York City*. : Oxford University Press, 2015. http://www.oxfordreference.com/view/10.1093/acref/9780199397020.001.0001/acref-9780199397020-e-677

p.114 "Voynich Manuscript." In *The Oxford Companion to the Book*. : Oxford University Press, 2010. http://www.oxfordreference.com/view/10.1093/acref/9780198606536.001.0001/acref-9780198606536-e-5129

p.129 "Berners-Lee, Sir Tim." In *A Dictionary of Computer Science*, edited by Butterfield, Andrew, and Gerard Ekembe Ngondi. : Oxford University Press, 2016. http://www.oxfordreference.com/view/10.1093/acref/9780199688975.001.0001/acref-9780199688975-e-6305

p.137 "Proverb." In *Concise Oxford Companion to the English Language*, edited by McArthur, Tom. : Oxford University Press, 1998. http://www.oxfordreference.com/view/10.1093/acref/9780192800619.001.0001/acref-9780192800619-e-997

p.147 "Pyramids of Giza." In *The Oxford Companion To Archaeology*. : Oxford University Press, 2012. http://www.oxfordreference.com/view/10.1093/acref/9780199735785.001.0001/acref-9780199735785-e-0363

p.147 "Bruce Springsteen." In *Oxford Essential Quotations*, edited by Ratcliffe, Susan. : Oxford University Press, http://www.oxfordreference.com/view/10.1093/acref/9780191843730.001.0001/q-oro-ed5-00010371

p.148 "Newspapers." In *Oxford Essential Quotations*, edited by Ratcliffe, Susan. : Oxford University Press, http://www.oxfordreference.com/view/10.1093/acref/9780191843730.001.0001/q-oro-ed5-00007862

p.149 "T. S. Eliot." In *The Oxford Dictionary of American Quotations*, edited by Rawson, Hugh, and Margaret Miner. : Oxford University Press, 2006. http://www.oxfordreference.com/view/10.1093/acref/9780195168235.001.0001/q-author-00008-00000509

p.150 "Andy Warhol." In *Oxford Dictionary of Quotations*, edited by Knowles, Elizabeth. : Oxford University Press, 2014. http://www.oxfordreference.com/view/10.1093/acref/9780199668700.001.0001/q-author-00010-00003350

p.151 "Martin Luther King." In *Oxford Dictionary of Political Quotations*, edited by Jay, Antony. : Oxford University Press, 2012. http://www.oxfordreference.com/view/10.1093/acref/9780199572687.001.0001/q-author-00002-00000883

p.152 "Coco Chanel." In *Oxford Essential Quotations*, edited by Ratcliffe, Susan. : Oxford University Press, http://www.oxfordreference.com/view/10.1093/acref/9780191843730.001.0001/q-oro-ed5-00012116

p.153 "The Mind." In *Oxford Dictionary of Humorous Quotations*, edited by Brandreth, Gyles. : Oxford University Press, 2013. http://www.oxfordreference.com/view/10.1093/acref/9780199681365.001.0001/q-subject-00008-00000195

p.154 "Andrew Grove." In *Oxford Dictionary of Quotations*, edited by Knowles, Elizabeth. : Oxford University Press, 2014. http://www.oxfordreference.com/view/10.1093/acref/9780199668700.001.0001/q-author-00010-00001449

p.155 "W. Somerset Maugham." In *Oxford Essential Quotations*, edited by Ratcliffe, Susan. : Oxford University Press, http://www.oxfordreference.com/view/10.1093/acref/9780191843730.001.0001/q-oro-ed5-00007179

p.156 "René Magritte." In *Oxford Essential Quotations*, edited by Ratcliffe, Susan. : Oxford University Press, http://www.oxfordreference.com/view/10.1093/acref/9780191843730.001.0001/q-oro-ed5-00012502

p.157 "Heraclitus." In *Oxford Essential Quotations*, edited by Ratcliffe, Susan. : Oxford University Press, http://www.oxfordreference.com/view/10.1093/acref/9780191843730.001.0001/q-oro-ed5-00005370

p.158 "Stephen Vincent Benét." In *Oxford Dictionary of Quotations*, edited by Knowles, Elizabeth. : Oxford University Press, 2014. http://www.oxfordreference.com/view/10.1093/acref/9780199668700.001.0001/q-author-00010-00000277

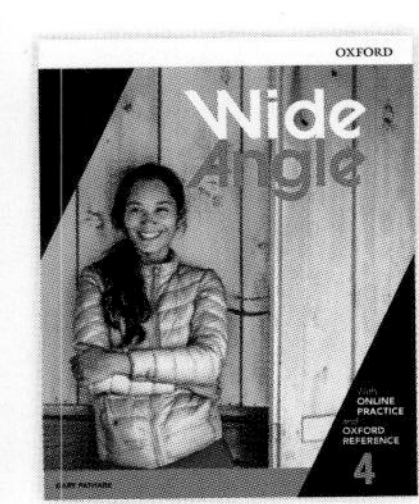

Cover photo by Quinn Ryan Mattingly.
Dalat, Vietnam, April 2017.

A portrait of Rolan Co Lieng, founder and owner of K'ho Coffee Company in Dalat, Vietnam. A member of the K'ho ethnic minority in Vietnam, her ancestors have been growing coffee in this region of Vietnam since the 1920s.

Contents

ENGLISH FOR REAL	GRAMMAR	VOCABULARY	PRONUNCIATION	REVIEW
Making inquiries	Simple present, present continuous, and present perfect State verbs *Each* and *every*	Personal development Collocations	Word stress in compound adjectives	see page 147
Giving and reacting to news	Narrative tenses: simple past, past continuous, and past perfect *all, both, either* *was/were going to*	Taking action (verbs) Comment adverbs	Stressed auxiliary verbs and form of *be*	see page 148
Interrupting and resuming	Verbs + *to* infinitive or *-ing* form Verbs + *-ing* form and verbs + *to* infinitive *so* and *such*	Exploration Suffixes for nouns	Shifting stress in suffix words	see page 149
Asking for and giving clarification	Present passive and past passive Present passive with modal verbs Adjectives with prepositions	Production (verbs) Explaining a process	Chunking	see page 150
Asking for and giving advice	Advice and warning with *should, ought to,* and *had better* Obligation with *must* and *have to* Intensifiers	Natural disasters (verbs) Extreme adjectives Phrasal verbs with *look*	Connected speech with words ending in /t/ or /d/	see page 151
Asking for and giving opinions	Time expressions with the present perfect and simple past *used to* and *be/get used to* *do* for emphasis	Fashion (adjectives) Work Adverbs and phrases for emphasis	*used to*	see page 152

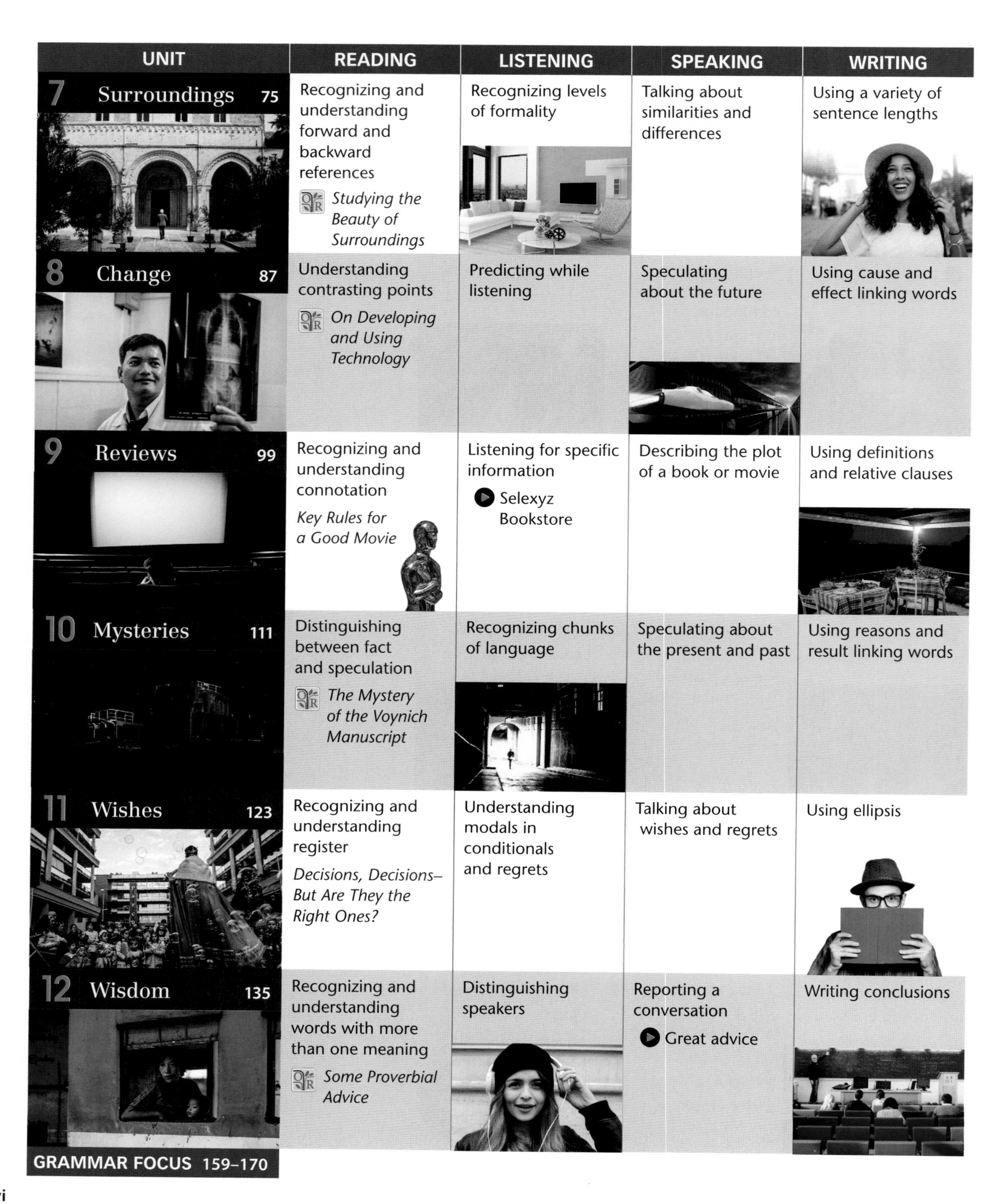

Acknowledgments

AUTHOR

Gary Pathare has a Master's in Education in TESOL from Newcastle University, England. He has been teaching English at the Higher Colleges of Technology in Dubai since 2001, after ten years teaching English and teacher training in Barcelona and Rome. Gary has spoken at international conferences on a wide range of topics, including spelling, literacy, writing, reading, grammar, metaphor, original uses of technology, memorization, materials writing, teacher training, and innovation in ELT.

SERIES CONSULTANTS

PRAGMATICS **Carsten Roever** is Associate Professor in Applied Linguistics at the University of Melbourne, Australia. He was trained as a TESOL teacher and holds a PhD in Second Language Acquisition from the University of Hawai'i at Manoa. His research interests include interlanguage pragmatics, language testing, and conversation analysis.

Naoko Taguchi is an Associate Professor of Japanese and Second Language Acquisition at the Dietrich College of Modern Languages at Carnegie Mellon University. She holds a PhD from Northern Arizona University. Her primary research interests include pragmatics in Second Language Acquisition, second language education, and classroom-based research.

PRONUNCIATION **Tamara Jones** is an instructor at the English Language Center at Howard Community College in Columbia, Maryland.

INCLUSIVITY & CRITICAL THINKING **Lara Ravitch** is a senior instructor and the Intensive English Program Coordinator of the American English Institute at the University of Oregon.

ENGLISH FOR REAL VIDEOS **Pamela Vittorio** acquired a BA in English/Theater from SUNY Geneseo and is an ABD PhD in Middle Eastern Studies with an MA in Middle Eastern Literature and Languages from NYU. She also designs ESL curriculum, materials, and English language assessment tools for publishing companies and academic institutions.

MIDDLE EAST ADVISORY BOARD **Amina Saif Al Hashami,** Nizwa College of Applied Sciences, Oman; **Karen Caldwell,** Higher Colleges of Technology, Ras Al Khaimah, UAE; **Chaker Ali Mhamdi,** Buraimi University College, Oman.

LATIN AMERICA ADVISORY BOARD **Reinaldo Hernández,** Duoc, Chile; **Mauricio Miraglia,** Universidad Tecnológica de Chile INACAP, Chile; **Aideé Damián Rodríguez,** Tecnológico de Monterrey, Mexico; **Adriana Recke Duhart,** Universidad Anáhuac, Mexico; **Inés Campos,** Centro de Idiomas, Cesar Vallejo University, Peru.

SPAIN ADVISORY BOARD **Alison Alonso,** EOI Luarca, Spain; **Juan Ramón Bautista Liébana,** EOI Rivas, Spain; **Ruth Pattison,** EOI, Spain; **David Silles McLaney,** EOI Majadahonda, Spain.

We would like to acknowledge the educators from around the world who participated in the development and review of this series:

ASIA Ralph Baker, Chuo University, Japan; **Elizabeth Belcour**, Chongshin University, South Korea; **Mark Benton**, Kobe Shoin Women's University, Japan; **Jon Berry**, Kyonggi University, South Korea; **Stephen Lyall Clarke**, Vietnam-US English Training Service Centers, Vietnam; **Edo Forsythe**, Hirosaki Gakuin University, Japan; **Clifford Gibson**, Dokkyo University, Japan; **Michelle Johnson**, Nihon University, Japan; **Stephan Johnson**, Rikkyo University, Japan; **Nicholas Kemp**, Kyushu International University, Japan; **Brendyn Lane**, Core Language School, Japan; **Annaliese Mackintosh**, Kyonggi University, South Korea; **Keith Milling**, Yonsei University, Korea; **Chau Ngoc Minh Nguyen**, Vietnam – USA Society English Training Service Center, Vietnam; **Yongjun Park**, Sangi University, South Korea; **Scott Schafer**, Inha University, South Korea; **Dennis Schumacher**, Cheongju University, South Korea; **Jenay Seymour**, Hongik University, South Korea; **Joseph Staples**, Shinshu University, Japan; **Greg Stapleton**, YBM Education Inc. – Adult Academies Division, South Korea; **Le Tuam Vu**, Tan True High School, Vietnam; **Ben Underwood**, Kugenuma High School, Japan; **Quyen Vuong**, VUS English Center, Vietnam

EUROPE Marta Alonso Jerez, Mainfor Formación, Spain; **Pilar Álvarez Polvorinos**, EOI San Blas, Spain; **Peter Anderson**, Anderson House, Italy; **Ana Anglés Esquinas**, First Class Idiomes i Formació, Spain; **Keith Appleby**, CET Services, Spain; **Isabel Arranz**, CULM Universidad de Zaragoza, Spain; **Jesus Baena**, EOI Alcalá de Guadaira, Spain; **José Gabriel Barbero Férnández**, EOI de Burgos, Spain; **Carlos Bibi Fernandez**, EIO de Madrid-Ciudad Lineal, Spain; **Alex Bishop**, IH Madrid, Spain; **Nathan Leopold Blackshaw**, CCI, Italy; **Olga Bel Blesa**, EOI, Spain; **Antoinette Breutel**, Academia Language School, Switzerland; **Angel Francisco Briones Barco**, EOI Fuenlabrada, Spain; **Ida Brucciani**, Pisa University, Italy; **Julie Bystrytska**, Profi-Lingua, Poland; **Raul Cabezali**, EOI Alcala de Guadaira, Spain; **Milena Cacko-Kozera**, Profi-Lingua, Poland; **Elena Calviño**, EOI Pontevedra, Spain; **Alex Cameron**, The English House, Spain; **Rosa Cano Vallese**, EOI Prat Llobregate, Spain; **Montse Cañada**, EOI Barcelona, Spain; **Elisabetta Carraro**, We.Co Translate, Italy; **Joaquim Andres Casamiquela**, Escola Oficial d'Idiomes – Guinardó, Spain; **Lara Ros Castillo**, Aula Campus, Spain; **Patricia Cervera Cottrell**, Centro de Idiomas White, Spain; **Sally Christopher**, Parkway S.I., Spain; **Marianne Clark**, The English Oak Tree Academy, Spain; **Helen Collins**, ELI, Spain; **María José Conde Torrado**, EOI Ferrol, Spain; **Ana Maria Costachi**, Centro de Estudios Ana Costachi S.I., Spain; **Michael Cotton**, Modern English Study Centre, Italy; **Pedro Cunado Placer**, English World, Spain; **Sarah Dague**, Universidad Carlos III, Spain; **María Pilar Delgado**, Big Ben School, Spain; **Ashley Renee Dentremont Matthäus**, Carl-Schurz Haus, Deutch-Amerikanisches-Institute Freiburg e.V., Germany; **Mary Dewhirst**, Cambridge English Systems, Spain; **Hanna Dobrzycka**, Advantage, Poland; **Laura Dolla**, E.F.E. Laura Dolla, Spain; **Paul Doncaster**, Taliesin Idiomes, Spain; **Marek Doskocz**, Lingwista Sp. z o.o., Poland; **Fiona Dunbar**, ELI Málaga, Spain; **Anna Dunin-Bzdak**, Military University of Technology, Poland; **Robin Evers**, l'Università di Modena e Reggio Emilia, Italy; **Yolanda Fernandez**, EOI, Spain; **Dolores Fernández Gavela**, EOI Gijón, Spain; **Mgr. Tomáš Fišer**, English Academy, Czech Republic; **Juan Fondón**, EOI de Langreo, Spain; **Carmen Forns**, Centro Universitario de Lenguas Modernas, Spain; **Ángela Fraga**, EOI de Ferrol, Spain; **Beatriz Freire**, Servicio de Idiomas FGULL, Spain; **Alena Fridrichova**, Palacky University in Olomouc, Faculty of Science, Department of Foreign Languages, Czech Republic, **Elena Friedrich**, Palacky University, **JM Galarza**, Iruñanko Hizkuntz Eskola, Spain; **Nancie Gantenbein**, TLC-IH, Switzerland; **Gema García**, EOI, Spain; **Maria Jose Garcia Ferrer**, EOI Moratalaz, Spain; **Josefa García González**, EOI Málaga, Spain; **Maria García Hermosa**, EOI, Spain; **Jane Gelder**, The British Institute of Florence, Italy; **Aleksandra Gelner**, ELC Katowice, Bankowa 14, Poland; **Marga Gesto**, EOI Ferrol, Spain; **Juan Gil**, EOI Maria Moliner, Spain; **Eva Gil Cepero**, EOI La Laguna, Spain; **Alan Giverin**, Today School, Spain; **Tomas Gomez**, EOI Segovia, Spain; **Mónica González**, EOI Carlos V, Spain; **Elena González Diaz**, EOI, Spain; **Steve Goodman**, Language Campus, Spain; **Katy Gorman**, Study Sulmona, Italy; **Edmund Green**, The British Institute of Florence, Italy; **Elvira Guerrero**, GO! English Granada, Spain; **Lauren Hale**, The British Institute of Florence, Italy; **Maria Jose Hernandez**, EOI de Salou, Spain; **Chris Hermann**, Hermann Brown English Language Centre, Spain; **Robert Holmes**, Holmes English, Czech Republic; **José Ramón Horrillo**, EOI de Aracena, Spain; **Laura Izquierdo**, Univerisity of Zaragoza, Spain; **Marcin Jaśkiewicz**, British School Żoliborz, Poland; **Mojmír Jurák**, Albi – jazyková škola, Czech Republic; **Eva Kejdová**, BLC, Czech Republic; **Turlough Kelleher**, British Council, Callaghan School of English, Spain; **Janina Knight**, Advantage Learners, Spain; **Ewa Kowalik**, English Point Radom, Poland; **Monika Krawczuk**, Wyższa Szkoła Finansów i Zarządzania, Poland; **Milica Krisan**, Agentura Parole, Czech Republic; **Jędrzej Kucharski**, Profi-lingua, Poland; **V. Lagunilla**, EOI San Blas, Spain; **Antonio Lara Davila**, EOI La Laguna, Spain; **Ana Lecubarri**, EOI Aviles, Spain; **Lesley Lee**, Exit Language Center, Spain; **Jessica Lewis**, Lewis Academy, Spain; **Alice Llopas**, EOI Estepa, Spain; **Angela Lloyd**, SRH Hochschule Berlin, Germany; **Helena Lohrová**, University of South Bohemia, Faculty of Philosophy, Czech Republic; **Elena López Luengo**, EOI Alcalá de Henares, Spain; **Karen Lord**, Cambridge House, Spain; **Carmen Loriente Duran**, EOI Rio Vero, Spain; **Alfonso Luengo**, EOI Jesús Maestro Madrid, Spain; **Virginia Lyons**, VLEC, Spain; **Anna Łętowska-Mickiewicz**, University of Warsaw, Poland; **Ewa Malesa**, Uniwersytet SWPS, Poland; **Klara Małowiecka**, University of Warsaw, Poland; **Dott. Ssa Kim Manzi**, Università degli Studi della Tuscia – DISTU – Viterbo, Italy; **James Martin**, St. James Language Center, Spain; **Ana Martin Arista**, EOI Tarazona, Spain; **Irene Martín Gago**, NEC, Spain; **Marga Martínez**, ESIC Idiomas Valencia, Spain; **Kenny McDonnell**, McDonnell English Services S.I., Spain; **Anne Mellon**, EEOI Motilla del Palacar, Spain; **Miguel Ángel Meroño**, EOI Cartagena, Spain; **Joanna Merta**, Lingua Nova, Poland; **Victoria Mollejo**, EOI San Blas-Madrid, Spain; **Rebecca Moon**, La Janda Language Services, Spain; **Anna Morales Puigicerver**, EOI TERRASSA, Spain; **Jesús Moreno**, Centro de Lenguas Modernas, Universidad de Zaragoza, Spain;

Emilio Moreno Prieto, EOI Albacete, Spain; **Daniel Muñoz Bravo**, Big Ben Center, Spain; **Heike Mülder**, In-House Englishtraining, Germany; **Alexandra Netea**, Albany School of English, Cordoba, Spain; **Christine M. Neubert**, Intercultural Communication, Germany; **Ignasi Nuez**, The King's Corner, Spain; **Guadalupe Núñez Barredo**, EOI de Ponferrada, Spain; **Monika Olizarowicz-Strygner**, XXII LO z OD im. Jose Marti, Poland; **A. Panter**, Oxford School of English, Italy; **Vanessa Jayne Parvin**, British School Florence, Italy; **Rachel Payne**, Academia Caledonian, Cadiz, Spain; **Olga Pelaez**, EOI Palencia, Spain; **Claudia Pellegrini**, Klubschule Migros, Switzerland; **Arantxa Pérez**, EOI Tudela, Spain; **Montse Pérez**, EOI Zamora, Spain; **Esther Pérez**, EOI Soria, Spain; **Rubén Pérez Montesinos**, EOI San Fernando de Henares, Spain; **Joss Pinches**, Servicio de Lenguas Modernas, Universidad de Huelva, Spain; **Katerina Pitrova**, FLCM TBU in Zlin, Czech Republic; **Erica Pivesso**, Komalingua, Spain; **Eva Plechackova**, Langfor CZ, Czech Republic; **Jesús Porras Santana**, JPS English School, Spain; **Adolfo Prieto**, EOI Albacete, Spain; **Sara Prieto**, Universidad Católica de Murcia, Spain; **Penelope Prodromou**, Universitá Roma Tre, Italy; **Maria Jose Pueyo**, EOI Zaragoza, Spain; **Bruce Ratcliff**, Academia Caledonian, Spain; **Jolanta Rawska**, School of English "Super Grade," Poland; **Mar Rey**, EOI Del Prat, Spain; **Silke Riegler**, HAW Landshut, Germany; **Pauline Rios**, Rivers, Spain; **Laura Rivero**, EOI La Laguna, Spain; **Carmen Rizo**, EOI Torrevieja, Spain; **Antonio F. Rocha Canizares**, EOI Talavera de la Reina, Spain; **Eva Rodellas Fontiguell**, London English School; **Sara Rojo**, EOI Elche, Spain; **Elena Romea**, UNED, Spain; **Ann Ross**, Centro Linguistico di Ateneo, Italy; **Tyler Ross**, Ingliese for you, Italy; **Susan Royo**, EOI Utebo, Spain; **Asuncion Ruiz Astruga**, EOI Maria Molinar, Spain; **Tamara Ruiz Fernandez**, English Today, Spain; **Soledat Sabate**, FIAC, Spain; **Maria Justa Saenz de Tejad**, ECI Idiomas Bailen, Spain; **Sophia Salaman**, University of Florence, Centro Linguistico de ATENEO, Italy; **Elizabeth Schiller**, Schillers Sprachstudio, Germany; **Carmen Serrano Tierz**, CULM, Spain; **Elizabeth R. Sherman**, Lexis Language Centre, Italy; **Rocio Sierra**, EOI Maspalomas, Spain; **David Silles McLaney**, EOI Majadahonda, Spain; **Alison Slade**, British School Florence, Italy; **Rachael Smith**, Accademia Britannica Toscana, Italy; **Michael Smith**, The Cultural English Centre, Spain; **Sonia Sood**, Oxford School Treviso, Italy; **Monika Stawska**, SJO Pigmalion, Poland; **Izabela Stępniewska**, ZS nr 69, Warszawa / British School Otwock, Poland; **Rocío Stevenson**, R & B Academia, Spain; **Petra Stolinova**, Magic English s.r.o., Czech Republic; **Hana Szulczewska**, UNO (Studium Języków Obcych), Poland; **Tim T.**, STP, Spain; **Vera Tauchmanova**, Univerzita Hradec Kralove, Czech Republic; **Nina Terry**, Nina School of English, Spain; **Francesca R. Thompson**, British School of East, Italy; **Pilar Tizzard**, Docklands Idiomes, Spain; **Jessica Toro**, International House Zaragoza, Spain; **Christine Tracey**, Università Roma Tre, Italy; **Loredana Trocchi**, L'Aquila, Italy; **Richard Twiggl**, International House Milan, Italy; **Natàlia Verdalet**, EOI Figueres, Spain; **Sergio Viñals**, EOI San Javier, Spain; **Edith von Sundahl-Hiller**, Supernova Idiomes, Spain; **Vanda Vyslouzilova**, Academia, Czech Republic; **Helen Waldron**, ELC, Germany; **Leslie Wallace**, Academia Language School, Switzerland; **Monika Wąsowska-Polak**, Akademia Obrony Narodowej, Poland; **Melissa Weaver**, TLC-IH, Switzerland; **Maria Watton**, Centro Lingue Estere CC, Italy; **Dr. Otto Weihs**, IMC FH Krems, Austria; **Kate Williams**, Oxford House Barcelona, Spain; **June Winterflood**, Academia Language School, Switzerland; **Ailsa Wood**, Cooperativa Babel, Italy; **Irene Zamora**, www.speakwithirene.com, Spain; **Coro Zapata**, EOIP Pamplona, Spain; **Gloria Zaragoza**, Alicante University, Spain; **Cristina Zêzere**, EOI Torrelavega, Spain

LATIN AMERICA **Fernando Arcos**, Santo Tomás University, Chile; **Ricardo Barreto**, Bridge School, Brazil; **Beth Bartlett**, Centro Cultural Colombo Americano, Cali, Colombia; **Julie Patricia Benito Lugo**, Universidad Central, Colombia; **Ana Luisa Bley Soriano**, Universidad UCINF, Chile; **Gabriela Brun**, I.S.F.D N 129, Argentina; **Talita Burlamaqui**, UFAM, Brazil; **Lourdes Leonides Canta Lozano**, Fac. De Ciencias Biolgicas UANL, Mexico; **Claudia Castro**, Stratford Institute – Moreno-Bs.As, Argentina; **Fabrício Cruz**, Britanic, Brazil; **Lisa Davies**, British Council, Colombia; **Adriana de Blasis**, English Studio Ciudad de Mercedes, Argentina; **Nora Abraira de Lombardo**, Cultural Inglesa de Mercedes, Argentina; **Bronwyn Donohue**, British Council, Colombia; **Andrea C. Duran**, Universidad Externado de Colombia; **Phil Elias**, British Council, Colombia; **Silvia C. Enríquez**, Escuela de Lenguas. Universidad Nacional de La Plata, Argentina; **Freddy Espinoza**, Universidad UCINF, Chile; **Maria de Lourdes Fernandes Silva**, The First Steps School, Brazil; **Doris Flores**, Santo Tomás English Program, Chile; **Hilda Flor-Páez**, Universidad Catolica Santiago de Guayaquil, Ecuador; **Lauriston Freitas**, Cooplem Idiomas, Brazil; **Alma Delia Frias Puente**, UANL, Mexico; **Sandra Gacitua Matus**, Universidad de la Frontera, Chile; **Gloria Garcia**, IPI Ushuaia-Tierra del Fuego, Argentina; **Alma Delia Garcia Ensastegui**, UAEM, Mexico; **Karina Garcia Gonzalez**, Universidad Panamericana, Mexico; **Miguel García Rojas**, UNMSM, Peru; **Macarena González Mena**, Universidad Tecnológica de Chile, Inacap, Chile; **Diana Granado**, Advanced English, Colombia; **Paul Christopher Graves**, Universidad Mayor, Chile; **Mabel Gutierrez**, British Council, Colombia; **Niamh Harnett**, Universidad Externado de Colombia, Colombia; **Elsa Hernandez**, English Time Institute, Argentina; **Reinaldo Hernández Sordo**, DUOC UC, Chile; **Eduardo Icaza**, CEN, Ecuador; **Kenel Joseph**, Haitian-American Institute, Haiti; **Joel Kellogg**, British Council, Colombia; **Sherif Ebrahim Khakil**, Chapingo Universidad Autonoma Chapingo, Mexico; **Cynthia Marquez**, Instituto Guatemalteco Americano, Guatemala; **Aaron McCarroll**, Universidad Sergio Arboleda, Colombia; **Milagro Machado**, SISE Institute, Peru; **Marta de Faria e Cunha Monteiro**, Federal University of Amazonas – UFAM, Brazil; **Lucía Murillo Sardi**, Instituto Británico, Peru; **Ricardo A. Nausa**, Universidad de los Andes, Colombia; **Andrea Olmos Bernal**, Universidad de Guadalajara, Mexico; **M. Edu Lizzete Olvera Dominguez**, Universidad Autonoma de Baja California Sur, Mexico; **Blanca Ortecho**,

Universidad Cesar Vallejo Centro de Idiomas, Peru; **Jim Osorio**, Instituto Guatemalteco Americano, Guatemala; **Erika del Carmen Partida Velasco**, Univam, Mexico; **Mrs. Katterine Pavez**, Universidad de Atacama, Chile; **Sergio Peña**, Universidad de La Frontera, Chile; **Leonor Cristina Peñafort Camacho**, Universidad Autónoma de Occidente, Colombia; **Tom Rickman**, British Council, Colombia; **Olga Lucia Rivera**, Universidad Externado de Colombia, Colombia; **Maria-Eugenia Ruiz Brand**, DUOC UC, Chile; **Gabriela S. Eguiarte**, London School, Mexico; **Majid Safadaran**, Instituto Cultural Peruano Norteamericano, Peru; **María Ines Salinas**, UCASAL, Argentina; **Ruth Salomon-Barkmeyer**, UNILINGUAS – UNISINOS, Brazil; **Mario Castillo Sanchez Hidalgo**, Universidad Panamericana, Mexico; **Katrina J. Schmidt**, Universidad de Los Andes, Colombia; **Jacqueline Sedore**, The Language Company, Chile; **Lourdes Angelica Serrano Herrera**, Adler Schule, Mexico; **Antonio Diego Sousa de Oliveira**, Federal University of Amazonas, Brazil; **Padraig Sweeney**, Universidad Sergio Arboleda, Colombia; **Edith Urquiza Parra**, Centro Universitario México, Mexico; **Eduardo Vásquez**, Instituto Chileno Britanico de Cultura, Chile; **Patricia Villasante**, Idiomas Católica, Peru; **Malaika Wilson**, The Language Company, Chile; **Alejandra Zegpi-Pons**, Universidad Católica de Temuco, Chile; **Boris Zevallos**, Universidad Cesar Vallejo Centro de Idiomas, Peru; **Wilma Zurita Beltran**, Universidad Central del Ecuador, Ecuador

THE MIDDLE EAST Chaker Ali Mhamdi, Buraimi University College, Oman; **Salama Kamal Shohayb**, Al-Faisal International Academy, Saudi Arabia

TURKEY M. Mine Bağ, Sabanci University, School of Languages; **Suzanne Campion**, Istanbul University; **Daniel Chavez**, Istanbul University Language Center; **Asuman Cincioğlu**, Istanbul University; **Hatice Çelikkanat**, Istanbul Esenyurt University; **Güneş Yurdasiper Dal**, Maltepe University; **Angeliki Douri**, Istanbul University Language Center; **Zia Foley**, Istanbul University; **Frank Foroutan**, Istanbul University Language Center; **Nicola Frampton**, Istanbul University; **Merve Güler**, Istanbul University; **H. Ibrahim Karabulut**, Dumlupınar University; **Catherine McKimm**, Istanbul University; **Merve Oflaz**, Dogus University; **Burcu Özgül**, Istanbul University; **Yusuf Özmenekşe**, Istanbul University Language Center; **Lanlo Pinter**, Istanbul University Language Center; **Ahmet Rasim**, Amasya University; **Diana Maria Rios Hoyos**, Istanbul University Language Center; **Jose Rodrigues**, Istanbul University; **Dilek Eryılmaz Salkı**, Ozyegin University; **Merve Selcuk**, Istanbul Kemerburgaz University; **Mehdi Solhi Andarab**, Istanbul Medipol University; **Jennifer Stephens**, Istanbul University; **Özgür Şahan**, Bursa Technical University; **Fatih Yücel**, Beykent University

UNITED KINGDOM Sarah Ali, Nottingham Trent International College, Nottingham; **Rolf Donald**, Eastbourne School of English, Eastbourne, East Sussex; **Nadine Early**, ATC Language Schools, Dublin, Ireland; **Dr. Sarah Ekdawi**, Oxford School of English, Oxford; **Glynis Ferrer**, LAL Torbay, Paignton Devon; **Diarmuid Fogarty**, INTO Manchester, Manchester; **Ryan Hannan**, Hampstead School of English, London; **Neil Harris**, ELTS, Swansea University, Swansea; **Claire Hunter**, Edinburgh School of English, Edinburgh, Scotland; **Becky Ilk**, LAL Torbay, Paignton; **Kirsty Matthews**, Ealing, Hammersmith & West London's college, London; **Amanda Mollaghan**, British Study Centres London, London; **Shila Nadar**, Twin ECL, London; **Sue Owens**, Cambridge Academy of English, Girton, Cambridge; **Caroline Preston**, International House Newcastle, Newcastle upon Tyne; **Ruby Rennie**, University of Edinburgh, Edinburgh, Scotland; **Howard Smith**, Oxford House College, London; **Yijie Wang**, The University of Edinburgh, Scotland; **Alex Warren**, Eurotraining, Bournemouth

UNITED STATES Christina H. Appel, ELS Educational Services, Manhattan, NY; **Nicole Bollhalder**, Stafford House, Chicago, IL; **Rachel Bricker**, Arizona State University, Tempe, AZ; **Kristen Brown**, Massachusetts International Academy, Marlborough, MA; **Tracey Brown**, Parkland College, Champaign, IL; **Peter Campisi**, ELS Educational Services, Manhattan, NY; **Teresa Cheung**, North Shore Community College, Lynn, MA; **Tyler Clancy**, ASC English, Boston, MA; **Rachael David**, Talk International, Miami, FL; **Danielle De Koker**, ELS Educational Services, New York, NY; **Diana Djaboury**, Mesa Community College, Mesa, AZ; **Mark Elman**, Talk International, Miami, FL; **Dan Gauran**, EC English, Boston, MA; **Kerry Gilman**, ASC English, Boston, MA; **Heidi Guenther**, ELS Educational Services, Manhattan, NY; **Emily Herrick**, University of Nebraska-Lincoln, Lincoln, NE; **Kristin Homuth**, Language Center International, Southfield, MI; **Alexander Ingle**, ALPS Language School, Seattle, WA; **Eugenio Jimenez**, Lingua Language Center at Broward College, Miami, FL; **Mahalia Joeseph**, Lingua Language Center at Broward College, Miami, FL; **Melissa Kaufman**, ELS Educational Services, Manhattan, NY; **Kristin Kradolfer Espinar**, MILA, Miami, FL; **Larissa Long**, TALK International, Fort Lauderdale, FL; **Mercedes Martinez**, Global Language Institute, Minneapolis, MN; **Ann McCrory**, San Diego Continuing Education, San Diego, CA; **Simon McDonough**, ASC English, Boston, MA; **Dr. June Ohrnberger**, Suffolk County Community College, Brentwood, NY; **Fernanda Ortiz**, Center for English as a Second Language at the University of Arizona, Tuscon, AZ; **Roberto S. Quintans**, Talk International, Miami, FL; **Terri J. Rapoport**, ELS, Princeton, NJ; **Alex Sanchez Silva**, Talk International, Miami, FL; **Cary B. Sands**, Talk International, Miami, FL; **Joseph Santaella Vidal**, EC English, Boston, MA; **Angel Serrano**, Lingua Language Center at Broward College, Miami, FL; **Timothy Alan Shaw**, New England School of English, Boston, MA; **Devinder Singh**, The University of Tulsa, Tulsa, OK; **Daniel Stein**, Lingua Language Center at Broward College, Miami, FL; **Christine R. Stesau**, Lingua Language Center at Broward College, Miami, FL; **David Stock**, ELS Educational Services, Manhattan, NY; **Joshua Stone**, Approach International Student Center, Allston, MA; **Maria-Virginia Tanash**, EC English, Boston, MA; **Noraina Vazquez Huyke**, Talk International, Miami, FL

A REAL-WORLD VIEWPOINT

Whatever your goals and aspirations, *Wide Angle* helps you use English to connect with the world around you. It empowers you to join any conversation and say the right thing at the right time, with confidence.

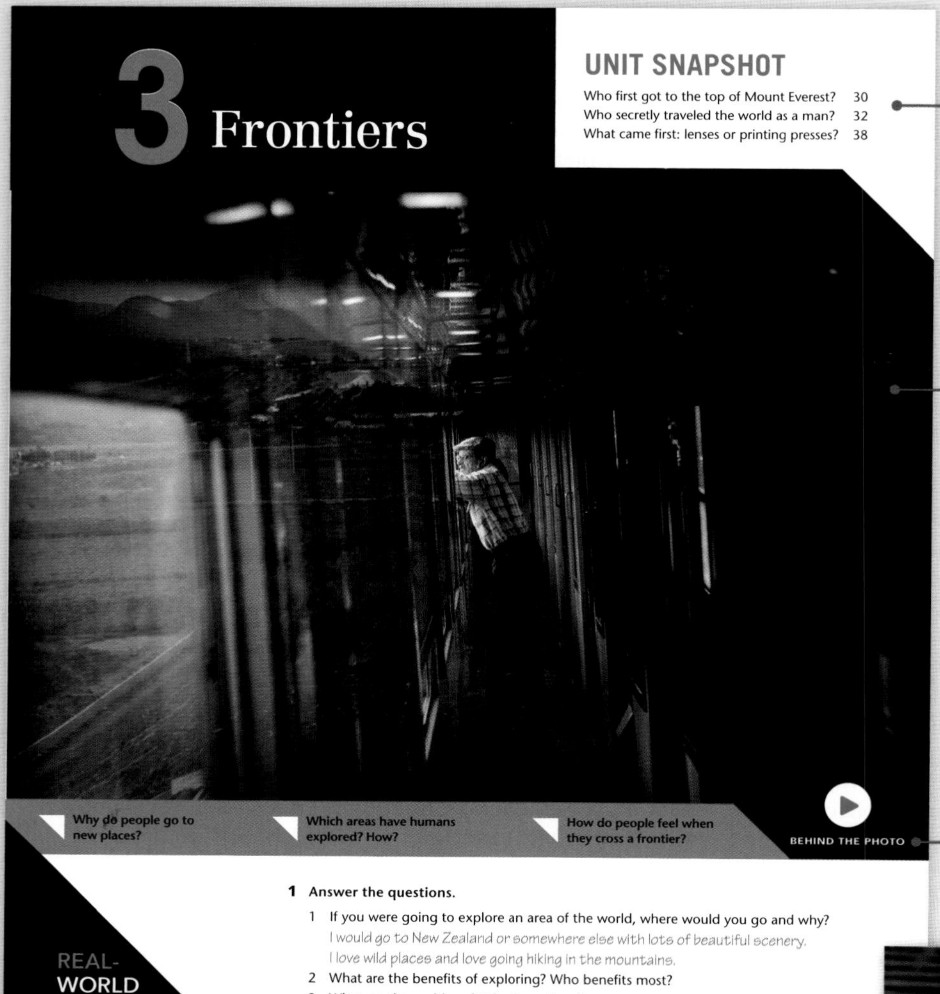

Start thinking about the topic with relevant, interesting **introduction questions**.

blink

Be inspired by the **vibrant unit opener images** from Blink photography. The international, award-winning photographers bring stories from around the world to life on the page.

Watch the **"Behind the Photo"** video from the photographer.

Apply learning to your own needs with **Real-World Goals**, instantly seeing the benefit of the English you are learning.

"People go to new places for a variety of reasons: to work, to study, to learn, relax, challenge themselves, or simply to discover something new. Travel is the ideal way to test yourself. It pushes people to their limits and gets them outside of their comfort zone."

Gianni Cipriano

Enjoy learning with the huge variety of **up-to-date, inventive, and engaging audio and video.**

3.4 Excuse Me…

Understand what to say and how to say it with **English For Real**.

These lessons equip you to choose and adapt appropriate language to communicate effectively in any situation.

ENGLISH FOR REAL

1 **ACTIVATE** Look at the pictures with a partner. What are the differences? Discuss the question in relation to the following.

location
situation
relationships between speakers

2 **IDENTIFY** Watch a conversation between Max, Andy, Phil, and Kevin about a lecture they have just attended. What do they keep doing?

3 **ASSESS** You are going to watch an extract of the lecture the friends were talking about in Exercise 2. Max wants to ask the speaker a question. What do you think Max's interruption will be like compared to the way the friends interrupted each other in their conversation? Why?

4 **ANALYZE** Watch the video and check your answers to Exercise 3.

REAL-WORLD ENGLISH Interrupting and resuming

Interrupting appropriately for the situation will get a better response from the speaker.

Sometimes it is necessary to interrupt a formal presentation to check understanding. You can raise your hand and then say you want to interrupt and why.

Excuse me for interrupting. Could I ask…?
I'm sorry to interrupt. Do you mind if…?
Excuse me for saying so, but I don't think…

With people you know in informal situations, you can use just one word like *but, so,* or *sorry* to show you want to say something.

So, why does…?
But what about…?
Sorry, but…?

When starting to speak again after an interruption, the speaker can use phrases to show it is their turn again.

Anyway, as I was saying…
Going back to what I was talking about…
So, where was I?

36

5 **IDENTIFY** Watch the complete video and take notes on the different ways of interrupting and resuming in each situation. Include phrases and actions. Compare your notes with a partner.

	In the lecture hall	Outside the lecture hall
Speakers	Max and lecturer	Max, Andy, Kevin, and Phil
To interrupt		
To resume		

6 **INTEGRATE** Work in pairs. Rewrite the interruptions so that they can be used for a more formal situation (e.g., the lecture hall situation in the video). Then listen and compare your answers. Did you rewrite them in the same way as the sentences in the audio?

1 But what about the start time?
2 So, we can finish early?
3 Actually, that's not right.
4 Sorry, but I need to say something here.

7 **INTERACT** Work in a group of three (A, B, and C) to do a role play. Choose situation 1 or 2, and prepare what you will say. Then role play the situation. Discuss what worked well in your role play. Then swap roles and repeat.

Situation 1: You join two friends in a café. They are having a conversation about a documentary they both saw. You need to tell them about the plans for that evening.

Situation 2: You and two friends meet outside the movie theater. They immediately start talking about the party last night. The movie is starting in ten minutes, and there is a line for tickets. You don't want to miss the start of the movie.

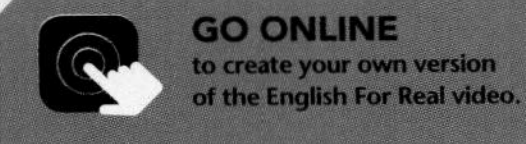

GO ONLINE to create your own version of the English For Real video.

37

Step into the course with **English For Real videos** that mimic real-life interactions. You can record your voice and respond in real time for out-of-class practice that is relevant to your life.

COMPREHENSIVE SYLLABUS

Ensure progress in all skills with a pedagogically consistent and appropriately leveled syllabus.

2 WHAT'S YOUR ANGLE? Imagine that you are on an exploration team. What skills do you have that would be useful?

3 VOCABULARY Complete the description of successful explorers with the words in the box.

independent	explore	quit	practical
survive	set off	keep going	flexible

Oxford 3000™

Successful explorers…

- ¹________ to ²________ with hope, energy, and positive feelings.
- know how to ³________ when things get tough.
- ⁴________ even when other people go back.
- don't like to ⁵________ but know that sometimes it is necessary.
- are ⁶________ and are not afraid of changing their plans.
- are ⁷________—they listen to others, but they make their own decisions.
- are ⁸________—they know how to take care of themselves and others.

LISTENING SKILL
Recognizing rephrasing in a talk

Speakers often use specific topic words and ideas that may not be familiar to the audience. They usually rephrase these to help the listener understand. Sometimes they do this immediately.

*Would you make **a good explorer**? Do you want to **find out about the world, push back frontiers, discover new places**?*

Sometimes they use signals to show they are rephrasing. Listen for these, for example:

in other words *that is* *by that I mean* *to put it another way*

6 IDENTIFY The speaker rephrases the three key points in the first part of her presentation. Can you remember how she did this? Match the original phrases to the rephrasing signals and to the rephrasing. Then listen again and check.

	Rephrasing signal	Rephrasing words
1 make a commitment	to put it another way	take in everything… going on around

VOCABULARY

The Oxford 3000™ is a word list containing the most important words to learn in English. The words are chosen based on frequency in the Oxford English Corpus and relevance to learners of English. Every word is aligned to the CEFR, guiding you on the words you should know at each level.

4 IDENTIFY Read the essay again. Find the topic sentence in each paragraph.

5 EXPAND Take notes of the supporting ideas and examples in paragraphs 2 and 3.

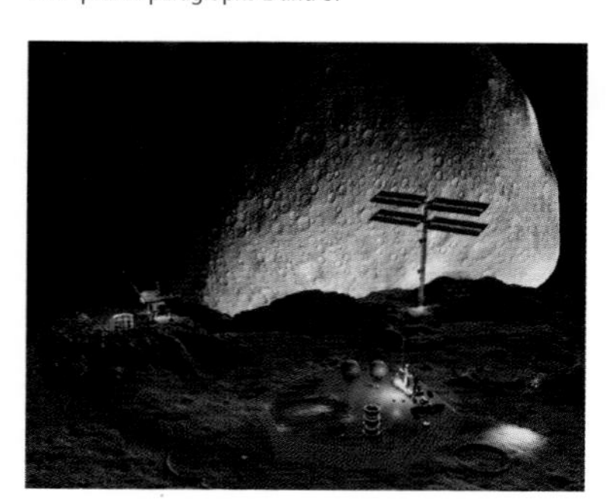

Paragraph 2: ________________

GRAMMAR IN CONTEXT *so* and *such*

We use *so* and *such* to emphasize what things are like.

so + adjective
so exciting

such (+ *a* / *an*) + adjective + noun
such a good idea

We don't need an adjective with *such* if the noun is something that is always good, bad, etc.
*It was **such** a problem.*

Also, we don't use *a* / *an* with *such* when the noun is uncountable.
*It was **such** bad weather.*

See Grammar focus on page 161.

7 IDENTIFY Find an example of *so* and *such* in the essay.

8 INTERACT Complete the sentences with *so*, *such*, or *such a* / *an*.

1 I understand why some people are ________ negative about space travel.
2 Space travel is ________ expensive activity. We should limit it.

GRAMMAR

The carefully graded grammar syllabus ensures you encounter the most relevant language at the right point in your learning.

Discovering explorers

What do Christopher Columbus, Captain Cook, and Marco Polo have in common? Yes, they were all famous explorers—and they were all male explorers, as are most of the well-known ones. However, women have a significant place in the history of **exploration**, and interest in female explorers has been rising since the 1980s. The very real achievements of female explorers, like Mary Kingsley, are finally getting the recognition they deserve.

Why have attitudes changed? One explanation is that the women's movement of the 20th and 21st centuries has increased interest in women's **accomplishments**. Also, their journals provide fascinating stories; these women appeared to enjoy facing danger, showing a willingness to confront wild animals, extreme weather, hostile natives, injury, and illness. Their confidence and commitment are an **inspiration** to today's women. It is often shocking to read about the attitudes they faced, especially in repressive Victorian Britain. For example, women were constantly denied recognition for their achievements. When the Liverpool Geographical Society wanted to learn about Mary Kingsley's explorations in West Africa, her paper was read aloud by a man while she sat in the background, as the organization would not allow women to speak. Equally shocking is the fact that membership of the New York Explorers' Club was male-only until 1981.

So, what were these women explorers like? Apart from having strong personalities and being intelligent and practical, they were usually middle-aged or beyond, having gained their independence after fulfilling family **obligations**, such as looking after elderly parents. In fact, one attraction for many women was the possibility of escape from a lifetime of service. They were usually unmarried, as few husbands would consider giving permission for their wives to pursue such a profession. They were also rich enough to afford to pay for their trips (**sponsorship** was usually not possible for women) and sufficiently educated and experienced to deal with the inevitable **complications** that arose. Mary Kingsley fits this profile. Unmarried, smart, and self-educated, Mary took care of her family while her father went on explorations. Only when both her parents died and her brother moved away was Mary finally able to begin her own explorations.

Now that the contributions of these women are finally revealed, in the context of their gender their achievements appear to be even more remarkable than those of their more famous male counterparts. While they didn't discover America, they made significant discoveries, but above all they showed that women can overcome impossible challenges to achieve **greatness**.

—adapted from *The Oxford Companion to World Exploration*, edited by David Buisseret

Oxford Reference is a trusted source of over two million authentic academic texts.

Free access to the Oxford Reference site is included with Student Books 4, 5, and 6.

Personalize the lesson topics and see how the language can work for you with **What's Your Angle?** activities.

3.1 End of the Road?

mountains

ice

underwater

underground

1 ACTIVATE What kind of people make good explorers? What are they like? What do they do?

2 WHAT'S YOUR ANGLE? Imagine that you are on an exploration team. What skills do you have that would be useful?

3 VOCABULARY Complete the description of successful explorers with the words in the box.

independent	explore	quit	practical
survive	set off	keep going	flexible

Oxford 3000™

Successful explorers…

- [1] ________ to [2] ________ with hope, energy, and positive feelings.
- know how to [3] ________ when things get tough.
- [4] ________ even when other people go back.
- don't like to [5] ________ but know that sometimes it is necessary.
- are [6] ________ and are not afraid of changing their plans.
- are [7] ________—they listen to others, but they make their own decisions.
- are [8] ________—they know how to take care of themselves and others.

4 INTERACT Discuss the questions with a partner.

1. Which ideas from the description in Exercise 3 did you mention in Exercises 1 and 2?
2. Which three ideas about explorers do you most agree with?

5 INTEGRATE Listen to the first part of a talk about modern-day exploration. Which skills and qualities from Exercise 3 are mentioned?

LISTENING SKILL
Recognizing rephrasing in a talk

Speakers often use specific topic words and ideas that may not be familiar to the audience. They usually rephrase these to help the listener understand. Sometimes they do this immediately.

*Would you make **a good explorer**? Do you want to **find out about the world, push back frontiers, discover new places**?*

Sometimes they use signals to show they are rephrasing. Listen for these, for example:

in other words   that is   by that I mean
to put it another way

6 IDENTIFY The speaker rephrases the three key points in the first part of her presentation. Can you remember how she did this? Match the original phrases to the rephrasing signals and to the rephrasing. Then listen again and check.

	Rephrasing signal	Rephrasing words
1 make a commitment	to put it another way	take in everything… going on around you…rather than just…looking ahead
2 be aware of your surroundings	by that I mean	the person to turn to…
3 be in control	in other words	make a decision…stick to it…get through the really bad times

7 INTEGRATE Review the key facts and predict the answers. Then listen to the rest of the talk and check.

Key facts

- Caves discovered in the world: about [1] ___%
- Earth's surface covered by ocean: about [2] ___%
- Unexplored ocean: about [3] ___%
- Life under Antarctic ice: up to [4] ___ million years old
- Money spent on brain research in Europe per year: over € [5] ___

GRAMMAR IN CONTEXT
Verbs + *to* infinitive or *-ing* form

Some verbs can take the *-ing* form or the *to* infinitive with little or no change in meaning. For example: *attempt, begin, can't stand, continue, hate, like, love, prefer, start.*

*Do you **like to be** in control? / Do you **like being** in control?*

Other verbs can take both the *-ing* form or the *to* infinitive but with a clear difference in meaning. For example: *stop, forget, remember.*

*Do you **stop to look**? (Do you stop doing something because you want to look?)*
*Do you **stop looking**? (Do you no longer look at what you were looking at before?)*

See Grammar focus on page 161.

8 IDENTIFY Work in pairs. Is there a difference in meaning in the sentences in each pair? What is it?

1. He stopped to talk to me. / He stopped talking to me.
2. She forgot meeting them. / She forgot to meet them.
3. I prefer traveling alone. / I prefer to travel alone.
4. He remembered visiting the place. / He remembered to visit the place.
5. She began to explain. / She began explaining.

9 INTEGRATE Read the extracts from the talk. Choose the verb form the speaker used. Then listen and check.

1. …we need to stop *to worry / worrying* about being the first to go somewhere.
2. …they forgot *to look / looking* and *learn / learning* about where they were.
3. … people will continue *to explore / exploring* forever, inward and outward…
4. …we should remember *to leave / leaving* the place as we find it…

10 WHAT'S YOUR ANGLE? Look at the areas for exploration in the pictures in this lesson and answer the questions.

1. Which areas should we continue exploring? Why?
2. Which should we definitely stop exploring? Why?
3. What other areas should we start to explore? Why?

the human mind

DNA

artificial intelligence

11 INTERACT Share your answers to the questions in Exercise 10 in a group. Try to agree on the top two areas for each answer.

READING AND LISTENING

Explicit reading and listening skills focus on helping you access and assimilate information confidently in this age of rapid information.

Build confidence with the **activation-presentation-practice-production** method, with activities moving from controlled to less controlled, with an increasing level of challenge.

WRITING SKILL
Writing paragraphs and topic sentences

Paragraphs with strong topic sentences help the reader to understand the organization of the text and the main ideas. This means the reader can:

- get a clear overview quickly.
- find the information they want more easily.
- understand the progression of the ideas.

Paragraphs should have one main idea, and the topic sentence usually presents this. Examples and more detailed information in the rest of the paragraph should support the main idea.

to live.

However, space travel also has signi
especially financial ones. Each missior
dollars, and many people are unhappy
money should be spent on problems v
change, poverty, and disease. All of th
from the billions of dollars that are curr
travel. There is also an environmental
in space, as we burn rocket fuel, use u
materials, and leave behind litter in spa

In conclusion, I feel there should be
question of space exploration because
uses too many resources. In today's w
sure that our money and effort are dire
most needed.

WRITING

The writing syllabus focuses on the writing styles needed for today, using a **process writing approach** of **prepare-plan-draft-review-correct** to produce the best possible writing.

SPEAKING Giving a presentation

The audience listens and learns more when a presentation is well organized and presented.

Give a clear, engaging introduction that tells your audience what you are going to talk about.

Today, I'm going to talk about…
First, I'll talk about…
Then I'll outline…
Finally, we will look at…
There will be time for questions at the end.

Then use signpost phrases to show the audience where you are in the presentation and to highlight changes of topic.

So, first of all,…   Moving on to…   In this final part,…

5 INTEGRATE Listen to the introduction again. Write a possible outline for the rest of the presentation.

6 ASSESS Listen to the opening parts for the other

5 relation—relationship
6 lazy—laziness

9 INTERACT Complete the noun
a suffix, and mark the stress on thes
check. Then listen again and repeat

1. I would like to look at other deve
2. …the simple lens gave us the po
3. …of raising the level of human ir
4. …the recogni________ of the in
5. …this will be an explora________ inventions…

10 PREPARE Choose an item you con
three most important inventions for
Write a list of reasons to support yo

11 DEVELOP Work in pairs. Review yo
invention and then together decide
presentation.

SPEAKING

Speaking and **pronunciation skills** build the functional language you need outside of class.

A BLENDED LEARNING APPROACH

Make the most of *Wide Angle* with opportunities for relevant, personalized learning outside of class.

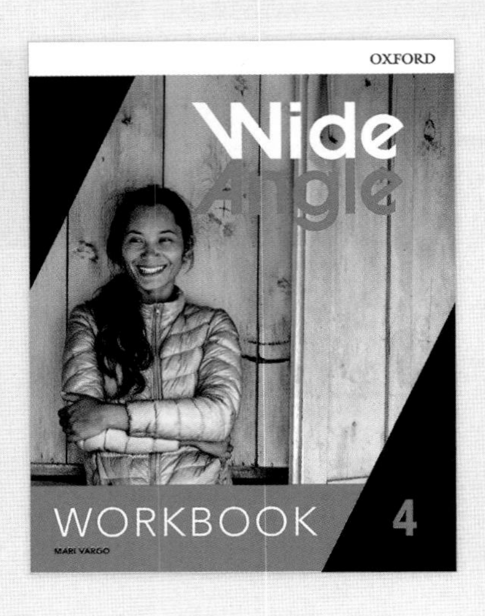

ONLINE PRACTICE

When you see this icon in your Student Book, go online to extend your learning.

With Online Practice you can:

- Review the skills taught in every lesson and get **instant feedback**.
- Practice grammar and vocabulary through **fun games**.
- Access **all audio and video** material. Use the Access Code in the front of this Student Book to log in for the first time at wideangle.oxfordonlinepractice.com.

WORKBOOK

Your Workbook provides additional practice for every unit of the Student Book.

Each unit includes:

- An entirely new reading with skill practice linked to **Oxford Reference**.
- Support for the **Discussion Board**, helping students to master online writing.
- Listening comprehension and skill practice using the **Unit Review Podcast**.
- Real-life English practice linked to the **English For Real** videos.
- **Grammar** and **vocabulary** exercises related to the unit topic.

Use your Workbook for homework or self-study.

FOCUS ON THE TEACHER

The Teacher's Resource Center at wideangle.oxfordonlinepractice.com saves teachers time by integrating and streamlining access to the following support:

- **Teacher's Guide**, including fun **More to Say** pronunciation activities and **professional development** materials.
- **Easy-to-use** learning management system for the student Online Practice, **answer keys**, **audio**, lots of **extra activities**, **videos**, and so much more.

The **Classroom Presentation Tool** brings the Student Book to life for heads-up lessons. Class audio, video, and answer keys, as well as teaching notes, are available online or offline and are updated across your devices.

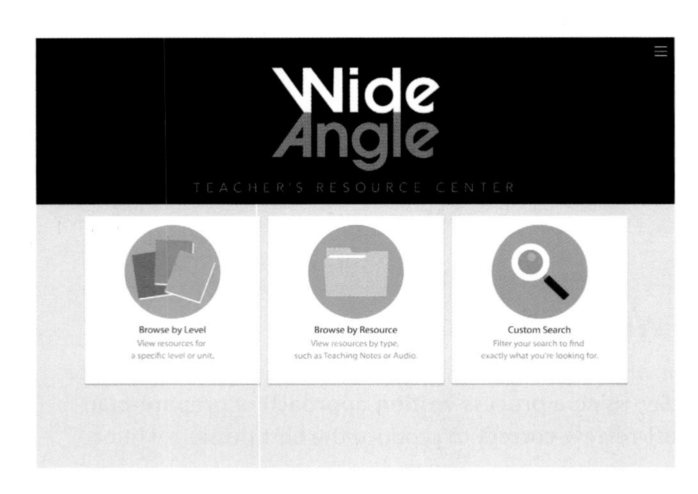

1 Achievements

UNIT SNAPSHOT

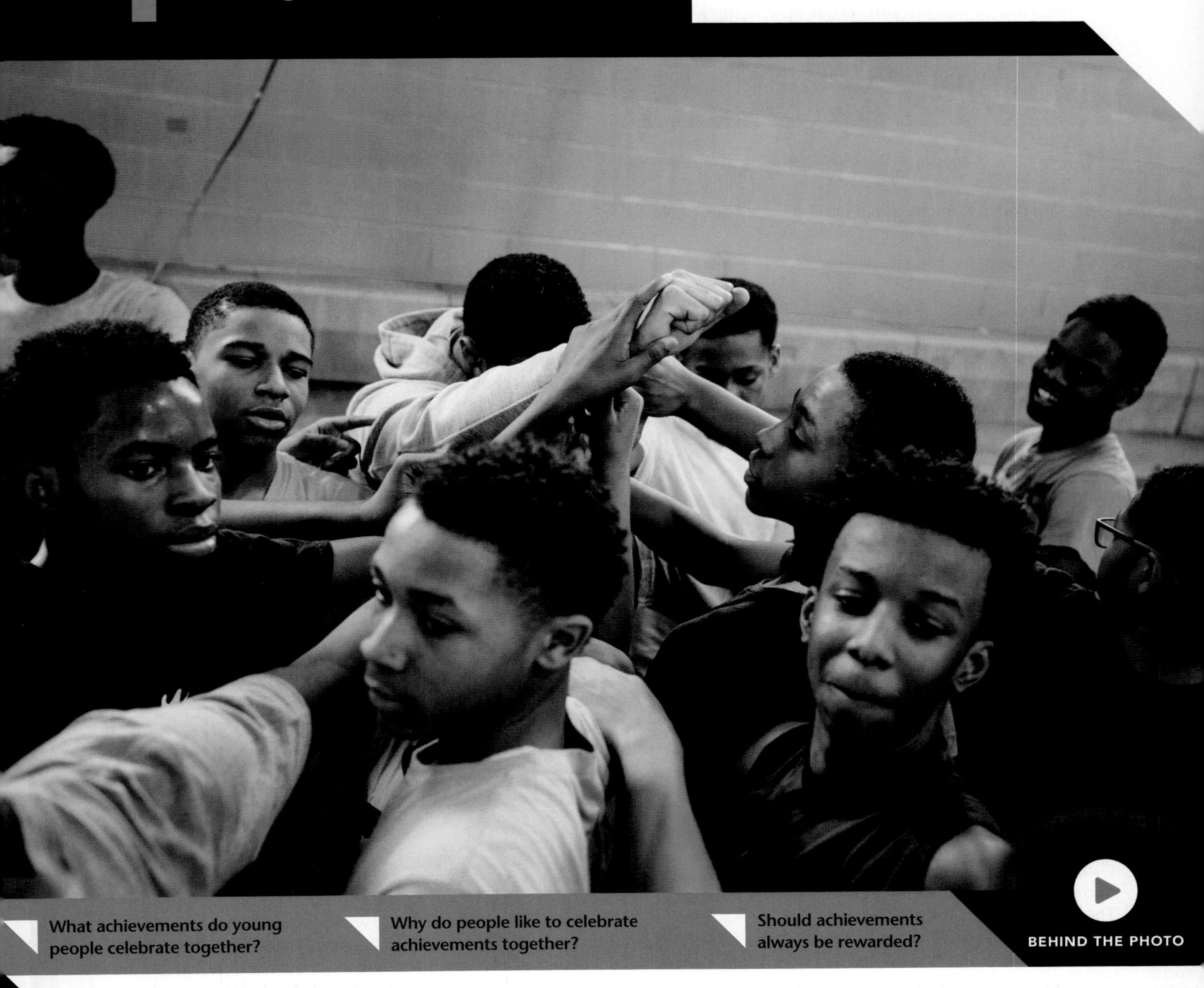

What achievements do young people celebrate together?

Why do people like to celebrate achievements together?

Should achievements always be rewarded?

BEHIND THE PHOTO

1 Which of these do you think is the greatest achievement? Put them in order. Add another achievement.

___ Quitting smoking
___ Raising a family
___ Forgiving yourself for a mistake
___ Doing a kind act without expecting reward
___ Finishing a marathon
___ Doing well on a test
___ Writing a novel
___ Other: ________________

2 Share your ideas with a partner. Do you agree?

REAL-WORLD GOAL

Watch a movie about a famous person

1.1 Getting to the Top

1 ACTIVATE Ask and answer the quiz questions with a partner. How similar are you? What do you think the quiz was trying to find out?

Do you…

1 write lists of things you want to achieve?	**Yes**	**No**
2 take classes to improve your skills?	**Yes**	**No**
3 finish everything that you start?	**Yes**	**No**
4 like people to tell you how good you are?	**Yes**	**No**
5 laugh when things go wrong?	**Yes**	**No**

READING SKILL Skimming and scanning

Readers approach texts in different ways to get the information they want quickly and effectively.

Skimming: To understand the general topic or "gist" of a text, look at the text quickly. Do not read every word. Instead, notice the title, headings, and pictures; the first sentences of paragraphs; and the repeated words, word families, and ideas. Skimming can help you decide if you want or need to read the complete text. It will also help you see how the text is organized and where to find information in it.

Scanning: To find specific information quickly, scan the text. Check what type of information you are looking for (e.g., a date or a name), and then scan for the correct form for the information (e.g., a number or a word starting with a capital letter).

2 IDENTIFY Skim the introduction to the blog article to find out what it is about.

Home | About | Articles | Search

Do you know any overachievers? My daughter Esmé does—Josh. Josh really annoys his classmates, including Esmé. According to her, Josh arrives each morning already knowing everything the teacher is about to present. Josh doesn't get A's, he gets A++'s. But will his early success continue? What qualities does he need to be an adult overachiever? I decided to find out, so this week's blog is all about people who overachieve as adults. Who are they, and what do they do?

1 ______________________________

Overachievers take risks, but when things go wrong, they don't feel bad. They use humor to laugh at their mistakes. They also make sure they enjoy their successes—after all, they have achieved their goals, so why not have fun and make the most of the experience? Laughter helps us be more relaxed and realistic, and it makes us popular with others.

2 ______________________________

Overachievers are not afraid to admit their own weak areas. They are, of course, certain that they have plenty of good points, too. But they never miss an opportunity to learn, train, and get experience to improve their skills.

3 ______________________________

Overachievers are highly organized. Their desks (and minds) are usually tidy. By the time everyone else is just starting their day, overachievers have already made lists and set goals.

4 ______________________________

Overachievers are very confident, and this helps them do their best even when things are difficult. But they also want people to notice and praise their hard work before they start on their next project. Around their desks, they like to display reminders of how they have made a difference in the world: photos, award certificates…anything that helps them stay motivated and also show the world how good they are.

5 ______________________________

Overachievers know there will always be new ideas, but ideas on their own mean nothing—you have to do something with them. Overachievers take advantage of this. When they bring an idea (even someone else's) to life, it becomes their own achievement.

My daughter is reading this over my shoulder as I write. "Yes, yes, yes, and yes," she is saying. "That's Josh." So, despite the fact that he annoys Esmé, it looks like Josh is developing the right skills for success in life.

3 INTEGRATE Skim the article, and match the article's subheadings to the sections.

A Organized and goal-driven
B Ready to turn ideas into action
C Confident but also need praise
D Have fun no matter what
E Know what they need to learn

4 IDENTIFY Review the subheadings in Exercise 3 and the words below. In which section of the article (1–5) do you think you will find each group of words (a–e)? Scan the article to check.

___ a positive feedback / hard work
___ b relaxed / popular
___ c new ideas / own achievement
___ d weak areas / good points
___ e tidy / lists

5 INTEGRATE Read the article in detail to complete the sentences with *Josh* or *Esmé*.

1 Other students don't like ________.
2 ________ is the child of the writer.
3 ________ gets excellent grades.
4 ________ is next to the writer.
5 ________ agrees that ________ is an overachiever.
6 ________ will probably be a success later in life.

6 WHAT'S YOUR ANGLE? Work in pairs. Review your answers to the quiz in Exercise 1. Is either of you an overachiever? Why? Why not? What about when you were children?

7 VOCABULARY Complete the phrases with the correct verb. Scan the article in Exercise 2 to check your answers.

do	make	make	miss	take	take

1 miss an **opportunity**
2 ________ **risks**
3 ________ the most of something
4 ________ a **difference**
5 ________ your best
6 ________ **advantage** of something

Oxford 3000™

8 BUILD Complete the sentences with the correct phrase from Exercise 7.

1 People who ________ are more successful in life.
2 I want to volunteer this summer to ________ in my community.
3 Never ________ to try something new.
4 My teacher told me to just ________ on the test.
5 If you want to achieve more, ________ any opportunities that appear, even small ones. You never know what they might lead to!
6 We have one hour to complete the assignment. Let's ________ of it.

9 INTEGRATE Choose four of the phrases in Exercise 7. Write a definition or example for each one. Then share your ideas with your group.

GRAMMAR IN CONTEXT Simple present, present continuous, and present perfect

We use the simple present to talk about:

- facts
  Laughter helps *us be more relaxed.*
- things that happen regularly
  Josh [1] ________ *A's.*

We use the present continuous to talk about:

- things happening now or around now
  My daughter [2] ________ *this over my shoulder.*
- things that are changing
  Josh [3] ________ *the right skills for success.*

We use the present perfect to talk about:

- experiences up to now
  They [4] ________ *a difference in the world.*
- things that have already or just happened
  They [5] ________ *already* ________ *lists.*

See Grammar focus on page 159.

10 IDENTIFY Scan the article for the Grammar in Context examples, and complete them in the box.

11 APPLY Choose the correct verb tenses to complete the profiles of these high achievers.

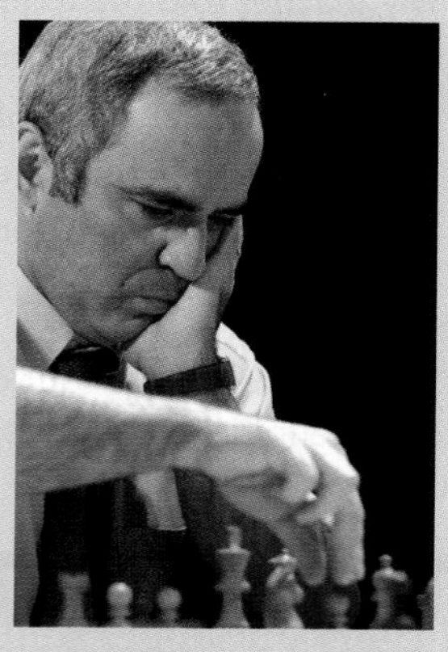

Garry Kasparov played his first game of chess at the age of six and won his first international tournament before he was 18. He [1] *is holding / holds* the record for being number one in the world of chess for the most years, and many [2] *are viewing / view* him as the best chess player of all time. Now middle-aged, he [3] *is still playing / has still played* chess with great success. He [4] *is recently playing / has recently played* against 30 chess players at the same time, winning all the games. He [5] *writes / has written* several books on chess.

Oprah Winfrey [6] *does / has done* many things over the years, including acting, hosting her own TV show, and running a company. She [7] *is even running / has even run* a marathon in under four and a half hours. Her childhood was difficult at times, but her experience [8] *shows / is showing* that difficulties can be overcome. The world is changing, and the number of women at the top of their profession [9] *increases / is increasing*. Many people say that Oprah [10] *has helped / helps* motivate many of these high-achieving women over the years.

12 IDENTIFY Find the sentences with incorrect verb forms, and correct them. There are four incorrect sentences.

1 I want to be a veterinarian ever since I visited my uncle's farm.

____

2 I'm afraid it is getting harder to get into top colleges.

____

3 Larry has exercised every morning to stay healthy and stress-free.

____

4 Diana has currently written a book about her volunteer work in Africa.

____

5 My sister is waiting for this promotion for more than a year.

____

6 I usually work until late on weekdays.

____

13 INTERACT Think of someone you know who has achieved a lot. Tell a partner about the person and their achievements. Do the people you both describe have the five qualities of overachievers described in the article in Exercise 2?

14 WHAT'S YOUR ANGLE? Complete the sentences with your own ideas. Then compare and discuss your sentences in a group. What can you learn from each other?

1 Taking risks makes life more...

exciting. I love not knowing what's going to happen next!

2 I never miss an opportunity to...

____

3 The best way to make a difference to other people is to...

____

4 It is more important to do your best than...

____

5 I have always made the most of...

____

6 Try to take advantage of every opportunity when you...

____

1.2 View from the Top

1 ACTIVATE Work in pairs. Complete the information about each structure with the cities and years in the box. Then match the structure to the view from its top (A–E).

Tokyo	Paris	New York City	Mecca	Dubai	2012	1931	1958	2010	1889

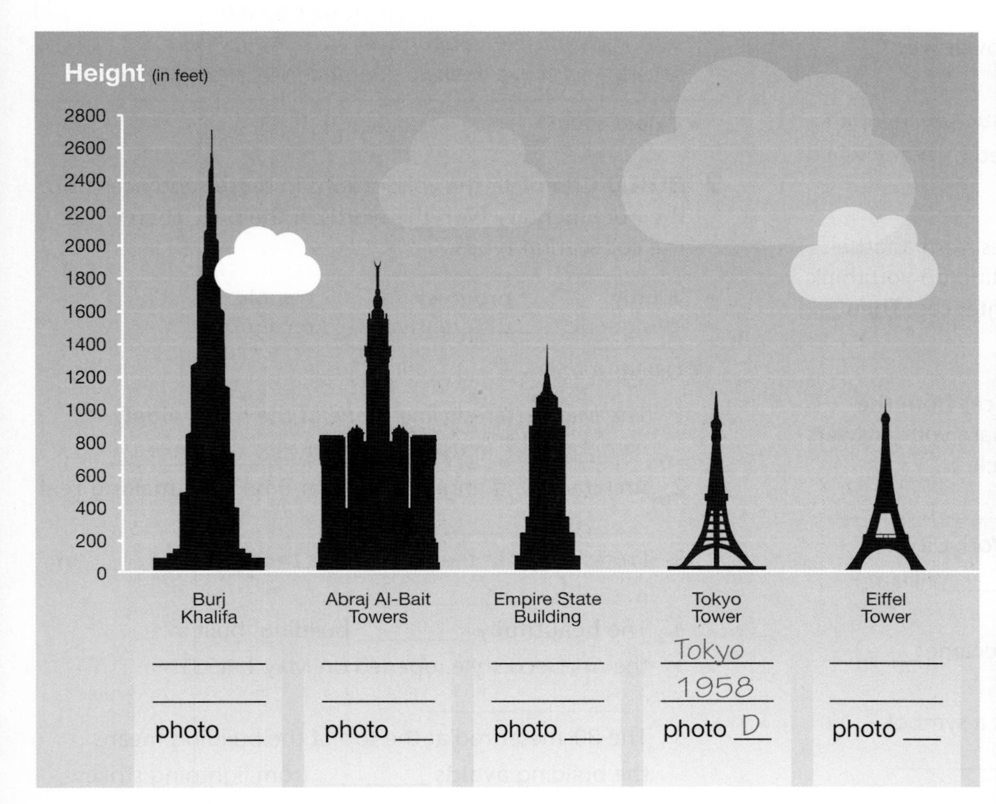

LISTENING SKILL Recognizing sentence stress and word boundaries

Speakers use sentence stress to make their message clearer. They stress the words that give the most important information. These words are often nouns, verbs, adjectives, and numbers.

Unstressed words are not usually as clear and easy to hear, and this can make word boundaries (where words start and end) difficult to hear. However, unstressed words (e.g., articles, prepositions, auxiliary verbs, etc.) are less important for the meaning of the sentences.

Sentence stress makes longer sentences sound shorter. The unstressed words between the important information are shortened. The number of stressed syllables usually indicates how long the sentence sounds.

It is still one of the tallest in New York.

2 ASSESS Now listen to part of a documentary about tall structures, and check your answers to Exercise 1.

3 WHAT'S YOUR ANGLE? Discuss the questions.

1. Have you or someone you know ever visited any of the towers mentioned in Exercise 2? When? Why? What did you or they do there?
2. Which towers would you like to visit? Put them in order of preference, and explain your reasons.

4 IDENTIFY Listen and write the sentences you hear.

5 **ASSESS** Read the sentences from the documentary. Predict the main stressed words. Then listen and check.

1 New York's Empire State Building held the title of the "world's tallest building."
2 The Burj Khalifa in Dubai became the world's tallest man-made structure in 2010.
3 The tallest of the towers is the third-tallest building in the world.
4 The design of this orange-and-white tower was influenced by the Eiffel Tower.
5 Built in 1958, it is the second-tallest structure in Japan.
6 Though much loved now, it was disliked by many when first built.

6 **INTEGRATE** Listen to three sentences from another part of the documentary. Which tall building do you think it is about? Listen again, and write the sentences. Then listen and underline the stressed words.

7 **IDENTIFY** Listen to five more sentences from the documentary, and complete them. Compare your answers with a partner. Then listen again and check.

1 _________ Empire State Building _________ _________ midtown Manhattan _________ New York City,
2 _________ _________ designed _________ William F. Lamb.
3 _________ 1933, _________ building became _________ worldwide icon.
4 The _________ _________ _________ is a symbol of both _________ _________ and the _________ _________.
5 Its _________ was a _________ _________, and it has _________ many around the _________.

8 **INTEGRATE** Watch the documentary, and complete the notes with numbers and dates.

VOCABULARY DEVELOPMENT Collocations

The English language has many collocations. These are combinations of words that go together more frequently and naturally than other words. Using these correctly helps your speech sound more natural.

Collocations are made with combinations of different word types. For example:

verb + noun: ***make contact*** *(NOT ~~do contact~~)*
verb + adverb: ***live dangerously*** *(NOT ~~live riskily~~)*
adverb + adjective: ***heavily guarded*** *(NOT ~~strongly guarded~~)*

Oxford 3000™

9 **BUILD** Complete the collocations in these sentences from the documentary with the words in the box. Then write the collocation types.

highly	progress	trouble
designed	differently	recognized

Oxford 3000™

1 The Manhattan skyline is one of the most **widely** recognized in the world. adverb + adjective
2 Architects and engineers at that time were **making real** _________. _________________
3 Professionals in the field always **thought** _________ **of** it. _________________
4 The **beautifully** _________ building, built in the Art Deco style, opened on May 1, 1931. _________________
5 The 20-meter rod at the top of the building means the building **avoids** _________ from lightning strikes. _________________
6 It has motivated many around the world to **think** _________ about what they too can do. _________________

The Empire State Building

Some basic facts

The location: Manhattan, New York
The year: 1931
The building: [1] ___ meters, [2] ___ floors
The people involved: William F. Lamb— the architect, more than [3] ___ workers ([4] ___ died)

Some interesting details

Construction: opened [5] ___ months ahead of schedule and [6] ___ million under budget.
Recognition: was world's tallest building for [7] ___ years. Ranked number [8] ___ on list by American Institute of Architects.
Movies: the movie King Kong used the building in [9] _________.
Tourists: [10] ___ million visit every year

10 **IDENTIFY** Choose the correct words to complete the collocations. Then listen and check.

1 Hard work does not *give* / *guarantee* / *take* success.
2 You should be *absolutely* / *obviously* / *heavily* certain you will succeed before you start.
3 Most people are *fully* / *perfectly* / *secretly* pleased when other people fail at something.
4 To achieve your academic goals, you have to take your studies *seriously* / *strongly* / *importantly*.
5 It is better to *make* / *find* / *acquire* knowledge rather than experience if you want to be successful.
6 We should stop worrying so much about achieving bigger and better things and learn to live *loosely* / *simply* / *easily*.

11 **WHAT'S YOUR ANGLE?** Explain which sentences from Exercise 10 you agree with and why.

GRAMMAR IN CONTEXT State verbs

Some verbs usually describe what we think, feel, experience, and possess. These are called state verbs, and we usually use them in simple tenses.

think: believe, agree, know, understand
Professionals always thought highly of it.
~~*NOT Professionals were always thinking highly of it.*~~
feel: like, love, hate, want
Tourists love the building.
~~*NOT Tourists are loving the building.*~~
experience: be, look, see, hear
Visitors see five different U.S. states.
~~*NOT Visitors are seeing five different U.S. states.*~~
possess: belong, have, own
The record belongs to an Australian.
~~*NOT The record is belonging to an Australian.*~~

See Grammar focus on page 159.

12 **IDENTIFY** Find the three sentences with state verb errors. Write the correct verbs.

1 The visitors love the design of the tower, but only two of them are wanting to go to the top. ______
2 More people are moving into tall buildings nowadays due to the rise in rents. ______
3 Some people are not believing it is healthy to live so high up. ______
4 The government wants to show how successful the country is by building the new tower. ______
5 Some companies like to rent office space in tall towers, but they aren't owning it. ______

13 **INTEGRATE** Complete the introduction to an article with the verbs in parentheses in the simple present, simple past, or present continuous.

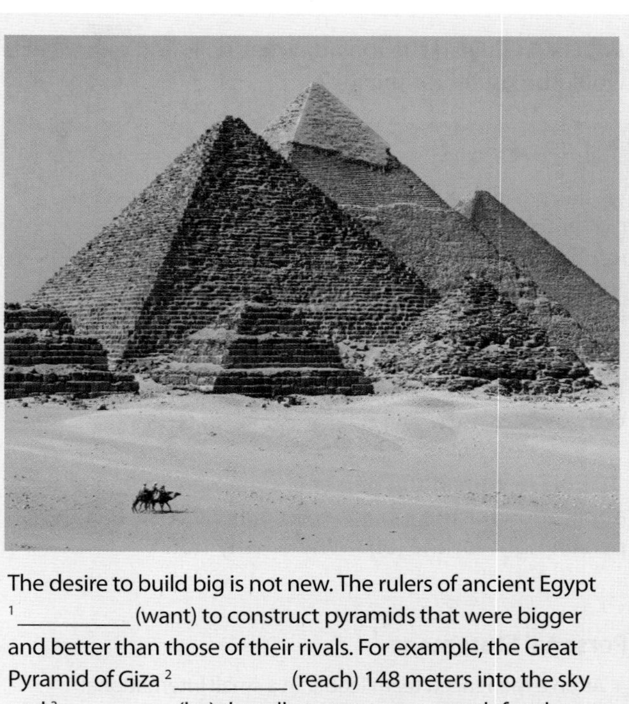

The desire to build big is not new. The rulers of ancient Egypt [1] ______ (want) to construct pyramids that were bigger and better than those of their rivals. For example, the Great Pyramid of Giza [2] ______ (reach) 148 meters into the sky and [3] ______ (be) the tallest structure on earth for almost 4,000 years.

Over the past 200 years, more and more people have moved to cities. City planners [4] ______ (know) from the start that the cheapest way to house all those people and the companies they worked in was to go upward. This [5] ______ (lead) to many unsafe buildings and dark streets in the developing industrial cities.

Today's cities [6] ______ (change) rapidly, but nowadays responsible planners [7] ______ (understand) more about the safety of buildings and the happiness of the people who live in them. Who [8] ______ (know) the design of our future buildings? Will they continue upward, or is there a new place for us to go, perhaps underground or even under the sea?

14 **WHAT'S YOUR ANGLE?** What do you think the next major engineering achievements will be? Write a list.

15 **INTERACT** Share your ideas from Exercise 14. Choose the two that are the most likely and tell the class.

1.3 Positive Impressions

1 ACTIVATE Read the job ad. What skills and experience would be useful for the job?

Project Planner

We are looking for a hardworking, well-organized person to manage a large project for our company. You will be responsible for planning the project, communicating with customers, and leading a team of twenty.

2 WHAT'S YOUR ANGLE? Would you apply for this job? Why or why not?

3 IDENTIFY Read the personal statement from an application for the job advertised in Exercise 1. Is the person right for the job? Why or why not?

Personal Statement

As an experienced team leader in a small international company, I have worked with several different teams, both within my department and in each of the company's international offices. Before entering the world of work, I studied business at the University of Michigan, graduating in 2015.

From my experience of planning and organizing demanding high-profile projects, I have developed strong skills in teamwork and people management. I can communicate effectively in English and Spanish, and I have used each language to build relationships and find solutions for customers on every project I have been involved with for the company.

My immediate goal is to gain a position in a larger company in which I can demonstrate and further develop my skills.

4 INTEGRATE Read the personal statement again, and check all the correct points in the checklist.

A personal statement…

- ☐ is a summary that goes with a job application or résumé.
- ☐ explains what is special about you.
- ☐ has clear sections focusing on different points.
- ☐ includes facts, experience, and future goals.
- ☐ can use *I* or *he* / *she*, but it must be consistent.
- ☐ should be about 100 to 150 words.

WRITING SKILL Using appropriate language

Using appropriate language with the correct tone helps your message be understood correctly.

To create a positive tone in a personal statement, use positive structures and words. Avoid negatives. Write about:

1. who you are
   As an experienced…
2. what you can offer
   I have a lot of experience…
3. what you want to do
   My immediate goal…

5 IDENTIFY Match the three points from the Writing Skill box to the paragraphs in the personal statement in Exercise 3.

First paragraph: ___
Second paragraph: ___
Third paragraph: ___

6 INTEGRATE Match the positive words and phrases from the personal statement to the less positive phrases.

LESS POSITIVE	POSITIVE
1 not a beginner ___	a further develop my skills
2 difficult and stressful ___	b gain a position in a larger company
3 had to learn how to work in groups ___	c developed strong skills in teamwork
4 deal with problems ___	d find solutions for
5 not work in a small company anymore ___	e experienced
6 learn the things I don't know now ___	f demanding, high-profile

GRAMMAR IN CONTEXT *Each* and *every*

1 We use *every* + singular noun to talk about all the people or things in a group of three or more.
Every job application *needs a personal statement.*

2 We use *each* + singular noun to talk about individual people or things in a group of two or more.
Each application *needs a specially written personal statement.*

3 We also use *every one* / *each* + *of* + *the* + plural noun/ pronoun with the same meaning as *each*. (However, we only use *every one* with three or more items.)
Each of the jobs *needs its own application.*
Every one of them *needs its own application.*

See Grammar focus on page 159.

7 IDENTIFY Find three examples of *each* and *every* in the personal statement in Exercise 3. Match them to the Grammar in Context points.

8 INTERACT Choose the correct words to complete the sentences. Then find examples of positive phrases in the sentences.

1 I have worked for several companies and learned a lot from *every* / *each* of them.
2 The job is demanding, but I have successfully dealt with each *challenge* / *challenges*.
3 Every *team* / *teams* needs a strong leader, and I believe I am that person.
4 I have received extremely positive comments about *every one of* / *every* project.
5 Every one of *them* / *they* is connected with business skills.

9 PREPARE Work in pairs. Tell your partner about a job you would like to have. Discuss skills and experience people need for the job. Take notes in the table.

Skills	Experience

10 WRITE Write your personal statement for the job you would like to have. Use the checklist to help.

☐ Use positive language.
☐ Include three sections (who you are, what you can offer, what you want to do).
☐ Match the statement to the job requirements.
☐ Write 100–150 words.

11 IMPROVE Review your partner's personal statement. Does it match each point on the checklist?

12 WHAT'S YOUR ANGLE? Read other classmates' personal statements. Which make a positive impression on you? Why?

Workers in a design workshop in Palermo, Italy

1.4 Asking the Right Questions

1

2

ENGLISH FOR REAL

1 ACTIVATE Look at the pictures. Guess the answers to the questions, and tell a partner.

1 Is the setting private or public?
2 Do the speakers know each other?
3 What is each speaker doing?
4 What is the purpose of the communication?

2 IDENTIFY Watch the video of an interaction at a career fair, and check your answers to Exercise 1. What information in the video did you use to check?

3 ASSESS Watch the video again, and take notes on what Kevin says to the company representative.

information Kevin gives ______________________

information Kevin inquires about ______________________

REAL-WORLD ENGLISH Making inquiries

We often make inquiries in a customer service or professional context. We usually don't know the other person in this situation. In these cases, we tend to use longer and more indirect ways of speaking than when talking to a friend. This is more polite and, therefore, more likely to get a good result.

I wonder if you could help.
Could / Can you help me please?
NOT ~~Help me.~~ / ~~I need help.~~

The person you are asking may also need background information. Clear, complete answers will make it easier for them to help you.

That's right. I'm a first-year student at Columbia University.
I'm a student, so I can only work evenings and weekends.

Be aware of the situation and the amount of time the inquiry is taking, especially if other people are waiting. Only ask the important questions, and go straight to the point.

Thanking the other person for their time ensures that you leave the person with a positive impression and more likely to follow up if necessary.

4 ANALYZE Work in pairs. Read the questions and sentences. Match them to functions A–D. How will the person listening to the question or sentence react?

A Making an inquiry
B Asking for help
C Thanking
D Giving information

1 I wonder if you could help. ___
2 Do you know how I can apply? ___
3 Thanks for your time. ___
4 Sorry to bother you again, but could you tell me the location? ___
5 I'm sorry, but that's not possible. They like to speak to the interviewee by phone. ___
6 Could the person text me instead? ___

5  **INTEGRATE** Work in pairs. The following questions are directed to a close friend. Rewrite them, so they become inquiries in a professional setting directed to someone you don't know. Then listen and compare.

1 Where is the office?
2 What time is the interview?
3 Call me tomorrow?
4 How do I get there?

6 PREPARE Work in pairs. Take turns making inquiries about job interviews. Ask for details about the information in the box. After you get the answer, thank the person for their time.

location	interview time
things to bring to the interview	name of interviewer
number of jobs available	deadline for application

7 INTERACT Work in pairs (A and B) to do a role play. Choose situation 1 or 2, and prepare what you will say. Then role-play the situation. Swap roles and repeat.

Situation 1

Student A: You are job hunting. You want to find out about the jobs a company is offering. You approach a company representative at a career fair.

Student B: Your company is hiring. You are one of the company representatives at a career fair. You are dealing with inquiries about the available jobs.

Situation 2

Student A: You want to learn a language. You need some information about a language course. You call a language school and talk to the manager.

Student B: You are the manager of a language school. One of your roles is to deal with course inquiries over the phone.

8 ANALYZE Get together with another pair, and repeat the role play. Get feedback.

9 WHAT'S YOUR ANGLE? When did you last make an inquiry? What was it about, and was the person you spoke to helpful?

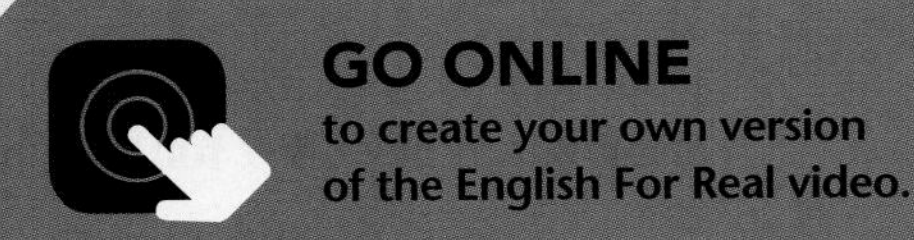

GO ONLINE
to create your own version of the English For Real video.

1.5 A Successful Interview

1 ACTIVATE Tell your partner about the last interview you had for work or study. Can you remember any questions from the interview?

2 IDENTIFY Listen to the job interview, and number the questions in the order you hear them.

___ a What do you consider your greatest achievement?
___ b Can you tell me about yourself?
___ c Where do you see yourself in five years?
___ d Could you tell us about something you have done to overcome a problem at work?

SPEAKING Answering interview questions

Interviews are usually formal situations, so formal language is necessary. Listen carefully to the question, and use similar language in your answer.

What do you consider your greatest achievement?
I think, to date, my greatest achievement has been to create an award-winning training course.

Answers normally require details and specific examples. If necessary, pause before answering to give yourself time to think, so your answers are clear and your language (tenses, use of articles, vocabulary, etc.) is accurate.

3 INTEGRATE Listen again, and take notes on how the candidate answers these questions. Compare your notes with a partner.

Can you tell me about yourself?

___

Could you tell us about something you have done to overcome a problem at work?

___

Where do you see yourself in five years?

___

PRONUNCIATION SKILL
Word stress in compound adjectives

Using the correct word stress with compound adjectives makes your English easier to understand and sound more natural.

Compound adjectives are usually stressed at the start when followed by a noun. When not followed by a noun, the stress is usually on the second part if the first word is an adverb or adjective.

He is a well-known person.	*It is a full-time job.*
He is well known.	*The job is full-time.*

4 IDENTIFY Find the stress on the compound adjectives in these sentences. Listen and check. Then listen again, and repeat the sentences.

1 I'd like to attend a part-time MBA program.
2 It's an award-winning course.
3 It's a five-hour session.
4 The company signed another two-year contract.
5 The clients were highly valued.

5 WHAT'S YOUR ANGLE? Use the compound adjectives in the box to make sentences about yourself. Remember to stress the words correctly.

part-time	full-time	hardworking
highly qualified	award-winning	open-minded
four-year	life-changing	

6 INTERACT Work in pairs. Listen to your partner's sentences from Exercise 5, and write the compound adjectives, marking the stress.

7 PREPARE Choose a job to interview for. Then review the questions in Exercise 2, and practice your answers. Think of two questions to ask the interviewer.

8 INTERACT Work in groups of three. Take turns playing the following roles.

A: You are the interviewer. Ask the four questions from Exercise 2. Then answer B's questions about the job.
B: You are the job candidate. Answer A's questions. Then ask two questions about the job.
C: Watch the interview and take notes of examples, numbers, success stories, and additional questions the candidate uses.

9 INTEGRATE In your group, share your notes on the interviews. Discuss the most successful answers.

What were they?
Why were they successful?

10 INTERACT Work with a new partner to do the interviews again. Which questions did you answer more successfully this time? Tell your partner.

Now go to page 147 for the Unit 1 Review

2 News

UNIT SNAPSHOT

What makes a news story?

Do you prefer to read, watch, or listen to the news?

Is 24/7 news good or bad for us? Why?

BEHIND THE PHOTO

REAL-WORLD GOAL

Find an interesting news story every day for a week

1 Which news do you follow most? Number the top three.

___ on my neighborhood
___ on my town or city
___ on my region of the country
___ other: ________________
___ on my country
___ on my continent
___ international

2 Why do you find news interesting? Compare and discuss your answers from Exercise 1 with a partner.

2.1 Read All About It

1 ACTIVATE Discuss the questions with a partner.

1 Which of these sections would you read first in a newspaper or on a news site?

2 Are there any parts of a newspaper you would never read? Why?

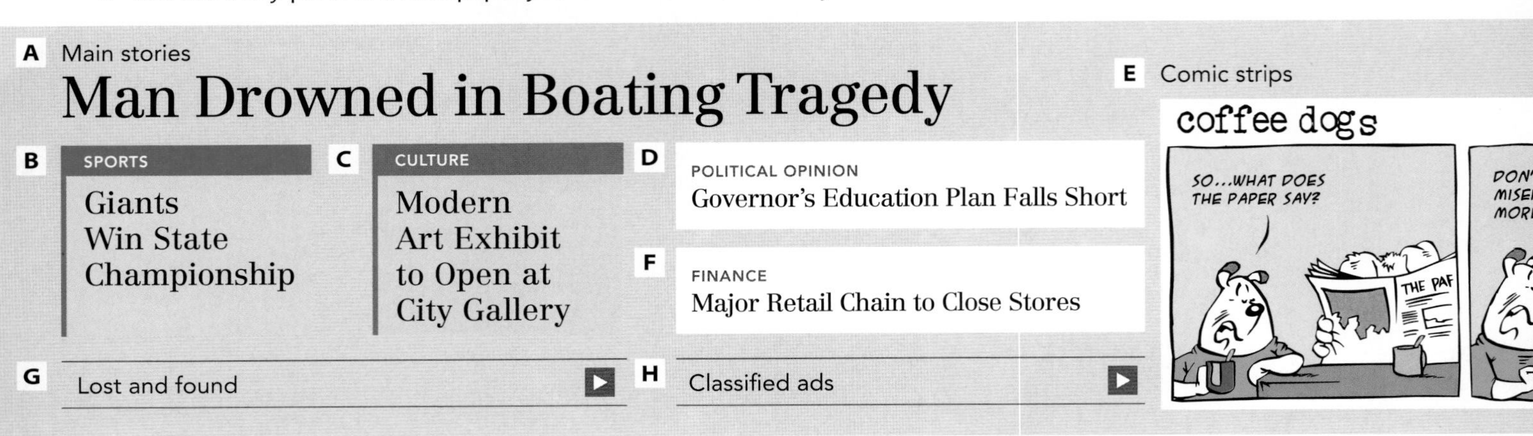

A Main stories

Man Drowned in Boating Tragedy

B SPORTS

Giants Win State Championship

C CULTURE

Modern Art Exhibit to Open at City Gallery

D POLITICAL OPINION

Governor's Education Plan Falls Short

E Comic strips

F FINANCE

Major Retail Chain to Close Stores

G Lost and found

H Classified ads

2 IDENTIFY When do you think the sections in Exercise 1 first appeared in newspapers? Write A–H on the timeline. Then scan the article to check your answers.

1800 ____________ 1900 ____________ 2000

The development of newspapers

1 ______________________________

Newspapers have changed the world. They have **brought down** governments, announced wars, and made people aware of issues like global warming. However, their reign may soon be over as sales fall and electronic news takes over. But how have they managed to be so important in our lives and for so long?

2 ______________________________

The story of modern newspapers started in Western Europe in the late 17th century. Newspapers came out weekly and mostly consisted of opinion pieces and some brief news items. Lost-and-found features were popular since up until then the main way of finding lost property had been to trust in magic. Later in the 18th century, advertisements were added, usually written in the same format as the news items.

3 ______________________________

Newspaper content, it seems, was initially fairly lightweight. However, at the time of the French Revolution at the end of the 18th century, newspaper content was becoming increasingly political. This led to a struggle between freedom and control. When they realized that newspapers were powerful and were forming opinion, governments acted by preventing radical and liberal journalists from expressing their political views. However, in the newly formed United States, cases such as John Peter Zenger's libel trial in 1735, after he had been in jail for almost a year, improved the freedom of the press. In France, the rulers attempted to stop newspapers from printing what they wanted, and this helped lead to the 1830 revolution in which journalists played an important part. Later, Karl Marx launched his career by writing newspaper articles in the 1840s, leading eventually to the Russian Revolution.

4 ______________________________

In the late 19th century, when the world was full of bad news, the newspapers started printing more stories to **distract** their readers—sensational stories such as sightings of the Loch Ness Monster in Scotland. By then, visuals had become important, starting with drawings and then photographs. Newspapers also began to include sports columns and, in North America, comic strips. By the middle of the 20th century, newspapers were becoming more or less what they are today.

5 ______________________________

But, in the era of multiple forms of media, will newspapers survive? It seems so. In fact, all the different forms of media seem to work together—we listen to the radio in the car, read a newspaper for more in-depth coverage, and watch television for dramatic pictures and light entertainment. Newspapers surely have a future even though they may be viewed on a screen rather than on paper.

—adapted from *Oxford Encyclopedia of the Modern World*, edited by Peter. N. Stearns

Oxford 3000™

READING SKILL Identifying topic sentences

The topic sentence indicates the main idea or point of a paragraph. Focusing on topic sentences first helps you understand the general theme and structure of the text more quickly. Then you can read for more detail.

The topic sentence is often the first in the paragraph. However, sometimes it is the second or final sentence. The other sentences in the paragraph provide supporting details, explaining and developing the topic further.

3 IDENTIFY Find the topic sentence in the first paragraph. Explain to a partner how you decided.

4 EXPAND Find the topic sentences in the other paragraphs. Compare your answers with a partner.

5 INTEGRATE Match the headings to each paragraph by skimming the paragraphs and using the topic sentences to help. (There is one extra heading.)

A A move toward entertainment
B The growing interest in ideas
C The importance of the paper
D The work and the writers
E A changing but successful future
F The early story

6 BUILD Read the text again. Focus on the supporting details, explanations, and examples. Decide if these sentences are true (T) or false (F) or if the information is not given (NG).

1 Early newspapers were mostly read by rich people. ___
2 The first newspaper was French. ___
3 Before newspapers, people often used magic to look for things they had lost. ___
4 John Peter Zenger went to prison for two years. ___
5 Comic strips first came out in South America. ___
6 Many thought people would stop reading newspapers because of television. ___

7 WHAT'S YOUR ANGLE? Discuss the questions.

1 Where do you get your news?
2 Has this news medium changed over the past few years? How? Why?
3 Where do you think we will get our news in the future?

8 VOCABULARY Review the highlighted verbs in the article. Then match the verbs to their definitions below.

Verbs	Definitions	Synonyms
1	to cause something to happen	
2	to make somebody lose power	
3	to begin an activity	
4	to tell people about something	
5	to direct someone's attention to something different	
6	to try to do something	
7	to become aware of something	
8	to make sure something doesn't happen	

9 IDENTIFY Match the synonyms to the verbs and definitions in Exercise 8.

cause	defeat	make known
aim to	set in motion	entertain
stop	recognize	

10 INTEGRATE Choose the correct verb to complete each question. Then ask your partner the questions. Use the verbs and synonyms from Exercises 8 and 9 to explain.

1 Which newspaper stories have *brought down* / *led to* / *attempted* changes in your country?
2 Who has successfully *launched* / *prevented* / *realized* their career through the media in your country?
3 How long do you think it will be before all newspapers *announce* / *distract* / *launch* that they are ending their print edition?
4 Can you think of news stories that have *brought down* / *distracted* / *attempted* high-profile personalities?
5 Do you think social media *leads to* / *distracts* / *announces* the public from real news stories?

GRAMMAR IN CONTEXT Narrative tenses: Simple past, past continuous, and past perfect

We use the narrative verb tenses to tell a story or talk about events in the past.

1 Main events—simple past:
*The story of newspapers **started** in Western Europe.*

2 Background events or longer actions interrupted by a shorter one— past continuous:
*When they realized newspapers **were driving** opinion, governments acted.*

3 Events happening earlier than the main events—past perfect:
*By then, visuals **had become** important.*

See Grammar focus on page 160.

11 IDENTIFY Match the narrative verb tense in bold in the extracts (a–c) with the rules (1–3) in the Grammar in Context box.

a ...by the middle of the 20th century, newspapers **were becoming** more or less what they are today. ___

b ...cases such as John Peter Zenger's libel trial in 1735, after he **had been** in jail for almost a year, established the freedom of the press. ___

c This **led** to a struggle between freedom and control. ___

12 EXPAND Find another example of each narrative tense in the article.

13 INTEGRATE Complete the story about someone hearing news for the first time. Use the correct form of the verb in parentheses. Then listen and check.

I [1] _________ (listen) to the radio in the kitchen. It was around seven, so I [2] _________ (make) breakfast. I [3] _________ (not sleep) well, so I was really tired, and I also remember that I [4] _________ (be) really hungry. (Funny what you remember about these moments when you look back!) And that's when I [5] _________ (hear) the news on the radio. I [6] _________ (not look) at the newspaper yet, so it [7] _________ (be) a total surprise. It's really strange because I [8] _________ (see) him on TV the day before. Anyway, I [9] _________ (make) my coffee and then [10] _________ (sit) down to read the newspaper to find out more.

14 WHAT'S YOUR ANGLE? Think of an example for each of the following types of news.

A major change in your country
The death of a famous person
An event that affected other countries

15 INTERACT Work in pairs. Share your examples from Exercise 14. Use the questions to find out more about your partner's news stories.

- Where were you when you heard the news?
- What were you doing?
- What had happened just before that?
- What did you do next?

School girls read a newspaper in Mbabane, Swaziland

2.2 Filling In the Detail

1 ACTIVATE For what reasons do famous people appear in the news? Think of at least three.

2 WHAT'S YOUR ANGLE? Which type of news involving famous people do you read? Why?

3 IDENTIFY Read the news report and choose the best headline in your opinion.

1 "We Are the Lucky Ones"
2 Help Goes to Those in Need
3 Billionaires to Give Away Fortunes

4 EXPAND Read the article again. Decide if the statements are True, False, or Not Given. Correct the false statements.

1 Judd Boyle and Antonia Benares are famous for giving their money to charity.

____

2 The couple has been traveling a lot to places that need help.

____

3 The motivation for giving away some of their fortune comes from the recognition that they are very lucky to be wealthy.

____

4 The couple intends to give lots of their money to hospitals because they have experience in the medical industry.

____

5 The couple will continue to travel to make sure the money reaches its destination.

____

NEWS

Home | Top news | World | Business | Science | Health

They have famous names, but they will never be seen in the same way again. Judd Boyle and Antonia Benares, the Internet billionaires well known for their parties and lifestyle, have announced that they will give away at least 50 percent of their fortune in the next ten years, starting in the next six months. Speaking at a news conference yesterday, they promised that the money would be spent on education or medicine. They said they are looking at either area in places that need the most help. Both billionaires have traveled a lot in the past year, visiting places in need, so the news was not a complete surprise.

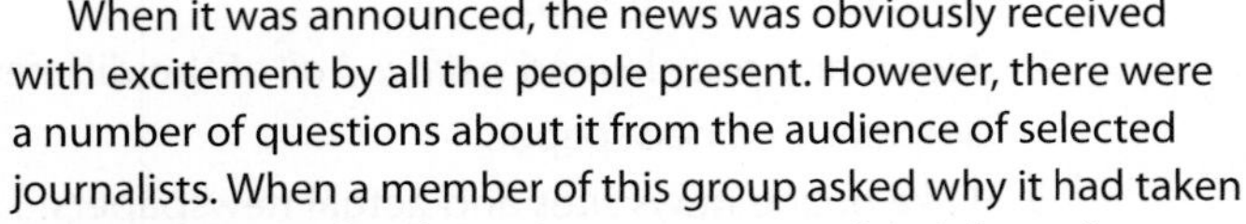

When it was announced, the news was obviously received with excitement by all the people present. However, there were a number of questions about it from the audience of selected journalists. When a member of this group asked why it had taken them so long to decide to give away some of their huge fortune, neither billionaire was prepared to answer. However, when asked about why they were doing it—were they doing it in order to help others or to improve their images—Antonia made a statement that explained their aim. "We both understand that we are the lucky ones. We both believe in the power of passion, and we want to use this to help those who are less fortunate than we are. To be honest, neither of us cares too much about our image. We know who we are, we know why we are doing it, so people can think whatever they like about us. It's really not important."

Boyle and Benares explained that they will give most of the money to projects in hospitals and schools. Either of these would be their first choice, but they are also thinking about helping local companies that work in these industries. The couple will also pay for the training of teachers and medical workers from local populations. Neither has experience in the medical or educational areas, so they are looking for experts to manage the work. However, the billionaires said they would work with the experts themselves, staying closely connected to make sure their donation has a real effect. Both want to ensure that all the money reaches its destination without any problems.

5 INTEGRATE Read the news report again and complete the notes in the plan for the report.

Section 1

Who: ____________ When: ____________
What: ____________ Where: ____________

Section 2

Reaction from others: ____________
Questions from others: ____________
Aims of the project: ____________

Section 3

The billionaires...
- will give money to ____________
- are looking for ____________
- will work with ____________
- want ____________

6 IDENTIFY Match the sections of the plan (1–3) in Exercise 5 to their content and purpose (a–c).

___ a Further information and closing—bringing the text to an end
___ b Reaction and quotes—helping readers to understand the context
___ c Lead information—the most important and interesting points

WRITING SKILL Using references and pronouns

Good writing avoids lots of repetition. Reference words and pronouns (e.g., *it, them, this, one*) help with this. Use these words to refer to nouns and phrases in the same sentence or other parts of the text.

*Boyle and Benares explained that **they** will give the money to projects...*
*When **it** was announced, the news was obviously received with excitement.*
*...the Internet billionaires well known for **their** parties and lifestyle...*

7 IDENTIFY Find the following words in the article. What do they refer to?

1 they (line 1) ____________
2 either area (line 8) ____________
3 it (line 13) ____________
4 this (line 14) ____________
5 us (line 20) ____________

8 EXPAND Find the following nouns in the article. What other words are used to refer to these?

1 hospitals and schools (line 21) ________
2 the couple (line 23) ________
3 all the money (line 26) ________

GRAMMAR IN CONTEXT
all, both, either, neither

We use the quantifiers *all, both, either,* and *neither* to identify the number of people or things we are referring to.

all: everything in a group of three or more
*The news was obviously received with excitement by **all** the people.*

both: two things in a pair
***Both** billionaires have traveled a lot in the past year.*

either: one or the other in a pair
***Either** of these would be their first choice.*

neither: not one and not the other in a pair
***Neither** billionaire was prepared to answer.*

See Grammar focus on page 160.

9 IDENTIFY Find another example of each quantifier in the news report. What does each quantifier refer to? How many people or things does each refer to?

10 INTEGRATE Choose the correct quantifier for each sentence.

1 I enjoyed reading *both / either* news stories, but yesterday's was better.
2 Not many people read *neither / all* of the different sections in a newspaper.
3 I like online news sites and actual newspapers. I read *neither / either*—it depends where I am.
4 *Neither / Either* news report had much detail about the story.
5 I get the news from *all / both* types of media, including radio and print.

11 APPLY Complete the sentences with the correct quantifier.

1 Can I borrow today's newspaper from ___ of you?
2 ___ reporter was present during the news conference.
3 The article was read by ___ the people in the department before it was published.
4 ___ the *Times* and the *Post* reported the same details.
5 I can't find the information I need. ___ source is reliable.

12 PREPARE Work in pairs. Think of a recent story in the news. With your partner, complete a plan similar to the one in Exercise 5. Can you remember any quotes about the news or find them online? If not, imagine what people said about the news.

13 WRITE Work on your own. Write the news report. Use the checklist to help.

- ☐ Follow the plan.
- ☐ Include a headline.
- ☐ Write three paragraphs.
- ☐ Use references and pronouns.
- ☐ Use *all*, *both*, *either*, and *neither*.
- ☐ Write 200–300 words.

14 IMPROVE Review your partner's report. Does it follow the plan?

15 SHARE Read other classmates' news reports. Which kept you reading to the end? Why?

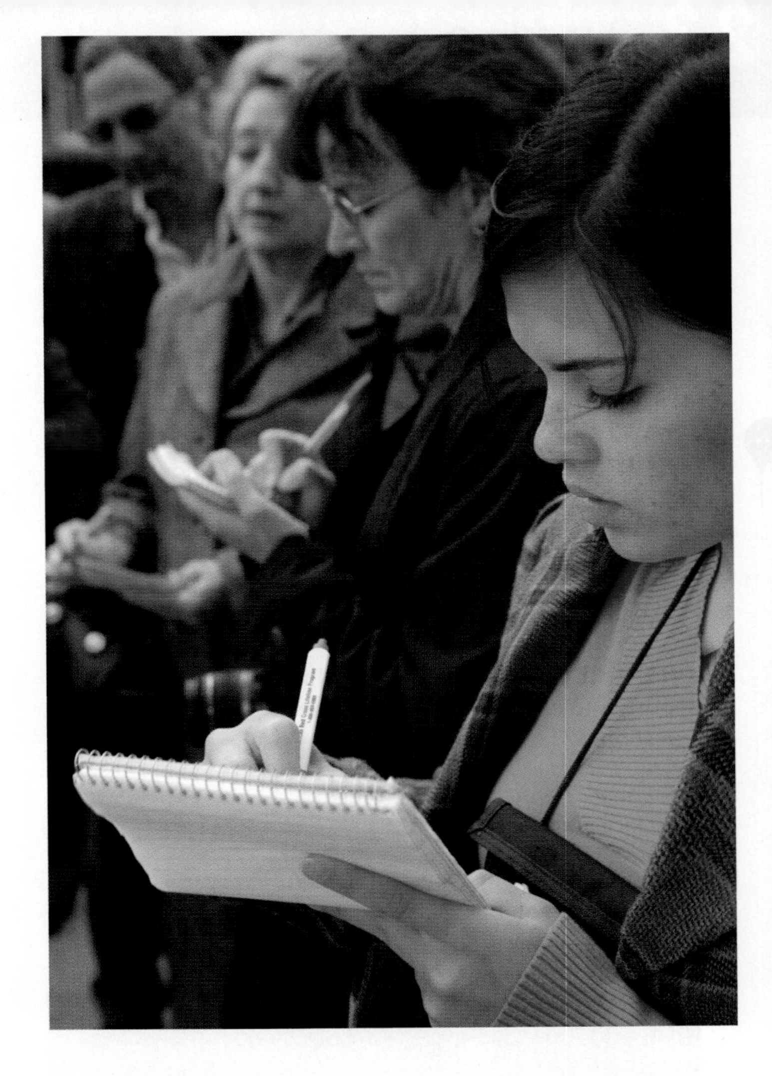

2.3 At the Scene

1 ACTIVATE Read the dictionary definition. What makes a news story newsworthy? List at least three things.

> **newsworthy**
>
> (ADJECTIVE)
>
> interesting and important enough to be reported as news

2 WHAT'S YOUR ANGLE? Discuss the questions.

1 When was the last time you discussed something in the news with anyone?
2 What was the news?
3 Why did you talk about it?

3 PREPARE Read the words and phrases from a news report, and look at the picture. Then answer the questions.

New Year's Eve	Dubai	tower
spectacular fireworks	flames and smoke	

1 Do you remember the story?
2 What (do you think) happened?
3 What (do you think) made the story newsworthy?

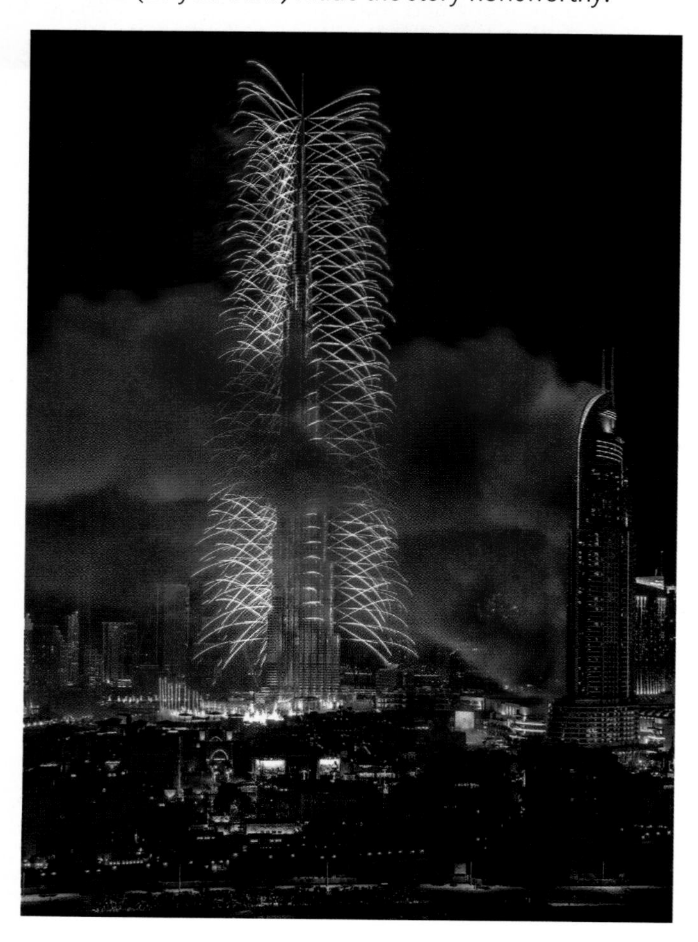

LISTENING SKILL
Recognizing linkers in fast speech

Recognizing linkers (e.g., *but, and, so, or, while, as*) helps you understand the connections between the speaker's ideas.

Linking phrases and words are sometimes unstressed in fast speech. This can make them less clear. Listen carefully for how the ideas are joined.

...it started just before midnight while we were waiting...
...we had a table reservation, but our plans obviously changed.

4 NOTICE Read the extracts from a news report and predict which linker is used. Then listen to the extracts and choose the correct linker.

1 ...they were shocked, *and* / *but* / *when* they realized they were looking at a...
2 ...been a disaster, *but* / *as* / *then* the good news is that there were apparently no serious injuries...
3 ...the fire services were able to clear the place *while* / *and* / *so* they put out the fire...
4 ...we were waiting for the fireworks to begin, and it was then *that* / *so* / *but* we saw people pointing.

5 EXPAND Read these extracts from the news report, and predict which linker is used. Then listen and complete the extracts.

1 ...out of the building and ________ we saw flames...
2 ...we saw people pointing, ________ we looked across...
3 I was worried about different things, for example, the traffic ________ how I was going to get home.
4 We were just making little movies to show our friends ________ we were waiting...

6 INTEGRATE Listen to the news report, and complete each sentence with one or two words you hear.

1 People watching the fireworks show were shocked to see a ________________.
2 Even though the building was very big, there were ________________ injuries.
3 Rosa was waiting in a ________________ to see the show.
4 Rosa was about ________________ from the actual fire.
5 Ronald and his wife had a ________________ at the hotel that evening.
6 Amir felt ________________ about going to see the event.
7 Amir spent the time before the show making ________________ for friends.

7 WHAT'S YOUR ANGLE? Have you ever seen a newsworthy event in real life? What happened?

GRAMMAR IN CONTEXT *was / were going to*

We can use *was / were going to* to talk about future events from a point of view in the past. The events may or may not actually happen.

*They **were going to** see a fireworks display.*

Using *but* shows the events definitely didn't happen.

*We **were going to** go, but, in the end, we stayed home.*

See Grammar focus on page 160.

8 ASSESS Read and listen to three extracts from the news report. Then answer the two questions for each extract.

A Yes, that's right…We were going to watch from inside the hotel because we had a table reservation, but our plans obviously changed…

B I wasn't going to come, you know…I was worried about different things, for example, the traffic and how I was going to get home, but, unfortunately, my friend persuaded me.

C Thousands of us had been waiting for hours at the site, knowing we were going to see something spectacular.

1 What was the original plan or idea?
2 Did it actually happen?

9 INTEGRATE Match the sentence parts. Did the event in the first part of each sentence happen or not? Or is it impossible to tell? Explain your answers to a partner.

1 The reporter was going to interview me, ___
2 The police were going to cancel the event ___
3 The hotel was going to be closed for a few months ___
4 Many people were planning to come later, ___
5 The hotel was going to have a big event the next day. ___

a to be redecorated.
b but they stayed home in the end.
c but she didn't have enough time.
d However, this was canceled.
e and send everyone home.

VOCABULARY DEVELOPMENT Comment adverbs

Comment adverbs give the speaker's point of view about an action or event. Other types of adverbs often describe the action or event itself. Compare the following:

*Comment adverb: **Luckily**, there were no injuries.*

*Other types of adverb: Many people **usually** go to the event. / They put out the fire **quickly**.*

Comment adverbs usually go at the start of sentences. They can sometimes go in the middle but less often at the end. They are usually separated from the sentence by commas or pauses.

*People, **apparently**, were making videos.*

*People were making videos, **apparently**.*

10 BUILD Read the sentences in each pair. Discuss with a partner the difference in their meaning.

1 **Unfortunately**, we were late. / **Luckily**, we were late.
2 **Naturally**, not many people went. / **Curiously**, not many people went.
3 **Surprisingly**, it was all over the news. / **Obviously**, it was all over the news.
4 **Apparently**, it cost a lot of money. / **Sadly**, it cost a lot of money.

Oxford 3000™

11 IDENTIFY Which adverb from Exercise 10 completes each of these extracts from the news report in Exercise 6? Listen and check.

1 There were, _________, no serious injuries.
2 _________, given the size of the building, the fire services were able to clear the place.
3 _________, we thought it was the fireworks.
4 It was scary, _________.
5 _________, everyone got out safely.
6 …but, _________, my friend persuaded me.

12 WHAT'S YOUR ANGLE? Rewrite each sentence with a comment adverb so that it shows your point of view. Use the correct punctuation.

1 We have 24/7 news coverage nowadays.
2 People are interested in finding out about famous people.
3 Most of the news we see is bad news.
4 People are more emotionally affected by local or national news.

13 INTERACT Compare your sentences from Exercise 12, and discuss your points of view with a partner.

2.4 You'll Never Guess What...

1

2

ENGLISH FOR REAL

1 ACTIVATE Look at the pictures. Guess the answers to the questions and tell a partner.

1 Do the speakers know each other?
2 Is this a professional call or an informal call?
3 Was the woman expecting the call?

2 IDENTIFY Watch the video and check your answers for Exercise 1. What clues (verbal or nonverbal) in the video helped you answer the questions?

3 ANALYZE Watch the video again. Take notes on the two pieces of news Andy gives Anna. Which news is good, and which is bad?

First piece of news: ______________________________
____

Second piece of news: ______________________________
____

REAL-WORLD ENGLISH Giving and reacting to news

How we share our news with people we know can depend on whether the news is good or bad. In both cases, we usually "set the scene" for the listener before we give the actual news.

Have you heard the good / bad news?
I've got to tell you something.

When the news is good, we often show our excitement to get the listener involved.

I've got some great news.
You'll never guess what... Something amazing has happened!

When the news is not good on a personal level, we may want to warn the person before giving the actual news. This can help to "soften" the bad news.

I'm afraid I've got some bad news.
I don't know how to say this, but...

When we react to news, we often start by showing our surprise and then follow with our reaction.

Reacting to good news: Really? That's great! / How exciting! / I'm so pleased for you.
Reacting to bad news: I don't believe it. How awful. / That's terrible. / I'm so sorry.

4 ▶ **ANALYZE** Watch the video again. Write the phrases Andy and Anna use to do the following:

1 give the good news ________________

2 react to good news ________________

3 break the bad news ________________

4 react to bad news ________________

5 **INTEGRATE** Work in pairs. Take turns using the same phrases from Exercise 4 that Andy uses to give his news and Anna uses to react to the news.

6 **INTERACT** Work in pairs. Take turns giving the following news. You are good friends: one of you breaks the bad news; the other reacts appropriately.

Classes today are canceled.

You have won a lot of money.

Your friend failed the exam.

The apartment you share was robbed.

Another friend is joining you both on a weekend trip.

Someone wants to buy your friend's car.

You won a prize both you and your friend were competing for.

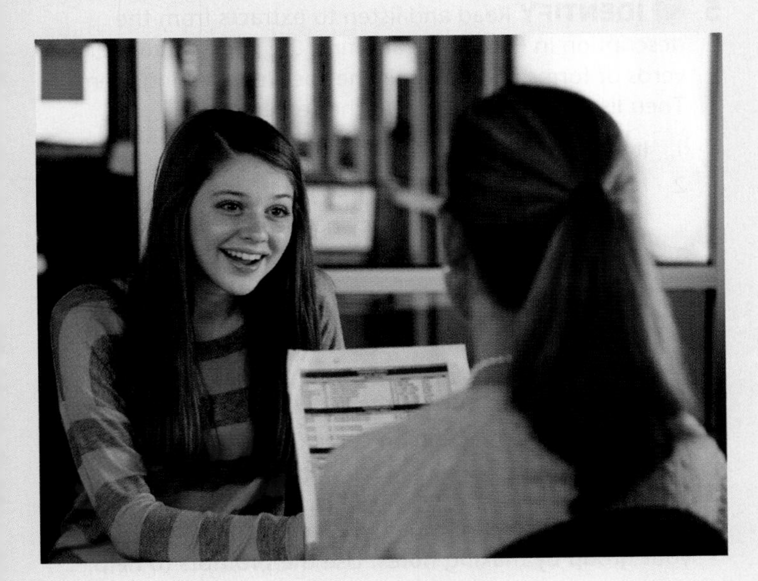

7 **PREPARE** Work in a new pair. Choose one of the situations from Exercise 6. Add more detail to the situation.

Decide:

- how long you have known each other
- how well you know each other
- how each of you feels about the situation (the same or different?)
- where you are when you share the news

8 **INTERACT** Work with another pair. Present the details of the situation you chose in Exercise 7, and do the role play while the other pair watches. Get feedback.

9 **WHAT'S YOUR ANGLE?** Think about the last piece of good news you received. What was it about, and who did it come from? How did you respond?

GO ONLINE
to create your own version of the English For Real video.

2.5 What an Experience!

1 ACTIVATE Look at the pictures. Discuss the questions.

1 Which of these activities have you done or would you like to do? Why?
2 Which one are you least likely to do in the future? Why?

snowboarding

riding a motorcycle

hot-air ballooning

skydiving

parasailing

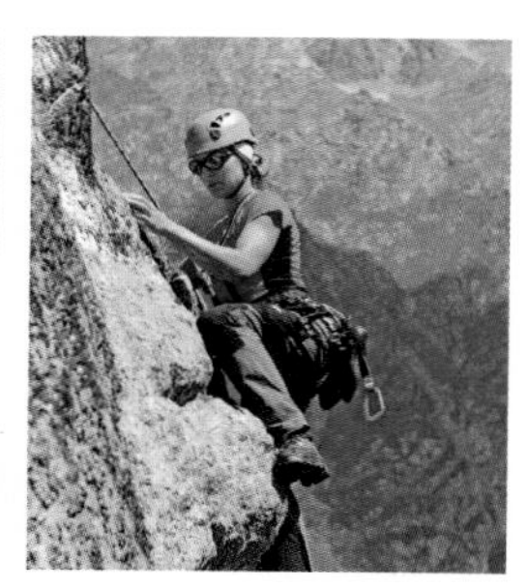

rock climbing

2 🔊 **IDENTIFY** Listen to someone describing an exciting experience. Which activity is she describing?

SPEAKING Describing an event

Different tenses are necessary to describe the background, details, and actions of an event. Use sequencing words to make the order of actions clear.

For actions before the event, use past perfect.

*…but actually, they **had bought** me something.*

Use past simple for facts and feelings and to describe the events or actions.

*It **was** my graduation. Anyway, I **was** a little bit down…*
*It **was** amazing…Once I **got over** feeling scared, the view **was** unbelievable.*

Use past continuous for events happening at the same time.

*My family **was watching** my reaction.*

3 🔊 **IDENTIFY** Listen again and note down details of the speaker's experience.

4 INTERACT Work in pairs. Use your notes to retell the story to your partner. If you are listening, check your notes for missing details. Then change partners and change roles.

PRONUNCIATION SKILL
Stressed auxiliary verbs and forms of *be*

Affirmative auxiliary verbs (e.g., *be*, *do*, *have*) are not usually stressed. However, we can stress them if we want to add to the meaning of the sentence, for example, to contradict or show surprise.

*I thought she hadn't booked the trip, but I was wrong. She **had** booked it.*

We can also add a stressed auxiliary where we don't usually use an auxiliary (e.g., in affirmative statements in the simple present or simple past) to make our point more clearly.

*You're wrong. He **did** want to go on the trip.*

And remember, we always stress auxiliary verbs or the verb *be* in short answers.

Did you go? *Yes, I **did**.*
Was it exciting? *Yes, it **was**.*

5 🔊 **IDENTIFY** Read and listen to extracts from the description in Exercise 2, and find the stressed auxiliary verbs or forms of *be*. Why is the speaker stressing them? Then listen again and repeat the sentences.

1 It was my birthday…Sorry, no, it wasn't.
2 I thought my family hadn't bought me a present to celebrate, but actually, they had bought something.
3 I thought it would be difficult to relax. But I did manage to.
4 Despite what people might say about the peace and quiet, it was noisy.
5 My family didn't go on the trip with me, but they were watching my reaction on camera back home.

6 PREPARE Think of an interesting experience you or someone you know has had. Get ready to describe it to your group by making notes. Use the prompts to help.

who/what/when/why/where
surprising or unexpected
adjectives

7 INTERACT Work in groups of three.

Take turns describing your experience. Make your description interesting with details, adjectives, and effective use of stressed words.
When it is your turn to listen, ask questions at the end to find out more detail and explore the person's feelings.

8 WHAT'S YOUR ANGLE? Did anyone have similar experiences? What was the most exciting/scary/funny experience?

Now go to page 148 for the Unit 2 Revie

3 Frontiers

UNIT SNAPSHOT

Why do people go to new places?

Which areas have humans explored? How?

How do people feel when they cross a frontier?

BEHIND THE PHOTO

1 Answer the questions.

1 If you were going to explore an area of the world, where would you go and why?
I would go to New Zealand or somewhere else with lots of beautiful scenery. I love wild places and love going hiking in the mountains.
2 What are the benefits of exploring? Who benefits most?
3 What are the problems? Who faces them?

2 Discuss your answers with a partner. Do you have similar views?

REAL-WORLD GOAL

Visit somewhere you have never been before

3.1 End of the Road?

mountains

ice

underwater

underground

1 ACTIVATE What kind of people make good explorers? What are they like? What do they do?

2 WHAT'S YOUR ANGLE? Imagine that you are on an exploration team. What skills do you have that would be useful?

3 VOCABULARY Complete the description of successful explorers with the words in the box.

independent	explore	quit	practical
survive	set off	keep going	flexible

Oxford 3000™

Successful explorers…

- [1] _________ to [2] _________ with hope, energy, and positive feelings.
- know how to [3] _________ when things get tough.
- [4] _________ even when other people go back.
- don't like to [5] _________ but know that sometimes it is necessary.
- are [6] _________ and are not afraid of changing their plans.
- are [7] _________—they listen to others, but they make their own decisions.
- are [8] _________—they know how to take care of themselves and others.

4 INTERACT Discuss the questions with a partner.

1 Which ideas from the description in Exercise 3 did you mention in Exercises 1 and 2?

2 Which three ideas about explorers do you most agree with?

5 INTEGRATE Listen to the first part of a talk about modern-day exploration. Which skills and qualities from Exercise 3 are mentioned?

LISTENING SKILL
Recognizing rephrasing in a talk

Speakers often use specific topic words and ideas that may not be familiar to the audience. They usually rephrase these to help the listener understand. Sometimes they do this immediately.

*Would you make **a good explorer**? Do you want to **find out about the world, push back frontiers, discover new places**?*

Sometimes they use signals to show they are rephrasing. Listen for these, for example:

in other words *that is* *by that I mean*
to put it another way

6 IDENTIFY The speaker rephrases the three key points in the first part of her presentation. Can you remember how she did this? Match the original phrases to the rephrasing signals and to the rephrasing. Then listen again and check.

	Rephrasing signal	Rephrasing words
1 make a commitment	to put it another way	take in everything… going on around you…rather than just…looking ahead
2 be aware of your surroundings	by that I mean	the person to turn to…
3 be in control	in other words	make a decision…stick to it…get through the really bad times

7 **INTEGRATE** Review the key facts and predict the answers. Then listen to the rest of the talk and check.

! Key facts

- Caves discovered in the world: about [1] ___%
- Earth's surface covered by ocean: about [2] ___%
- Unexplored ocean: about [3] ___%
- Life under Antarctic ice: up to [4] ___ million years old
- Money spent on brain research in Europe per year: over € [5] ___

GRAMMAR IN CONTEXT
Verbs + *to* infinitive or *-ing* form

Some verbs can take the *-ing* form or the *to* infinitive with little or no change in meaning. For example: *attempt, begin, can't stand, continue, hate, like, love, prefer, start.*

*Do you **like to be** in control? / Do you **like being** in control?*

Other verbs can take both the *-ing* form or the *to* infinitive but with a clear difference in meaning. For example: *stop, forget, remember.*

*Do you **stop to look**? (Do you stop doing something because you want to look?)*
*Do you **stop looking**? (Do you no longer look at what you were looking at before?)*

See Grammar focus on page 161.

8 **IDENTIFY** Work in pairs. Is there a difference in meaning in the sentences in each pair? What is it?

1. He stopped to talk to me. / He stopped talking to me.
2. She forgot meeting them. / She forgot to meet them.
3. I prefer traveling alone. / I prefer to travel alone.
4. He remembered visiting the place. / He remembered to visit the place.
5. She began to explain. / She began explaining.

9 **INTEGRATE** Read the extracts from the talk. Choose the verb form the speaker used. Then listen and check.

1. …we need to stop *to worry* / *worrying* about being the first to go somewhere.
2. …they forgot *to look* / *looking* and *learn* / *learning* about where they were.
3. … people will continue *to explore* / *exploring* forever, inward and outward…
4. …we should remember *to leave* / *leaving* the place as we find it…

10 **WHAT'S YOUR ANGLE?** Look at the areas for exploration in the pictures in this lesson and answer the questions.

1. Which areas should we continue exploring? Why?
2. Which should we definitely stop exploring? Why?
3. What other areas should we start to explore? Why?

the human mind

DNA

artificial intelligence

11 **INTERACT** Share your answers to the questions in Exercise 10 in a group. Try to agree on the top two areas for each answer.

3.2 Who Went Where?

1 ACTIVATE Match the dates, nationalities, and areas of exploration to the people shown in the pictures.

1934–1968	1903–1941	1910–1997
1868–1926	1866–1955	1914–1986
Soviet	British	French
American	British	Nepalese
desert	the Arctic	space
air	sea	mountains

1 Amy Johnson
1903–1941
British
air

2 Jacques Cousteau

3 Matthew Henson

4 Yuri Gagarin

5 Tenzing Norgay

6 Gertrude Bell

2 IDENTIFY Work in pairs. Match the sentences (a–f) to the people in Exercise 1 (1–6). Then discuss the meaning of the words in bold.

a He was a **pioneer** in marine exploration and filmmaking, making the first French underwater film and helping to develop modern diving techniques. ___

b She was a brilliant **aviator**, being the first woman to fly solo from Britain to Australia. ___

c He was the first human to go into outer space and around the Earth, completing an **orbit** on April 12, 1961. ___

d She explored many areas of the Middle East, making friends and developing strong **bonds** with many leaders there. ___

e He made several **voyages** to the Arctic and was part of one of the first teams to reach the Geographic North Pole. ___

f He is one of the most famous climbers in history and the first person to reach the **summit** of Mount Everest. ___

READING SKILL
Working out meaning from context

Knowing how to use context to deal with new words will help your reading become faster as you will need to look up words less often.

Use the text around the new word to figure out its meaning. What is the topic of the sentence and the paragraph? What other words are linked to the new one?

*He was a **pioneer** in marine exploration and filmmaking, making the first French underwater film and helping to develop modern diving techniques.*

Use the word form and the grammar of the sentence to understand the function of the word. Does it have a prefix or suffix? Is it a verb, a noun, etc.?

*She was a brilliant **aviator**.* (*-or* = noun suffix often indicating the noun is a person)

Avoid using a dictionary to check the meaning of a lot of words, especially the first time you read. Use the context and improve your deduction skills. Check in a dictionary later to get a more precise definition.

3 EXPAND Review your answers to Exercise 2. Then use a dictionary to check the precise meaning of the words in bold.

4 WHAT'S YOUR ANGLE? From the facts in Exercise 2 and any information you know about the people in Exercise 1, which person would you most like to have been?

5 INTEGRATE Skim the topic sentences in the article below to help.

1 What kind of explorers is the article about?
2 What kinds of difficulties did these explorers face?

6 APPLY Work in pairs. Find the words in the box in the article. Then use the steps to figure out the meaning of each word.

fascinating (line 12)	obligations (line 30)
confront (line 14)	self-educated (line 39)
repressive (line 17)	

1 Read the sentences around the word, and decide on the topic and key words.
2 Identify the part of speech of the word and its use in the sentence.
3 Discuss the possible meaning of the word.
4 Check the precise meaning in a dictionary.

7 EXPAND Find three more words you do not know in the article. Use the steps in Exercise 6 to figure out their meaning.

8 INTEGRATE Read the article in detail, and write short answers to the questions.

1 What change has happened over the past 40 years?
2 What did the women's movement do?
3 What did the female explorers' journals show?
4 What were some practical ways in which women explorers were ignored?
5 What factors did many female explorers share?
6 What does the writer conclude about male and female explorers?

Discovering explorers

What do Christopher Columbus, Captain Cook, and Marco Polo have in common? Yes, they were all famous explorers—and they were all male explorers, as are most of the well-known ones. However, women have a significant place in the history of **exploration**, and interest in female explorers has been rising since the 1980s. The very real achievements of female explorers, like Mary Kingsley, are finally getting the recognition they deserve. (5)

Why have attitudes changed? One explanation is that the women's movement of the 20th and 21st centuries has increased interest in women's **accomplishments**. Also, their journals provide fascinating stories; these women appeared to enjoy facing danger, showing a willingness to confront wild animals, extreme weather, hostile natives, injury, and illness. Their confidence and commitment are an **inspiration** to today's women. It is often shocking to read about the attitudes they faced, especially in repressive Victorian Britain. For example, women were constantly denied recognition for their achievements. When the Liverpool Geographical Society wanted to learn about Mary Kingsley's explorations in West Africa, her paper was read aloud by a man while she sat in the background, as the organization would not allow women to speak. Equally shocking is the fact that membership of the New York Explorers' Club was male-only until 1981. (10, 15, 20, 25)

So, what were these women explorers like? Apart from having strong personalities and being intelligent and practical, they were usually middle-aged or beyond, having gained their independence after fulfilling family **obligations**, such as looking after elderly parents. In fact, one attraction for many women was the possibility of escape from a lifetime of service. They were usually unmarried, as few husbands would consider giving permission for their wives to pursue such a profession. They were also rich enough to afford to pay for their trips (**sponsorship** was usually not possible for women) and sufficiently educated and experienced to deal with the inevitable **complications** that arose. Mary Kingsley fits this profile. Unmarried, smart, and self-educated, Mary took care of her family while her father went on explorations. Only when both her parents died and her brother moved away was Mary finally able to begin her own explorations. (30, 35, 40)

Now that the contributions of these women are finally revealed, in the context of their gender their achievements appear to be even more remarkable than those of their more famous male counterparts. While they didn't discover America, they made significant discoveries, but above all they showed that women can overcome impossible challenges to achieve **greatness**. (45)

—adapted from *The Oxford Companion to World Exploration*, edited by David Buisseret

Oxford 3000™

VOCABULARY DEVELOPMENT Suffixes for nouns

Recognizing suffixes can help you identify nouns and understand their meaning.

*explora**tion***	*personal**ity***	*achieve**ment***
*confid**ence***	*member**ship***	*willing**ness***

Using suffixes to make nouns will increase your vocabulary by allowing you to create new words from the basic ones you know (such as verbs and adjectives).

*However, women have a significant place in the history of **exploration**, and interest in female **explorers** has been rising since the 1980s.*

9 IDENTIFY Find all the examples of nouns with these suffixes in the article. Which suffixes are mainly added to verbs? Which to adjectives? Which to other nouns?

1 *-tion*: ________________
mainly added to ____________
2 *-ment*: ________________
mainly added to ____________
3 *-ness*: ________________
mainly added to ____________
4 *-ence*: ________________
mainly added to ____________
5 *-ity*: ________________
mainly added to ____________
6 *-ship*: ________________
mainly added to ____________

10 BUILD Add suffixes to the words in the box, and complete the sentences with the best word.

contribute	different	encourage

1 With _________, everyone can achieve their goals.
2 We all want to be recognized for our _________ to the world.
3 The ways we are the same are more important than our _________.

happy	friend	secure

4 We should focus on safety and _________, not adventure and exploration.
5 Family and _________ are more important than money and fame.
6 To have _________ we must have freedom.

11 WHAT'S YOUR ANGLE? Which sentences from Exercise 10 do you agree with? Why?

GRAMMAR IN CONTEXT
Verbs + *-ing* form and verbs + *to* infinitive

We use the *-ing* form only after certain verbs, for example:

admit, avoid, consider, deny, finish, practice, suggest

*Few husbands would **consider giving** permission for their wives to do this.*

We use the *-ing* form after verbs that talk about likes and dislikes, for example:

can't stand, enjoy, hate, like, (don't / doesn't) mind, prefer

*These women appeared to **enjoy facing** danger.*

We can also use the *to* infinitive with some of these verbs, for example:

like, hate, love

*She **liked to travel** to new places.*

We use the *to* infinitive after other verbs, for example:

afford, agree, aim, allow, choose, decide, demand, expect, hope, manage, need, offer, plan, want

*They were also rich enough to **afford to pay** for their trips.*

See Grammar focus on page 161.

12 INTEGRATE Complete the article about a female explorer with the correct forms of the verbs in parentheses.

Jeanne Baret (1740–1807)

Jeanne Baret managed [1] _________ (do) something no woman had done before: she completed a voyage around the world. However, she did this dressed as a man since no women were allowed [2] _________ (travel) on French Navy ships in those days. So, to avoid [3] _________ (be) thrown off the ship, Baret put on men's clothes and became Jean instead of Jeanne.
It is not clear when Baret's true identify was discovered and whether she admitted [4] _________ (be) a woman or others on the ship had become suspicious and demanded [5] _________ (know). However, it is clear that she chose [6] _________ (live) life on her own terms and will forever have a place in the history books.

13 IDENTIFY Find the sentences with incorrect verb forms and correct them.

1 I really enjoy to visit new countries.
2 I can't stand traveling to places I have been before.
3 I hope visiting every continent in my lifetime.
4 I avoid to go to crowded travel destinations.
5 I have a list of travel destinations that I aim to visit in the next few years.
6 I'm planning going on an unusual trip soon.

14 WHAT'S YOUR ANGLE? Which sentences in Exercise 13 are true for you? Compare with a partner and explain your answers.

3.3 Inner or Outer Space?

1 ACTIVATE Work in pairs. Write a list of pros and cons of exploring space.

Pros	Cons

2 WHAT'S YOUR ANGLE? Decide whether you are for or against space exploration. Explain your view to your group. Who has the most similar view to yours?

3 INTEGRATE Read the essay. Are any of your ideas from Exercise 1 included?

WRITING SKILL
Writing paragraphs and topic sentences

Paragraphs with strong topic sentences help the reader to understand the organization of the text and the main ideas. This means the reader can:

- get a clear overview quickly.
- find the information they want more easily.
- understand the progression of the ideas.

Paragraphs should have one main idea, and the topic sentence usually presents this. Examples and more detailed information in the rest of the paragraph should support the main idea.

Although it has been more than four decades since the last manned moon landing, humankind has not stopped exploring space. Almost daily we read reports of new rocket launches and landings on Mars, each costing millions of dollars. Many people do not agree with this; they say we need the money for solutions to problems on our own planet. In this essay, I will discuss the benefits and drawbacks of space exploration.

Starting with the benefits, there are several general advantages. The first is that space exploration helps to improve technology. This improvement eventually reaches consumers on earth. Many people also believe that humans are designed to explore and expand our knowledge, and space is the ultimate place to do this. This is such a strong argument that many governments are happy to fund projects with little short-term benefit. There are also some practical benefits, for example, the discovery of new resources in space or the possible discovery of a new place for humans to live.

However, space travel also has significant disadvantages, especially financial ones. Each mission costs millions of dollars, and many people are unhappy with this. They say the money should be spent on problems we face, like climate change, poverty, and disease. All of these would benefit from the billions of dollars that are currently spent on space travel. There is also an environmental cost both on earth and in space, as we burn rocket fuel, use up expensive and rare materials, and leave behind litter in space.

In conclusion, I feel there should be more discussion on the question of space exploration because it is so expensive and uses too many resources. In today's world, we need to make sure that our money and effort are directed where they are most needed.

4 IDENTIFY Read the essay again. Find the topic sentence in each paragraph.

5 EXPAND Take notes of the supporting ideas and examples in paragraphs 2 and 3.

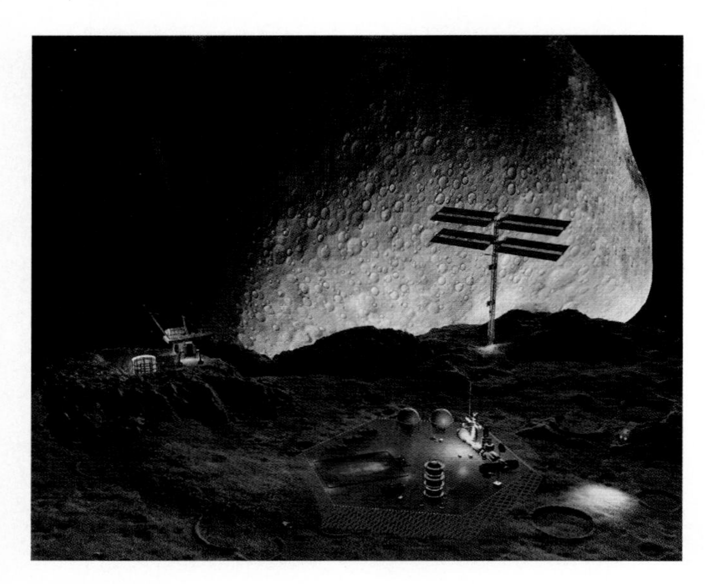

Paragraph 2:

____

____

____

Paragraph 3:

____

____

____

6 WHAT'S YOUR ANGLE? Review the essay. Has it changed your mind about space exploration? Why or why not?

GRAMMAR IN CONTEXT *so* and *such*

We use *so* and *such* to emphasize what things are like.

so + adjective

so exciting

such (+ *a* / *an*) + adjective + noun

such a good idea

We don't need an adjective with *such* if the noun is something that is always good, bad, etc.

*It was **such** a problem.*

Also, we don't use *a* / *an* with *such* when the noun is uncountable.

*It was **such** bad weather.*

See Grammar focus on page 161.

7 IDENTIFY Find an example of *so* and *such* in the essay.

8 INTERACT Complete the sentences with *so*, *such*, or *such a* / *an*.

1 I understand why some people are _________ negative about space travel.
2 Space travel is _________ expensive activity. We should limit it.
3 We should focus on the problems on earth only because they are _________ serious.
4 Finding enough money for every issue is _________ challenge for most governments.
5 We shouldn't stop space exploration because it gives us _________ good knowledge.
6 Space travel is _________ opportunity for a country to show its scientific and technology skills.

9 INTEGRATE Rewrite the sentences to replace *so* with *such*, or *such* with *so*.

1 It is such an expensive program that some people think it should be shut down.
The program is so expensive that some people think it should be shut down.
2 The university was so interested in his research that they decided to hire him.
____
3 His discoveries were so valuable that many study his contributions today.
____
4 You have such a strong argument in favor of space exploration.
____
5 She has such a unique perspective on the issue.
____

10 WHAT'S YOUR ANGLE? Discuss the statements in Exercise 8. Which do you agree with?

11 PREPARE Choose one of the topics to write a for-and-against essay about. Should we spend money on the research into these areas nowadays? Write your notes in the table.

oceans	the human mind	underground
cures for diseases	the North or South Pole	
artificial intelligence	DNA	

Topic	
Arguments for/ advantages	
Arguments against/ disadvantages	
Conclusion	

12 WRITE Write a for-and-against essay of up to 300 words. Include an introduction, a paragraph "for," a paragraph "against," and a conclusion. Remember to use strong topic sentences and clear supporting details and examples.

13 IMPROVE Review your partner's essay.

Does the essay…

- include four paragraphs with strong topic sentences?
- include clear supporting ideas and examples?
- use *so* and *such* correctly?

14 SHARE Read other classmates' essays. Which have arguments you hadn't thought of before?

Satellite antennas on the grounds of the Fucino Space Center in Abruzzo, Italy

3.4 Excuse Me...

ENGLISH FOR REAL

1 ACTIVATE Look at the pictures with a partner. What are the differences? Discuss the question in relation to the following.

location
situation
relationships between speakers

2 IDENTIFY Watch a conversation between Max, Andy, Phil, and Kevin about a lecture they have just attended. What do they keep doing?

3 ASSESS You are going to watch an extract of the lecture the friends were talking about in Exercise 2. Max wants to ask the speaker a question. What do you think Max's interruption will be like compared to the way the friends interrupted each other in their conversation? Why?

4 ANALYZE Watch the video and check your answers to Exercise 3.

REAL-WORLD ENGLISH Interrupting and resuming

Interrupting appropriately for the situation will get a better response from the speaker.

Sometimes it is necessary to interrupt a formal presentation to check understanding. You can raise your hand and then say you want to interrupt and why.

Excuse me for interrupting. Could I ask...?
I'm sorry to interrupt. Do you mind if...?
Excuse me for saying so, but I don't think...

With people you know in informal situations, you can use just one word like *but*, *so*, or *sorry* to show you want to say something.

So, why does...?
But what about...?
Sorry, but...?

When starting to speak again after an interruption, the speaker can use phrases to show it is their turn again.

Anyway, as I was saying...
Going back to what I was talking about...
So, where was I?

5 **IDENTIFY** Watch the complete video and take notes on the different ways of interrupting and resuming in each situation. Include phrases and actions. Compare your notes with a partner.

	In the classroom	Outside the classroom
Speakers	Max and lecturer	Max, Andy, Kevin, and Phil
To interrupt		
To resume		

6 **INTEGRATE** Work in pairs. Rewrite the interruptions so that they can be used for a more formal situation (e.g., the classroom situation in the video). Then listen and compare your answers. Did you rewrite them in the same way as the sentences in the audio?

1 But what about the start time?
2 So, we can finish early?
3 Actually, that's not right.
4 Sorry, but I need to say something here.

7 **INTERACT** Work in a group of three (A, B, and C) to do a role play. Choose situation 1 or 2, and prepare what you will say. Then role-play the situation. Discuss what worked well in your role play. Then swap roles and repeat.

Situation 1: You join two friends in a café. They are having a conversation about a documentary they both saw. You need to tell them about the plans for that evening.

Situation 2: You and two friends meet outside the movie theater. They immediately start talking about the party last night. The movie is starting in ten minutes, and there is a line for tickets. You don't want to miss the start of the movie.

8 **INTERACT** Now work in pairs (A and B). Review situations 3 and 4. How do they differ from situations 1 and 2 in Exercise 7? Choose situation 3 or 4. Decide on the details, and prepare what you will say. Then role-play the situation.

Situation 3: The lecturer is talking to a large group about the assignment that is due next week. You have some questions about it. Decide on course name, type of assignment, and so on.

Situation 4: It is your first day at work. You and ten other new people are in a training session with the manager. She hasn't answered your questions about the new job. Decide on the type of company, new job title, and so on.

9 **ANALYZE** Discuss what worked well in your role play in Exercise 8. How could you make your language more appropriate? Then swap roles and repeat.

10 **WHAT'S YOUR ANGLE?** Have you ever wanted to interrupt but didn't? Why not?

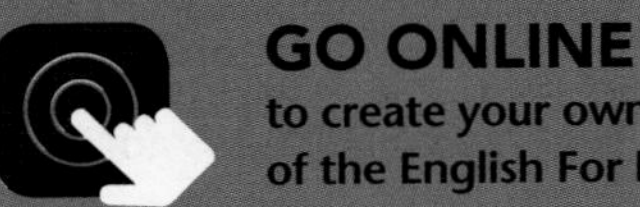

GO ONLINE
to create your own version of the English For Real video.

3.5 Moving On

1 ACTIVATE Discuss the questions.

1 Which of these things have you used or benefited from this week?
2 How important is each one in your life?

compass	printing press	airplane
Internet	telephone	corrective eye lenses
paper money	mechanical clock	

2 ASSESS Answer the questions.

1 In which century were the items in Exercise 1 probably invented?
2 Which have been the most important in the development of human knowledge? Choose your top three.

3 INTERACT Discuss your answers in Exercise 2 in a group. Decide on the top three inventions.

4 IDENTIFY Listen to the start of a presentation. Which of the items from Exercise 1 is the speaker going to talk about?

SPEAKING Giving a presentation

The audience listens and learns more when a presentation is well organized and presented.

Give a clear, engaging introduction that tells your audience what you are going to talk about.

Today, I'm going to talk about…
First, I'll talk about…
Then I'll outline…
Finally, we will look at…
There will be time for questions at the end.

Then use signpost phrases to show the audience where you are in the presentation and to highlight changes of topic.

So, first of all,… *Moving on to…* *In this final part,…*

5 INTEGRATE Listen to the introduction again. Write a possible outline for the rest of the presentation.

6 ASSESS Listen to the opening parts for the other sections of the presentation, and check your answers to Exercise 5.

7 IDENTIFY Listen again and complete the phrases used to introduce or change the topic.

1 So, ________________, the question is how…
2 ________________ the history of…
3 In ________________, I would like to look at…
4 ________________ questions…

PRONUNCIATION SKILL
Shifting stress in suffix words

Correct word stress helps the listener understand key nouns.

When certain suffixes are added to adjectives or verbs to form nouns, the stress moves to a different syllable in the noun. For example, with the suffixes *-ity* and *-tion*, the stress moves to the syllable before the suffix.

***per**sonal—perso**nal**ity* *ad**mire**—admi**ra**tion*

Some suffixes don't affect the stress when they are added, for example: *-ment*, *-ness*, *-ship*, and *-ence*.

*a**chieve**—a**chieve**ment* *__hap__py—__hap__piness*
***mem**ber—**mem**bership* ***con**fident—**con**fidence*

8 IDENTIFY Notice the stress in the first word. Then identify the suffix in the noun form, and find the main stress. Listen and check.

1 disappoint—disappointment
2 available—availability
3 differ—difference
4 apply—application
5 relation—relationship
6 lazy—laziness

9 INTERACT Complete the nouns in the extracts with a suffix, and mark the stress on these nouns. Listen and check. Then listen again and repeat the extracts.

1 I would like to look at other develop__________s…
2 …the simple lens gave us the possibil__________…
3 …of raising the level of human intellig__________…
4 …the recogni__________ of the importance of this item…
5 …this will be an explora__________ of important inventions…

10 PREPARE Choose an item you consider to be in the top three most important inventions for human knowledge. Write a list of reasons to support your view.

11 DEVELOP Work in pairs. Review your partner's choice of invention and then together decide how to organize each presentation.

12 IMPROVE Practice your presentation. Ask your partner for feedback on the organization and delivery.

13 SHARE Give your presentation to a group. Answer questions from other students at the end of the presentation.

14 WHAT'S YOUR ANGLE? After listening to the other speakers in your group, have you changed your choice of important invention? Why or why not?

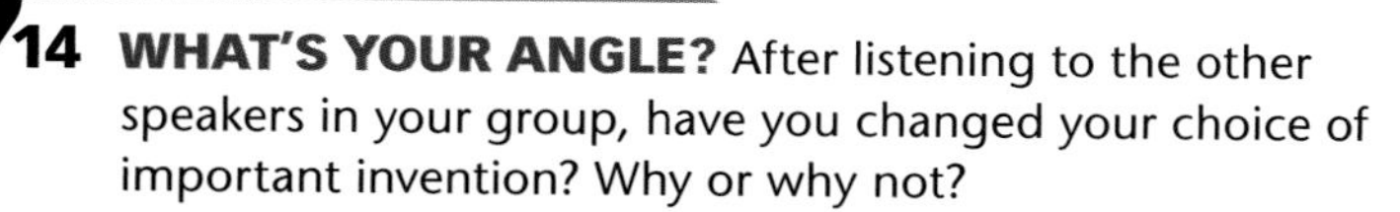
Now go to page 149 for the Unit 3 Review

4 Processes

UNIT SNAPSHOT

What kind of work requires processes?

Why are processes important?

What can happen if we don't follow a process?

BEHIND THE PHOTO

1 In which of these areas of life do you think we use these processes? Write A, B, or C next to each process. Then compare your answers with a partner. Do you agree?

A. work B. leisure C. education

Applying for a job	___	Preparing for a sports competition	___
Learning a skill	___	Preparing for a party	___
Learning a sport	___	Planning a wedding	___
Redecorating a room	___	Teaching someone a skill	___
Preparing for an exam	___	Applying for college	___

2 In pairs, choose two of the processes from Exercise 1. How many steps can you think of for each?

REAL-WORLD GOAL

Learn a new process from an online video

4.1 Proudly Made

1 ACTIVATE Complete each picture label with a verb and a noun from the box.

cake	wool scarf	paper plane	clay pot	knit	fold	mold	bake

1 ________ a ________

2 ________ a ________

3 ________ a ________

4 ________ a ________

2 WHAT'S YOUR ANGLE? Look at the photos in Exercise 1. Answer the questions.

1 Which of the items can you make?
2 Which would you like to be able to make? Why?

VOCABULARY DEVELOPMENT
Explaining a process

Ordinal numbers and signpost words and phrases can be used to make the steps of a process clear.

The first / second / third stage is...
Firstly,... / Secondly,...

These signposts usually come at the beginning of the sentence to make the step immediately clear. Make sure you understand the part of speech of the word or phrase and check that it fits with the grammar and punctuation of the sentence.

Following that, knit two more rows in blue wool.
Finally, pour the mixture into a cake tin.
Once the cake is cooked, remove it from the oven.
The last step is to sew the sides of the hat together.

Oxford 3000™

3 IDENTIFY Which of the things in Exercise 1 is the person making? Number the steps in the correct order.

___ a The last step is to decorate it.
___ b Once it is the right shape, make the bottom flat.
___ c Then make a hole in the ball with your thumb.
___ d After that, mold the sides into the correct shape.
___ e The first stage is to make a ball of clay.

4 INTEGRATE Listen and check your answers to Exercise 3. Underline the phrases in Exercise 3 that show the stages.

LISTENING SKILL
Using visual information while listening

Visual information can help you better understand what you are listening to. It can help you understand more complex language as well as learn new language.

Before you listen, review any images that accompany the listening. Look for items in the images that you know the words for. Check the vocabulary for items shown in the images that you don't know the words for.

While listening, use the images to follow what the speaker is saying and to support your understanding. Do this by focusing on sections of images highlighted by the speaker, considering how images shown relate to what is being said, and listening carefully for language you know that refer to elements in the image.

Listen a second time and make a note of unknown language you hear or see on any images used. Use a dictionary to check their meaning afterward.

5 IDENTIFY You are going to watch a video of people making a special type of fabric called Harris Tweed. Look at these images from the video. Label the items you know in English.

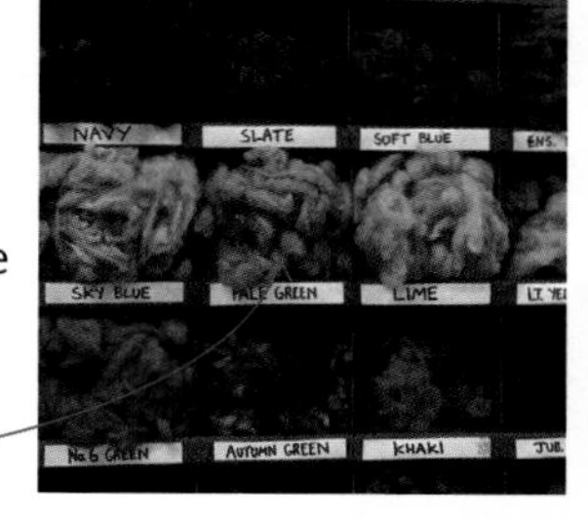

shades of blue

6 **NOTICE** Watch the video. Choose the phrases you hear.

- ☐ a dyed a few different colors
- ☐ b mix the base colors
- ☐ c complicated colors and shades
- ☐ d Chinese textile company
- ☐ e highly skilled weavers
- ☐ f the fabric and the patterns
- ☐ g old-style foot-operated looms
- ☐ h woven by hand
- ☐ i small industry
- ☐ j high-quality
- ☐ k stamped
- ☐ l Orb Mark trademark
- ☐ m traditional brand
- ☐ n modernized its operations

7 **IDENTIFY** Discuss the meaning of the words and phrases in Exercise 6 with a partner. Use the images from Exercise 5 and a dictionary to find out the meaning of any words you don't know. Which can you guess from the visuals?

8 **INTEGRATE** Watch the description of the process of making Harris Tweed, and match the two parts of the sentences.

1 The first stage of ___
2 The result of this ___
3 Following that, ___
4 During this stage, ___
5 The last step is for ___
6 Once ___

a old-style foot-operated looms are used, and the tweed is woven by hand.
b making the tweed is to mix the base colors of the wool to a specific recipe.
c the weavers create the fabric and the patterns.
d they're happy that it is high quality, the material is stamped with the Orb Mark trademark.
e the Harris Tweed Authority to inspect the material.
f more complicated colors and shades.

9 **INTEGRATE** Watch the complete video and answer the questions.

1 Who made and still makes the cloth?
2 Which material gets the special Orb Mark trademark?
3 What kind of wool do the mills use?
4 How does the tweed get its color?
5 What kinds of things are made of Harris Tweed nowadays?
6 Where do people buy the cloth?
7 Which country has invested in the production of this cloth?
8 Where does the wool come from nowadays?

GRAMMAR IN CONTEXT
Present passive and past passive

We use the passive form to focus on what happens to someone or something rather than who or what does the action. We make the passive with a form of *be* and the past participle of the verb.

*active: The worker **stamps** the material.*
*passive: The material **is stamped**.*

To change the time we are talking about, we change the tense of *be*.

*Cloth **was** developed.*

We use *by* + noun if we want to include who or what did the action.

*Harris Tweed was handmade **by people from the islands**.*

We often use the passive to continue talking about a particular thing.

*Harris Tweed has been one of the most famous names in the British textile industry for more than 150 years, and it **is** now **known** all over the world.*

See Grammar focus on page 162.

10 **IDENTIFY** Complete the sentences from the video with the correct passive form of the verb in parentheses.

1 Harris Tweed _________ (make) in the Outer Hebrides.
2 This quality cloth _________ first _________ (export) in the 1840s.
3 The Orb Mark trademark _________ (develop) to protect the brand.
5 Three mills _________ (license) to produce Harris Tweed.
6 Three years ago, half a million meters of Harris Tweed _________ (produce) every year.

11 **INTEGRATE** Rewrite the answers to Exercise 9 in the passive. (Use the questions to help you.)

1 The cloth was made and is still made by people from the islands.

12 **APPLY** Rewrite the sentences using the passive. Then listen to the extract from a cooking show and check.

1 We chose this week's recipe from a traditional cookbook.
2 In the past, people served this cake on special occasions.
3 People eat it at any time nowadays.
4 You combine all the ingredients in a large bowl.
5 You mix the eggs separately at first.
6 You bake the cake for 40 minutes.

13 **WHAT'S YOUR ANGLE?** What was the last thing you made / cooked / painted / grew / created?

4.2 Making It to the Big Screen

1 ACTIVATE Complete the information about movies with the numbers in the box.

11	38.6	71	245	718	164,000

In 2016:

- The global box office for all movies released in each country around the world reached $____ billion.
- Movie theater screens increased to ____ worldwide.
- ____ movies were released in the United States and Canada.
- ____% of U.S. and Canadian populations (about ____ million people) went to the movies at least once. ____% went at least once a month.

2 WHAT'S YOUR ANGLE? Answer the questions.

1 How often do you go to the movies? Why?
2 How often do you watch movies at home?

3 VOCABULARY Review the process for making a movie in *Got a Good Idea for a Film.* Complete the process with the correct form of the verbs in the box.

film	promote	produce	select
design	solve	revise	create

 Oxford 3000™

4 WHAT'S YOUR ANGLE? Look at the process in *Got a Good Idea for a Film.* Answer the questions.

1 Which do you think is the most difficult stage of making a movie? Explain your reasons.
2 Which stage would you like to be involved in? Why?

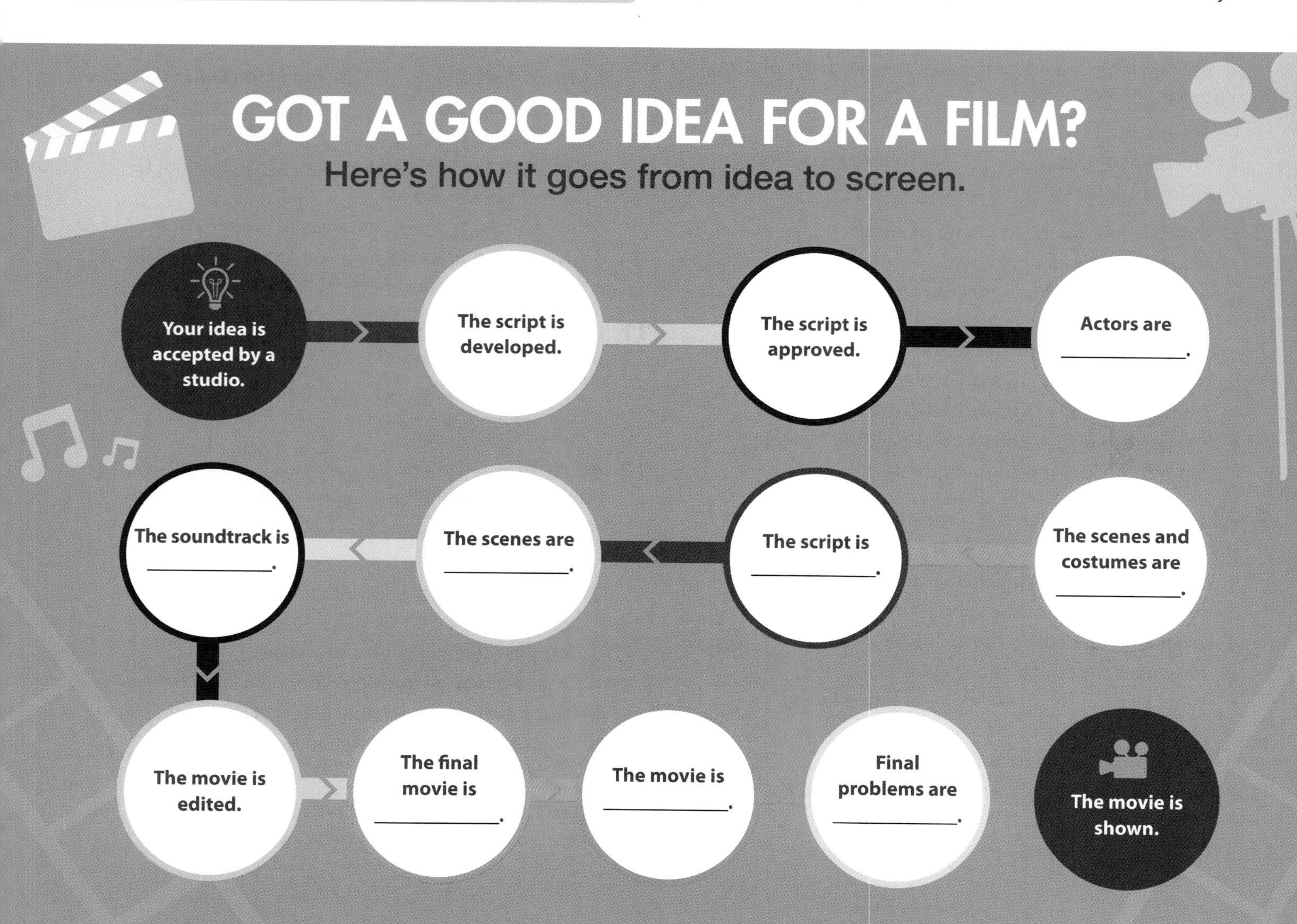

5 ASSESS You are going to read an article about the history of the movies. Number these in the order you think they happened.

___ a the first 3D movie process
___ b U.S. weekly attendance fell from 90 to 51 million
___ c Audion vacuum tube invented
___ d *Toy Story* movie
___ e first movies with sound and color
___ f start of electrical recording
___ g problems with color solved
___ h *Avatar* movie
___ i the increased use of computer-generated images (CGI)
___ j *The Lord of the Rings* movies

READING SKILL
Classifying information from a text

We can use diagrams to develop reading skills. Selecting and classifying information helps the reader understand the content and organization of a text. Diagrams are also useful for summarizing information, so they are good review tools.

Flow charts show steps in a process.

Step 1 ⟶ Step 2 ⟶ Step 3

Timelines show when events happened.

1850 1900 1950 2000

Mind maps show connections between ideas.

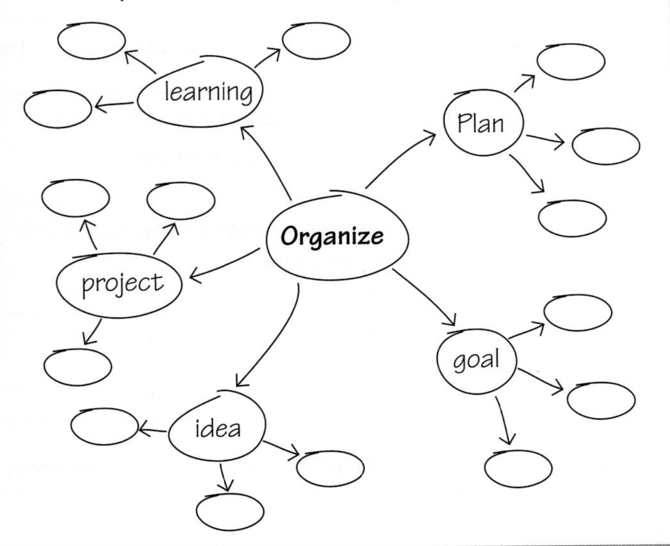

Technology and the big screen

When we watch a movie at the theater, unlike with many other arts, we see a pure product of technology. Without technology, no movie can be created since no sound can be recorded and no moving images filmed. However, for more than a hundred years, the development of motion picture technology has been a slow and irregular process.

The development of cinematic technology dates back to the late 19th century, and even though it took another century to evolve, many of the ideas were already in place in the early years. In the 1890s, for example, the initial movies were already made with sound and color, although it must be noted that these were very basic. British inventor William Friese-Greene even designed a 3D film process back in 1893.

The technology behind sound progressed quickly with the invention of the Audion vacuum tube in 1906, which enabled the amplification of sound, and the first electrical recordings around 1924. The technology behind color developed more slowly. It wasn't until the 1950s, for example, that complex technical problems in getting true color were solved by Kodak Eastman's new Eastmancolor process.

Movie technology accelerated in the middle to late 20th century. One reason was that between 1948 and 1952, the average weekly attendance at U.S. movie theaters fell from 90 to 51 million, largely because many people started preferring more active leisure activities, such as playing golf and traveling. For passive entertainment, they now had television. In response, the movie industry decided that moviegoers should be made to feel that they were actually participating in the movie action, so they developed technologies such as curved screens, which made the audience feel surrounded by the images, and powerful sound systems.

In recent times, digital technology dominates mainstream production, including the widespread use of 3D filming. In 1995, *Toy Story* was the first movie that showed that digital technology can be used to produce entire films. By the end of that decade, digital cameras were already used to film authentic-looking battle scenes, like those in the *Star Wars* episode *The Phantom Menace* in 1999.

In the 21st century, studios believe that audiences must be treated to amazing computer-generated special effects if they are to attend in mass numbers. In the past few decades, the studios have used them to produce spectacular blockbusters like *The Lord of the Rings* trilogy (2001–2003) and *Avatar* (2009). However, it should be remembered that there has been over a century of development to arrive at this point.

—adapted from *The Oxford Encyclopedia of the History of American Science, Medicine, and Technology*, edited by Hugh Richard Slotten

6 IDENTIFY Scan the article to find when the events in Exercise 5 happened. Write them in the correct place on the timeline.

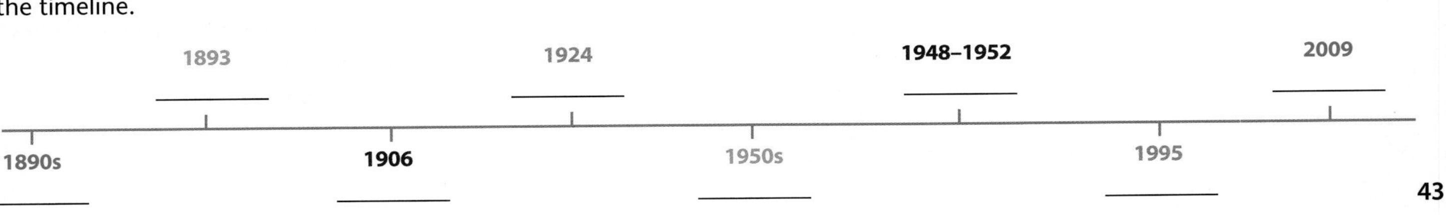

7 INTEGRATE Use the article and the words in the box to complete mind map blanks 1–8.

color	entertaining	images	leisure activities	screens	sound	sound systems	television

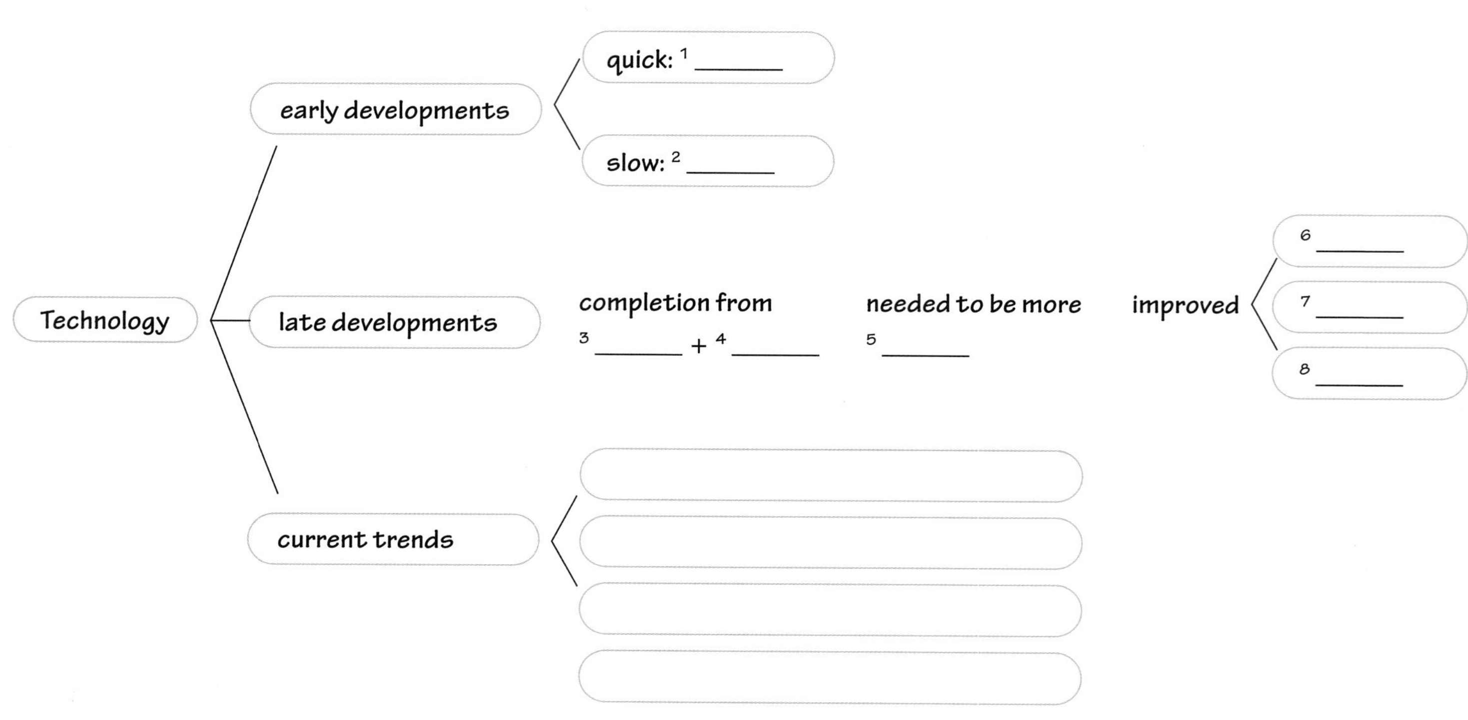

8 EXPAND Add information about current trends to the mind map. Use ideas from the article and your own.

GRAMMAR IN CONTEXT
Present passive with modal verbs

We can use the passive with modal verbs such as *can, could, might, should, must*, and so on.

Subject + modal verb + *be* + past participle

*...no sound **can be recorded**...*
*It **must be noted** that...*

See Grammar focus on page 162.

9 IDENTIFY Find more examples of the present passive with modal verbs in the article. For each example, discuss with a partner who or what does the action.

10 APPLY Put the words in the correct order to make sentences in the present passive with a modal verb.

1 have to / nowadays, audiences / entertained / by more and more special effects / be

____

2 shouldn't / replaced / real actors / by digital avatars / be

____

3 be / more money / could / making movie theaters better / spent on / to attract bigger audiences

____

4 to be active, / children / encouraged / should / rather than sit and watch movies / be

____

5 banned / should / cell phones / be / from movie theaters

____

11 INTERACT Do you agree or disagree with the sentences in Exercise 10? Discuss your views with a partner.

12 WHAT'S YOUR ANGLE? Imagine you have a good idea for a movie. Answer the questions in a group.

1 Who would you select to act in it?
2 Who would you want to develop the script and direct it?
3 Where would you want it filmed?
4 Who would create the soundtrack?

4.3 What's the Difference?

1 ACTIVATE Discuss the items and match the words to the pictures. More than one may be possible for each picture.

handmade	machine-made	homemade	store-bought

2 WHAT'S YOUR ANGLE? What's your first choice for each of the following? Would you prefer them to be handmade, homemade, machine-made, or store-bought?

a birthday card	a cake	a special outfit	a car	a bag

3 IDENTIFY Read the introduction to the essay. Which two types of products are compared and contrasted?

4 ASSESS Read the essay. Complete the diagram with the information about handmade and machine-made products. Which information applies to each type of product? Which information applies to both?

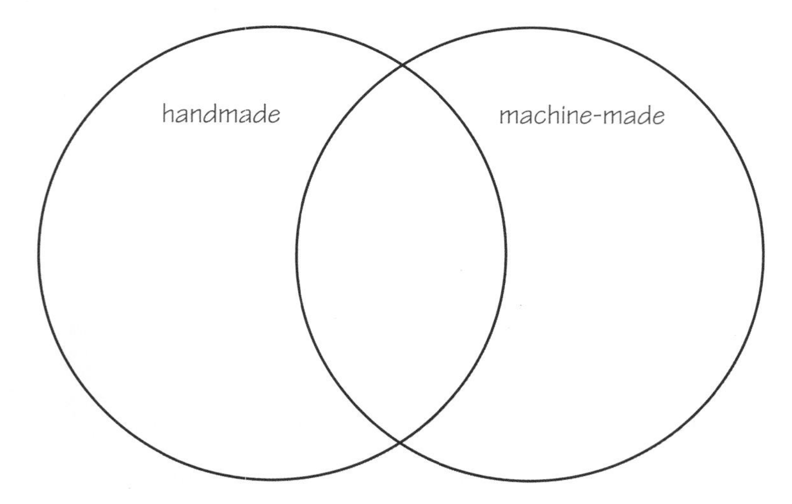

WRITING SKILL
Using example and explanation linking words

To help the reader, use examples and explanation to make your points clear. Use signpost words and phrases to show the reader you are doing this.

To introduce examples:

for instance, for example, such as like

***For instance**, most people are not interested in learning about how their washing machine was made.*

To introduce explanations:

this means, that is (to say), in other words, to put it another way,

***That is to say**, people are often prepared to pay extra for a handmade item because it makes them feel special.*

We live in an age of shopping. One aspect that separates the thousands of available items to buy is how they are produced—in general, things can be made by hand or by machine. In this essay, I will compare and contrast the two types of products.

Starting with the similarities between the two types of products, the first point is that a good-quality item can be produced by either method. Actually, for many buyers, the fact that one item is made by hand and another by machine may not be important, especially if their quality is considered similar. For instance, most people are not interested in learning about how their washing machine was made—only if it works well. Most modern factories use machines to make excellent products, and customers, in general, are satisfied with such machine-made products. Another point in common is that both types of product are actually often made by highly skilled people. For instance, machine-made electrical equipment is frequently made by people who are very good at operating machines. This is the same for handmade items; in other words, items made by hand or by machine are typically made by workers who are excellent at their job.

However, there are also differences between the two types of items. The main difference is the level of quality. Handmade products are usually made more slowly and carefully. For example, many people consider that a handmade car, such as a McLaren, is finished to a higher quality than a mass-produced car like a Toyota. Secondly, handmade products are made in smaller numbers. This smaller production means that these items are usually more expensive since they cost more to produce in this way. Finally, a handmade item is seen to be better than a mass-produced one, which also increases the price. That is to say, people are often prepared to pay extra for a handmade item because it makes them feel special.

In conclusion, when we compare and contrast handmade and machine-made products, we can see that some things are the same and some are different. The quality of most machine-made products is excellent, and it is usually good enough for most people. However, there will always be a market for quality handmade products.

5 INTEGRATE Match the points to the examples, and add the linking words used in the essay.

1 difference between machine-made and handmade is not important *for instance* (→ d)
2 both types are made by highly skilled people ________
3 handmade products take more time and care to make ________
4 a handmade car ________
5 not a handmade car ________

a machine-made equipment is made by people who are good at operating machines
b many people think that handmade cars are better quality than machine-made ones
c a Toyota
d people are not interested in how washing machines are made
e a McLaren

6 IDENTIFY Find the two linking phrases for explanations in the essay. Identify the point that is explained and the explanation that is given.

GRAMMAR IN CONTEXT
Adjectives with prepositions

We use prepositions after adjectives to talk about feelings, abilities, etc.

surprised by	*bad at*	*bored with*	*pleased about*
1 ________	2 ________	3 ________	4 ________

We can use an *-ing* form after some prepositions.

Most people are interested in learning about…

5 ________________________________

See Grammar focus on page 162.

7 INTEGRATE Use a preposition and a phrase from the box to complete the sentences.

baking	their response	my performance
people finding out	the bad quality	

1 My cousin is good ________ homemade desserts.
2 I'm fed up ________ of mass-produced clothes.
3 My teacher was pleased ________ this semester.
4 I was surprised ________ to my speech.
5 Kate was worried ________ it was a store-bought dish.

8 IDENTIFY Complete the Grammar in Context box with more examples from the text.

9 WHAT'S YOUR ANGLE? Answer the questions. Explain your answers to your partner, giving explanations and examples to help.

What are you…

- good at?
- interested in?
- pleased about?
- surprised by?

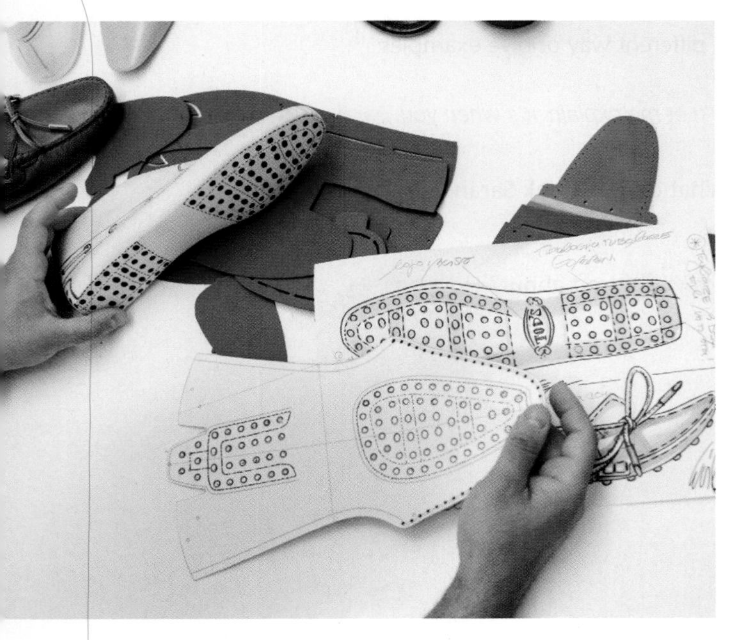

10 PREPARE Work in pairs. Choose one of these topics for a compare-and-contrast essay. Complete a diagram for the two items you are comparing.

- a hand-painted picture and a photograph
- a store-bought gift and a handmade gift
- a homemade meal and a takeout meal

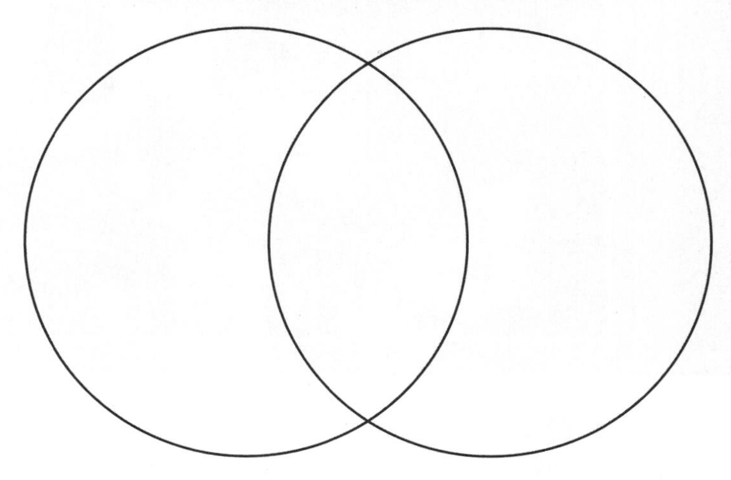

11 WRITE Write a compare-and-contrast essay individually. Use the checklist to help.

- ☐ Include an introduction explaining what you are comparing/contrasting.
- ☐ Include similarities and differences.
- ☐ Include explanations.
- ☐ Include examples.
- ☐ Use adjectives with prepositions.
- ☐ End with a conclusion.
- ☐ Write 200–300 words.

12 IMPROVE Compare your essay with your partner's. Do both essays match each point on the checklist?

13 SHARE Read other classmates' essays. Make a note of any new ideas and arguments you strongly agree or disagree with.

A technician shows the various designing steps in the creation of a Tod's shoe, at the Tod's headquarters in Sant'Elpidio a Mare, Italy

4.4 I Get It Now!

1 **ACTIVATE** Watch the first part of the video and answer the questions. What information in the video helped you answer them?

1 Where are Andy, Max, and Sarah from?
2 Where are the people in the movie that Andy and Max watched from?
3 Who is not sure about things in the movie?

REAL-WORLD ENGLISH Asking for and giving clarification

In conversation, we sometimes need to ask for clarification. This can be for different reasons; for example, we may not understand the information, we can't hear the person clearly, or we may not understand the language used.

Could you say that again? *I didn't understand the part about…* *What do you mean by…?*

When you ask for clarification,

- say what point you are asking about.
  Could you explain the part about…? *What exactly is…?*
- indicate when you understand.
  I get it now. *OK, that makes sense.*

When giving clarification, you can repeat the information in a different way or give examples to help the person understand.

I mean that… / It means that… *To give you an example…* *Let me explain. It's when you…*

2 **ASSESS** What did Max ask for clarification about? What do you think Sarah will say? Watch and check.

3 **IDENTIFY** Watch the complete video. What else is Max confused about? How do Sarah and Andy respond?

ENGLISH FOR REAL

4 ANALYZE Review the phrases from the video and decide if they are asking for clarification (1), indicating understanding (2), or giving clarification (3).

_1_ I didn't get some of the jokes.
___ I never saw a scarf!
___ Why was he the best?
___ OK, let me explain.
___ I get it now.
___ A muffler is part of a car.
___ Why is that funny?

5 EXPAND Work in pairs. Take turns asking for and giving clarification about these things mentioned in the video.

a "best boy"	a silencer	a muffler	a scarf

I didn't understand the part about a "best boy."
OK, let me explain. A "best boy"...

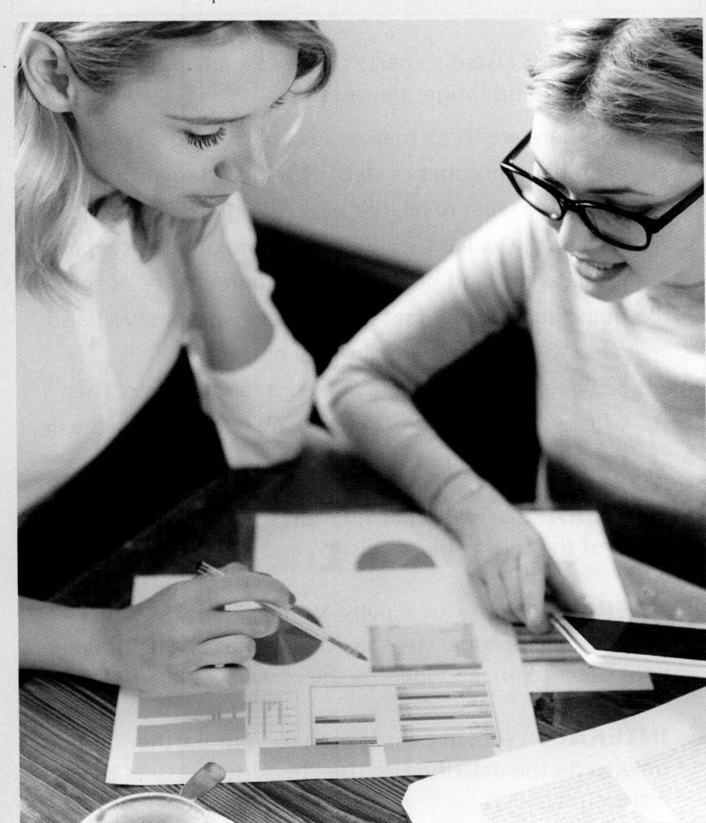

6 INTERACT Work in pairs and decide who is Student A and who is Student B. Read the situation and make notes on your role. Then act out the situation with your partner.

You had a different teacher for English class last week. There are some things you aren't clear about. Ask your partner for clarification and answer their questions.

Student A: You aren't sure what the homework was or how to spell the new teacher's name, but you know the topic of the test for the next class and what time you need to be in class.

Student B: You understood the homework, and you wrote down the new teacher's name, so you're confident you know how to spell it, but you're confused about the test in the next class. You don't know what the topic is or what time you need to be in class.

7 WHAT'S YOUR ANGLE? Think about two times you asked for or gave clarification. What were the situations? What language did you use? Why?

GO ONLINE
to create your own version of the English For Real video.

4.5 It's Quite Simple, Really

1 ACTIVATE Discuss the questions.

1 What kinds of games are popular in your country?
2 What makes a good game?

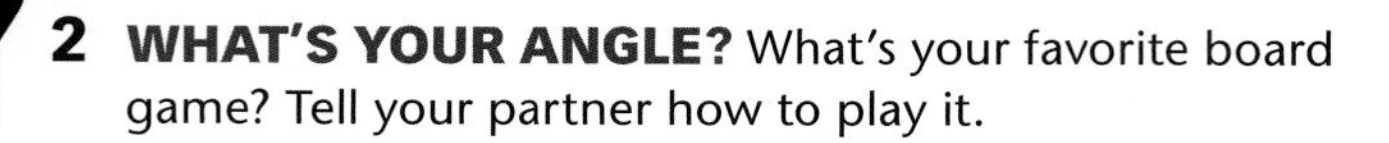

2 WHAT'S YOUR ANGLE? What's your favorite board game? Tell your partner how to play it.

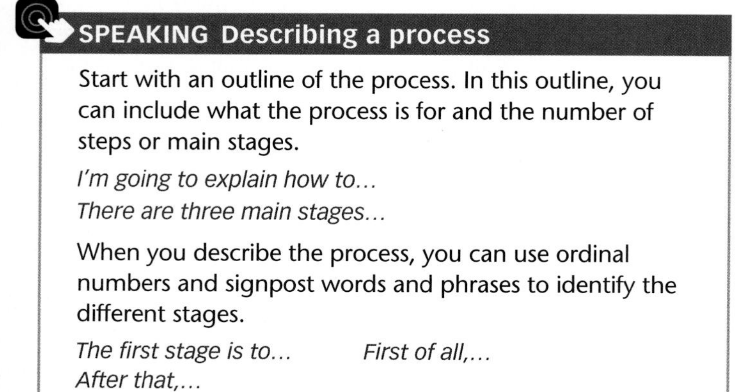

SPEAKING Describing a process

Start with an outline of the process. In this outline, you can include what the process is for and the number of steps or main stages.

I'm going to explain how to...
There are three main stages...

When you describe the process, you can use ordinal numbers and signpost words and phrases to identify the different stages.

The first stage is to... *First of all,...*
After that,...

3 ASSESS Review the steps for making a board game. Which stage of making a game does each step belong to? Which order would you put the steps in?

Making a board game	Initial concept	Developing the first version	Making the final version
___ make a simple version	☐	☐	☐
___ choose the basic design	☐	☐	☐
___ try the game	☐	☐	☐
___ decide on number of players	☐	☐	☐
___ identify the goals of the game	☐	☐	☐
___ choose the level of difficulty	☐	☐	☐
___ make the final game	☐	☐	☐
___ decide how players will interact or move	☐	☐	☐

4 IDENTIFY Listen to someone describing how to make a board game, and check the order of the steps in Exercise 3. Does it match the order you suggested?

PRONUNCIATION SKILL Chunking

Speech can be difficult to understand when the speaker doesn't use natural chunks.

OK, so I'm going to explain how to make a board game.

We use pauses between groups of words—or "chunks"—to help our listener understand our message.

OK, | so I'm going to explain | how to make a board game.

We use longer pauses between sentences and stages in a talk.

OK, | so I'm going to explain | how to make a board game. | You might think | it's going to be complicated, | but it's quite simple, really.
So, | there are three main stages...

5 NOTICE Listen to parts of the talk again, and mark the shorter and longer pauses.

1 So, there are three main stages of making a game, and each has a number of steps. The first stage is to plan the game. First of all, the basic design must be chosen.
2 And finally, will it be a difficult game or an easy game for all ages? And how long will a game take? At some point during this first stage of development, you also need to identify the main goal of the game.
3 See how long it lasts, and look out for problems. Then, when you are sure it works, you are ready to plan the final product. So, the last stage is to make that final version.

6 INTEGRATE Work in pairs. Listen to your partner give parts of the talk from Exercise 5, and check the pauses.

7 PREPARE Choose an activity. Write a list of the main stages and individual steps needed to make or do it. Prepare your description, and identify the chunks and pauses.

8 INTERACT Work in pairs. Listen to your partner describe how to do the activity. Use the checklist to assess the instructions.

☐ Are the main stages clear?
☐ Are the steps clear?
☐ Were the pauses and chunks helpful?

9 IMPROVE Get feedback from your partner on your description. Can you improve it?

10 SHARE Work in a group. Listen to each other's descriptions. What new information did you learn?

Now go to page 150 for the Unit 4 Review.

5 Survival

UNIT SNAPSHOT

What problems do people encounter in this environment?

What do they do to survive?

In what other environments is it difficult for people to survive?

BEHIND THE PHOTO

REAL-WORLD GOAL

Help someone with an everyday disaster

1 Answer the questions.

1. How do friends and family help each other survive everyday difficult situations?
   Friends and family can offer advice and emotional support. They can do things for each other and spend time together.
2. How do countries work together when natural disasters occur?
3. Why do many people want to help when they hear about problems?

2 Discuss your answers with a partner. Think of reasons and examples to support your opinions.

5.1 Everyday Disasters

1 ACTIVATE Look at the problems. Discuss the questions.

1 Which of these things have you ever done?
2 Which would be the worst thing for you to do?
3 Which would you know how to deal with?

sent a message to the wrong person

locked yourself out

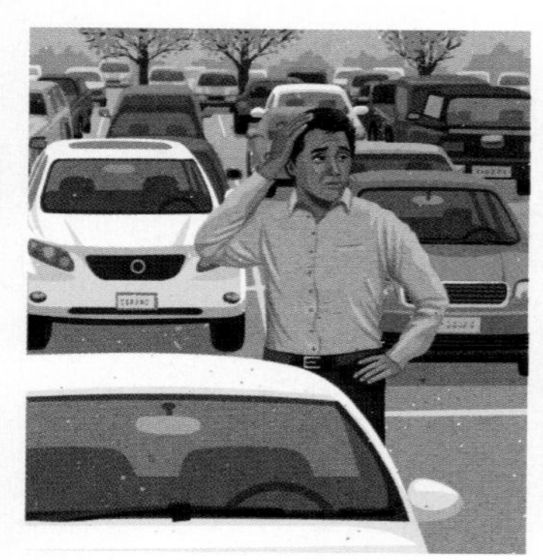

forgotten where you parked the car

missed an important deadline

spilled a drink on a carpet

had a child repeat something bad you said

2 ASSESS Listen to the start of a radio show. Which problems from Exercise 1 do you think each expert could deal with?

3 IDENTIFY Listen to the show. Identify the three problems from Exercise 1.

LISTENING SKILL
Interpreting changes in volume, speed, and pitch

Our words give information, but our voices also change according to what we are trying to communicate. We often change the volume, speed, and pitch (up and down). Listen for these changes and stressed words to understand the speaker better.

Stressing words or slowing them down tells the listener how important particular ideas are and how strongly the speaker feels about them. For example, when:

- giving advice:
  *I **really** think you should do that.*
- feeling frustrated:
  *I **reeeeeally** need to get rid of it before my parents see it.*

The intonation going down at the end of a sentence can show that the speaker is sure. For example, when:

- giving a warning:
  People never enjoy the result of that.

Slowing speech can show that the speaker wants you to listen carefully or that the speaker is thinking carefully while speaking. For example, when:

- realizing something as you say it:
  But if you do that—then—we—will—lose.

4 IDENTIFY Listen to and read the extracts from the show. Decide what the speaker is doing: warning (W), realizing (R), or giving advice (A).

1 But the most important thing is not to lie to her. People never like that. ___
2 You really should look out when you have any kind of food or drink and white carpets... ___
3 Yes, there was. Uh...does that matter? ___

5 APPLY Listen again. Mark the stresses, speed, and pitch changes. Compare with a partner.

6 IDENTIFY Listen to more extracts, and decide what the speaker is doing.

1 ________ 3 ________ 5 ________
2 ________ 4 ________ 6 ________

7 **INTEGRATE** Complete the notes for the three everyday disasters and the advice Tom and Penny gave. Then listen again, and check your notes.

Caller	Everyday disaster	Advice
Chloe	What? When?	
Lana	What? When?	
Phil	What? When?	

8 **WHAT'S YOUR ANGLE?** Look at your notes in Exercise 7. Answer the questions.

1 Do you have any more advice for Chloe and Lana?
2 What advice would you give Phil?

GRAMMAR IN CONTEXT Advice and warning with *should, ought to,* and *had better*

We use *should, ought to,* and *had better* to give and ask for advice.

We can use *should* in statements and questions.

*You **should** always listen.*
*He **shouldn't** say anything.*
***Should** I do that? Yes, you **should**. / No, you **shouldn't**.*

Ought to is more formal. We generally don't use *ought to* with *not* or in questions.

*You **ought to** try.*

Had better gives a stronger warning. We don't usually use it in questions.

*He'**d better** say something.*
*You'**d better** not do that.*

See Grammar focus on page 163.

9 **APPLY** Discuss these extracts from the radio show with a partner. Complete them with a form of *should, ought to,* or *had better.* Then listen and check.

1 _________ I try again?
2 You _________ give up yet.
3 You _________ tell her the truth as soon as possible.
4 Any parents listening out there _________ remember this.

VOCABULARY DEVELOPMENT Phrasal verbs with *look*

We can use *look* in many phrasal verbs. For example:

look into *look forward to* *look up from* *look out*

1 Sometimes the meaning of the phrasal verb can be easily inferred from the individual meaning of its parts.

***look around** somewhere—visit all different parts of a place*

2 Sometimes the meaning of the phrasal verb is less clear from its parts.

***look after something**—make sure that something is safe*

Oxford 3000™

10 **INTEGRATE** Review the definitions below for the phrasal verbs from group 2 in the Vocabulary Development box. Then listen to the extracts from the radio show, and complete the phrasal verbs.

1 look _________ something—to take care of something
2 look _________—be careful
3 look _________ something—to examine something
4 look something _________—to look for information in a book or on the computer
5 look _________ somebody—respect somebody

11 **INTEGRATE** Complete the sentences with the correct words from the boxes.

around up from through forward

1 I often look _________ my home to check on safety.
2 I always look _________ the safety instructions when I get on a plane.
3 The fire alarm goes off so often at work that I don't look _________ my computer now.
4 I look _________ things going wrong because I love helping to fix things.

out up to into after up

5 If I hear a strange noise at night, I get out of bed and look _________ the situation immediately.
6 When I have a practical problem, I look _________ the solution on the Internet.
7 I look _________ my phone and wallet very carefully when I'm in a big city.
8 When I'm out with friends, I'm always the one looking _________ for everyone else.
9 I look _________ to people who are very good at dealing with practical problems.

12 **WHAT'S YOUR ANGLE?** Which sentences in Exercise 11 are true for you?

5.2 Unexpected Consequences

1

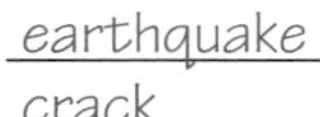

2

3

4

5

6

1 ACTIVATE Match the words in the box to the pictures of natural disasters. Then write four key words related to each picture. Use a dictionary to help.

earthquake	drought	hurricane
volcanic eruption	wildfire	flood

2 WHAT'S YOUR ANGLE? Which of the natural disasters in Exercise 1 have you seen on the news recently?

3 ASSESS Match the years to the four natural disasters. What do you know about these disasters? Then scan the article to check the dates.

1	Great Lisbon Earthquake	___	a	1918
2	Eruption of volcano Krakatoa	___	b	1976
3	Spanish flu epidemic	___	c	1883
4	Great Tangshan Earthquake in China	___	d	1755

The Great Lisbon Earthquake

A natural disaster with unnatural consequences

Natural disasters, such as earthquakes, hurricanes, floods, drought, and fires, are natural events that destroy large areas, often cause loss of life, and have a major economic impact.

One way of assessing the impact of a natural disaster is to look at how many people died and how much property was destroyed. Of the hundreds of natural disasters that have happened in modern times, a few are more famous for the extent of the destruction they caused. The eruption of the volcano Krakatoa in 1883 changed the weather of the northern hemisphere for a while and destroyed more than 300 communities. Similarly, the Spanish flu epidemic of 1918 killed about 30 million people. However, the impact of a disaster sometimes is not measured only in terms of loss of life and property—history can be affected as well.

One of the most important natural disasters to shake the course of history was the Great Lisbon Earthquake of 1755. Its center was about 200 miles from the coast of Portugal, and its effects were felt far and wide—the shock destroyed parts of Spain, Morocco, and Algeria. However, it was Portugal that suffered the most losses. About 30,000 people died from the earthquake and up to 70,000 more from floods and fires. In addition, the Portuguese capital was almost completely destroyed.

Although the Lisbon earthquake is still considered one of the most powerful and destructive in European history, it is so important not because of its physical effects—the Great Tangshan Earthquake in China in 1976 killed more than 240,000 people—but because it changed the way we view and respond to such events. After the Lisbon earthquake, thinkers such as the French philosopher Voltaire started to question—and eventually gave up—the belief that such natural disasters had metaphysical causes and started looking for scientific explanations. Seismology, the study of earthquakes, became popular, as scientists and governments realized that they had to learn to forecast earthquakes. They developed the idea that to protect a place, people must prepare rather than react. In addition, the Lisbon earthquake had a major effect on politics. The terrible financial and human losses probably contributed to the end of Portugal as a great global power, leading to changes in the world order.

As a result of the Lisbon earthquake, we now recognize that we can't only assess natural disasters for their physical effects; they can change human thought and society, too.

—adapted from the *Oxford Encyclopedia of the Modern World*, edited by Peter N. Stearns

READING SKILL
Recognizing and understanding exemplification

The writer often give examples to help readers understand the points they are making.

Sometimes writers use signpost phrases for this:

Natural disasters, ***such as*** *earthquakes, hurricanes, floods, drought, and fires, are natural events that destroy large areas.*

However, sometimes readers need to recognize the relationship without a signpost phrase. This often involves making connections across sentences: sentences expressing a more general idea are sometimes followed by sentences or phrases providing more specific or detailed information or examples.

Of the hundreds of natural disasters that have happened in modern times, a few are more famous for the extent of the destruction they caused. ***The eruption of the volcano Krakatoa*** *in 1883…*

4 IDENTIFY Find examples of each of these things in the text.

1. where the effects of the Great Lisbon Earthquake were felt
2. the losses that Portugal suffered
3. an earthquake that had a greater physical impact than the Lisbon one
4. a philosopher that changed his way of thinking after the Lisbon earthquake
5. a change in people's view of natural disasters
6. a change in politics after the earthquake

5 INTEGRATE Read the article again. How was the Great Lisbon Earthquake different from other disasters?

GRAMMAR IN CONTEXT
Obligation with *must* and *have to*

We use *must* or *have to* to say that something is necessary.

We often use *must* to talk about the feelings and wishes of the speaker.

*...people **must** prepare...*

We usually use *have to* to talk about rules that come from someone else. We also usually use *have to* in questions.

*...scientists **have to** look at all the potential causes of a disaster...*
*Do they **have to**...?*

We use *can't* to say it is necessary not to do something.

*...we **can't** only assess natural disasters for their physical effects...*

We use *don't have to* to say that something isn't necessary.

*...scientists **don't have to** feel the ground shake to know that an earthquake is starting...*

Must doesn't have a past tense form, so we use *had to* instead.

*...they **had to** learn to forecast earthquakes.*

See Grammar focus on page 163.

6 APPLY Complete the sentences, so they reflect views from the article. Use *must*, *can't*, or the correct form of *have to*.

1 We _________ think about people, buildings, and history when studying natural disasters.
2 For natural disasters to be on worldwide news, there _________ be extensive damage.
3 We _________ only think about earthquakes after they happen. We _________ prepare for them.
4 Designers _________ think about natural disasters when planning new cities.
5 We _________ feel we are powerless against natural disasters. We can plan and prepare.

Neighbors help rescue a car which went off the road in Valls d'Aguilar, Catalonia, Spain

7 VOCABULARY Find the verbs in the article. Then match them to the definitions.

destroy	react	affect
forecast	protect	prepare

Oxford 3000™

1 _________: to do or say something because of something that happened
2 _________: to say something will happen in the future using information you have now
3 _________: to damage something very badly so it doesn't work or exist anymore
4 _________: to make sure something is safe
5 _________: to get ready for something
6 _________: to produce a change in something

8 EXPAND Use your own ideas to answer the questions.

1 What types of buildings are often **destroyed** in earthquakes?
2 What can be done to **protect** people after a natural disaster?
3 If a natural disaster, like a hurricane, is **forecast**, how can people prepare?
4 How do natural disasters **affect** decisions governments make?
5 How do people usually **react** when they see natural disasters on the news?

9 WHAT'S YOUR ANGLE? Complete the sentences, so they show your views about natural disasters.

1 We have to protect...
2 These types of disasters mostly affect...
3 We must prepare for...
4 Governments must spend more money on forecasting...
5 We must react quickly when...

10 INTERACT Tell a partner your sentences from Exercise 9. Does your partner agree with your views?

5.3 Absolutely Essential

1 ACTIVATE What are the advantages and disadvantages of getting advice from these different people and places?

family	online discussion boards
colleagues	friends
professional advisers	magazine advice columns

2 WHAT'S YOUR ANGLE? What people and places do you go to for advice on the following topics?

money	career	relationships	travel

3 INTEGRATE Read the online advice column. Summarize the problem in a sentence. Then summarize the advice in a list of steps.

AdviceZone

Search

Home | About | Advice | News | Sign in

A problem shared...

The problem:

Life is so busy right now. I am moving to another apartment next week, I just got a promotion and a whole new team to work with, and my exams for my business course start next month. And although I'm absolutely exhausted the whole time, I can't sleep at night. What should I do to survive the next few months?

—Ana

The advice:

Thank you for writing in with your problem. I'm extremely pleased you have decided to get help at this time when things are a little difficult. Remember: a problem shared is a problem halved.

Your basic problem is time—like many people, you see it as your enemy, not your friend. However, that is not the case. So, as well as helping you, I hope this answer will help many of our readers.

First of all, it is absolutely essential that you change the way you think about time. There is always enough time if we use it in the right way. Right now, you should make time to sit down and write a list of things you have to do. In addition to helping you get organized, this will help you relax. Get the problems out of your head and on paper.

Next, look through your list and congratulate yourself. Many of the things you have listed are really good—a promotion, a lovely new home, finishing your business course. Yes, you have to do some work to get there, but you will manage.

Now you need to write *A*, *B*, or *C* next to each thing on the list: *A* is for very important, *B* for fairly important, and *C* for things that are hardly important at all. At this point, you shouldn't feel you have to keep everything on the list. Besides, you might not actually be the best person to do them. For example, yes, you need to move your things to your new home. However, perhaps a team with a van would do a better job than you and your very small car.

The final step is to decide the order to do the A things. You will find there is plenty of time as well as a natural order. The B and C things will follow naturally.

Comments:

cityboy123

You really should try this. I use this solution all the time. And the absolutely amazing thing about C things is that they often disappear by the time you get to them!

happytohelp

In addition to this advice, you should make sure you are eating well and exercising. You say you're really tired but can't sleep—that's a sign that you need to take care of yourself. It's hard to deal with problems when you're feeling absolutely awful.

WRITING SKILL
Using addition and contrast linking words

Use linking words to show the relationship between parts of your writing.

Addition linking words show when you are adding more information.

in addition (to)   *as well as*   *besides*

***In addition to** helping you get organized, this will help you relax.*

Contrasting linking words show when you are presenting different, sometimes opposing, ideas.

but   *however*   *although*

*You see it as your enemy, not your friend. **However**, that is not the case.*

4 IDENTIFY Find each idea from the first column in the text. Then write the linking word used in the text, and match the idea to the connected one from the second column.

1 Ana can't sleep, although ___ e
2 The advice will help Ana ___________ ___
3 The advice will help Ana organize ___________ ___
4 It is going to be hard work, ___________ ___
5 Ana doesn't have to do everything. ___________, ___
6 Ana needs to move her things. ___________, ___

a a group of people might be better.
b there might be someone else better.
c help other people.
d helping her relax.
e she is very tired.
f she will be able to do it.

5 APPLY Rewrite these sentences, adding the best word from the parentheses and changing the grammar and punctuation as necessary.

1 He advised me to stop. I didn't want to. (as well as / however)
2 I need help with the project. I need help with my assignment. (as well as / but)
3 You shouldn't try to do everything. You should try to do as much as you can. (besides / although)
4 You don't have to offer to help. They may not want any help. (besides / however)
5 It will be difficult. That shouldn't stop you from trying. (as well as / but)
6 They worked very well together. They gave an amazing presentation. (although / in addition to)

6 VOCABULARY Match the adjectives in the first column to the ones with similar meanings in the second column. There may be more than one possibility for some of them.

1	tired	d	a	amazing
2	bad	___	b	huge
3	small	___	c	**terrified**
4	afraid	___	d	**exhausted**
5	good	___	e	**freezing**
6	pleased	___	f	extraordinary
7	surprising	___	g	awful
8	important	___	h	tiny
9	special	___	i	terrible
10	silly	___	j	delighted
11	big	___	k	essential
12	cold	___	l	ridiculous

Oxford 3000™

GRAMMAR IN CONTEXT Intensifiers

We can use an adverb before an adjective to make the adjective stronger or weaker.

*I'm **extremely** pleased.*
*Things are **a little** difficult.*

Some adjectives are "ungradable." They often express perfection or its opposite. We use *absolutely* with ungradable adjectives only.

*I'm **absolutely** exhausted.*
~~*I'm very exhausted.*~~
~~*I'm absolutely tired.*~~

See Grammar focus on page 163.

7 EXPAND Find nine more adverb + adjective pairs in the text. Complete the table.

Adverb	Gradable adjective	Ungradable adjective
absolutely		exhausted
extremely	pleased	

8 ASSESS Review the text, and write the adverbs from Exercise 7 on the scale showing how the adverb changes the adjective.

to the highest degree ______________

to a high degree ______________
____
____

to some degree ______________

to a low degree ______________

to a very low degree ______________

9 PREPARE Choose one of these problems to give advice on, or use your own idea. Then discuss your ideas with a partner, and make notes of any additional ideas.

You sent a text message to the wrong friend. In the message, you (correctly) complained about them. Now this friend won't speak to you.

Your boss doesn't recognize the good work you do. Instead, she praises another team member and thinks that person is responsible for your team's success.

Your new neighbor makes a lot of noise at night. You get up early in the morning, so you like to be asleep by 9:30 p.m. You haven't said anything yet, but the situation is getting worse.

10 WRITE Write a response of up to 300 words giving advice on the problem. Use intensifiers and ungradable adjectives.

11 IMPROVE Review your partner's advice with the checklist.

Did your partner...

- give clear and helpful advice?
- include additional and different ideas?
- use intensifiers with adjectives?
- write up to 300 words?

12 WHAT'S YOUR ANGLE? Read the advice from some of your other classmates. Do you have any additional or different ideas? Add comments.

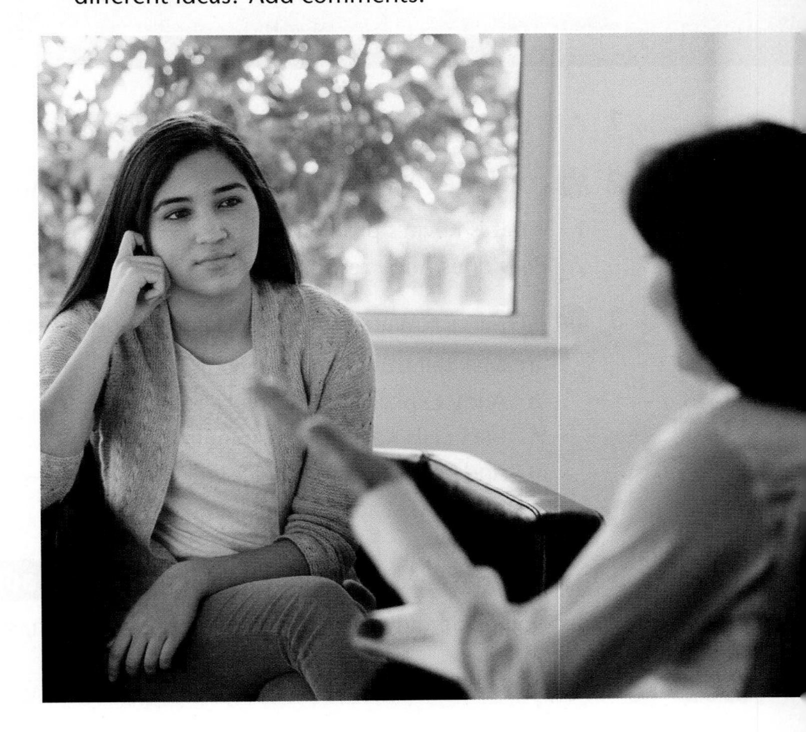

5.4 What's the Problem?

ENGLISH FOR REAL

1 ACTIVATE Look at the pictures. What do you think the problem is?

2 IDENTIFY Watch the first part of the video. Answer the questions with a partner.

1. What is Kevin's problem?
2. How does Andy respond to Kevin?

3 ANALYZE Watch the second part of the video. Choose the things that happen.

- ☐ a Max tells Andy about Kevin.
- ☐ b Andy explains the problem to Max.
- ☐ c Max calls Kevin to give him advice.
- ☐ d Andy asks Max for advice.
- ☐ e Max makes some suggestions.

REAL-WORLD ENGLISH Asking for and giving advice

When you ask for advice, give background information, so the person understands the situation.

Well, the problem is I missed the assignment deadline... What do you think I should do?

You can use modal verbs to ask for advice.

What would you do if you were me? *What should I do?*

Effective advice is often in the form of suggestions rather than instructions for what to do. Use modal verbs and phrases like *I think*.

I think you should... *You could...* *Maybe you can...*

Imperatives are stronger, and so is *had better*. They might sound more like instructions. Avoid these in more formal and delicate situations.

Speak to him. *Just tell him...* *You'd better call.*

When we give advice, we often show we are thinking from the other person's point of view.

If I were you, I would... *It's up to you, but I think...*

The language used to ask for and give advice is different when the situation is more serious, if the context is more formal, or if the speakers don't know each other, for example, between a doctor and patient or in a professional context such as an employee speaking to their manager. In these situations, the language is less direct.

I'm trying to lose weight. Can you advise on what kind of diet I should follow?

I'd recommend that you try to... It might be a good idea to...

4 **ANALYZE** Watch the second part of the video again, and answer the questions. Then discuss the answers with a partner.

1 What is Max's suggestion? How does he express it the first time?
2 Did Andy accept the suggestion? Why or why not?
3 What does Max think is the problem with Kevin staying?
4 How does Max express his suggestion the second time? How is it different from the first time?

5 **IDENTIFY** Listen to extracts from the video, and complete the phrases for asking for and giving advice.

Asking for advice	Giving advice
1 What ________ do?	3 I think ________ call Phil.
2 ________ invite him to stay?	5 ________ invite him.
4 What ________ do if you were me?	6 ________ call Phil.

6 **WHAT'S YOUR ANGLE?** What would you do in Andy's situation?

7 **INTERACT** Work in pairs. Use the phrases in the Real-world English box and in Exercise 5 to ask for and give advice on the following situations.

an argument with a friend
not getting a good grade
what to wear on a night out
buying a new phone
trying to get fit

8 **PREPARE** Work in pairs. Review the problem. Discuss different advice to give.

A friend wants to borrow $30. You have the cash, but your friend hasn't paid you back $20 from last month. You ask your roommate for advice.

9 **INTERACT** Work with a new partner. Decide on your roles. Prepare what you will say. Then role-play the situation.

10 **ASSESS** How helpful was the advice? Did you accept or decline it? Why? What will you do?

11 **INTERACT** Change roles. Follow the same steps with the problem below.

A good friend is having some problems and needs somewhere to stay for a month. You have important exams coming up, and you are not supposed to have anyone to stay in your dorm room for longer than two nights. You ask another friend for advice.

GO ONLINE to create your own version of the English For Real video.

5.5 Don't Panic!

1 ACTIVATE If you had to do the following things, how would you find out what to do? Discuss your ideas with a partner. Use the list below to help.

rescue your phone from water	change a tire
find your keys	change an electric plug
get nail polish off the furniture	

Watch an online video.

Call a friend.

Read instructions in the manual or online.

Try to figure it out for yourself.

Something different.

2 IDENTIFY Listen to someone starting to give instructions. Answer the questions.

1 What will the instructions be for?

2 What problems does Dan have?

3 ASSESS Work in pairs. Number the steps in order to make instructions for changing a bicycle tire.

___ new tube in and tire on

___ air in new tire

___ bike upside down

___ wheel back on bike

___ wheel off bike

___ tube and tire off wheel

4 IDENTIFY Listen to the instructions.

1 Is the order the same as yours?

2 Do you agree with the instructions, or would you suggest something different?

SPEAKING Giving practical instructions

Instructions need to be clear and easy to follow.

Use imperatives and simple sentences.

First, turn the bike upside down.

Use signposting phrases to show the order.

After that, you put the tube in.
Finally, put the wheel back on.

If you're face-to-face with the person, you can use *this*, *that*, *here*, and *there* with gestures to show what you mean.

Look, hold this part here. Then turn that handle.

5 IDENTIFY Listen and complete the extracts from the instructions with verbs and sequencing expressions.

1 So, ________, ________ the bike upside down.

2 ________ ________, ________ the levers.

3 ________ ________ the tire and the tube off.

4 And, ________, ________ the wheel back on.

PRONUNCIATION SKILL
Connected speech with words ending in /t/ or /d/

Sounds can change in connected speech. We often miss /t/ and /d/ at the end of words when the next word starts with a consonant sound.

aroun(d) the　　*firs(t) turn*

However, when the next word starts with a vowel sound, we hear /t/ and /d/ more clearly at the start of that word.

outside edge → *outsi dedge*
flat tire → *fla tire*

6 INTEGRATE Identify the words ending in /t/ and /d/ in these instructions, and predict how to say them in connected speech. Listen and check. Then practice.

1 …turn the bike upside down.

2 After that, turn the levers…

3 Then take the tire and the tube off.

4 …you're going to put the new tube in…

5 …it's hard work, but if you keep trying…

6 And, finally, put the wheel back on…

7 …the opposite way from how you took it off.

8 …call me if you get stuck…

7 IDENTIFY Listen to the summary of the instructions, and complete it. Then identify the words ending with /t/ and /d/, and predict how to say them. Listen again and check. Then practice.

Don't panic. You can do it! Just remember the steps—[1] ________ the bike upside down, [2] ________ the wheel off, [3] ________ the tire off, [4] ________ the tube, [5] ________ the tire, [6] ________ the wheel back on. It's not hard at all.

8 PREPARE Work in pairs. Make a list of everyday disasters. Then choose a disaster from your list or from Exercise 1, and plan instructions for how to deal with it.

9 IMPROVE Practice giving your instructions. When you listen to your partner, use the checklist to give feedback.

☐ Are the instructions clear and easy to follow?

☐ Is there enough (but not too much) detail?

☐ Does your partner use imperatives and signposts?

☐ Are the instructions summarized at the end?

10 INTERACT Give your instructions to a group. Did they find them clear and easy to follow?

11 WHAT'S YOUR ANGLE? What's the most useful thing you learned from your group's instructions?

Now go to page 151 for the Unit 5 Review.

6 Trends

UNIT SNAPSHOT

What is the appeal of tradition?

How do traditions change to reflect the times?

Why do people follow fashion?

BEHIND THE PHOTO

1 Work in pairs. What do you think will be the biggest trend in each of the following areas in the next 20 years?

clothes	food	buildings	transportation	education

I think sustainable fashion will be the biggest trend in clothes. People will buy fewer clothes, but they will last longer, and they will be made from environmentally-friendly materials.

2 Share your ideas with another pair, and choose the most likely trend.

REAL-WORLD GOAL

Read a fashion blog

6.1 Always in Fashion

1 ACTIVATE Discuss these questions with a partner.

1. What's your favorite piece of clothing?
2. Where did you get it?
3. When do you wear it?
4. How do you feel when you wear it?

READING SKILL Using questions when reading

Before you read, review the title, pictures, and general layout of the text. Ask yourself questions about the source, genre, and topic of the text and what you already know about it. This will help focus your mind on the topic and activate your knowledge of it.

Where is the text from?
What do I already know about this topic?

Then read the introduction and think about the questions the text might answer.

Who…? What…? Where…? When…? Why…? How…?

As you read, look for answers to these questions. These will help you understand the main ideas and facts in the text as well as the author's attitude and point of view.

After you finish reading, use the questions to summarize the main ideas. This will help you recall and retain the information better. If there is a question you can't answer, go back to the text and read more carefully.

What were the main points?
What events or actions were described?

2 IDENTIFY Look at the title, pictures, and layout of the text. Then discuss the questions with a partner.

1. Where do you think the text is from—a blog, an encyclopedia, a magazine for teenagers, or a newspaper?
2. What can you see in the pictures?
3. What do you know about the topic of the text (facts, history, etc.)?

3 ASSESS Read the introduction, and write three questions you think the rest of the text might answer. Then compare your questions with a partner. Which three questions do you both think the article is most likely to answer?

4 IDENTIFY Read the text. Are any of your questions answered?

Blue jeans

Blue jeans are the most famous item of clothing ever invented and one of the world's most long-lasting trends. They have been fashionable for more than 50 years. Not only that, as they have traveled around the world, jeans have spread ideas about America as the land of the free and independent—not bad for what started out as cheap work pants.

The story of jeans began about 170 years ago when people went to California to look for gold in the desert. In 1853, Levi Strauss, a 24-year-old from far-off Bavaria, traveled to California to join his family in their San Francisco store. There they sold goods, including tents made of strong canvas, to workers in the gold fields.

Levi saw an opportunity; he had the idea of using the tents to make cheap, tough pants. Later, he changed the material to denim, and he dyed it blue so that dirt marks wouldn't show. Twenty years after this, Jacob Davis, a Latvian tailor, added metal rivets at places where the jeans needed to be stronger, such as by the pockets where the men put the heavy rocks containing gold. The red label on the left back pocket was created in 1936 to identify Levi jeans at a distance since there were now many other makers of jeans, like Lee and Wrangler.

Movies in the 1950s led to jeans becoming fashionable. These films showed exciting young actors, like James Dean, refusing to follow the normal rules of society. The actors and their uniform of tight jeans became symbols of change for younger people. The look was very different from the unfashionable loose pants that their parents wore then, and young people around the world started copying it. In 1957, *Jailhouse Rock*, starring Elvis Presley, spread the trend further, and hippie culture, rock and roll, and hip-hop have all added to it.

Jeans are now worn all over the world. Comfortable and long-lasting, they can be both casual and elegant depending on what they are worn with. They are, however, not always cheap—jeans designed in Milan and Paris are worn as high-fashion items by women in stylish high heels and expensive tops and jewelry.

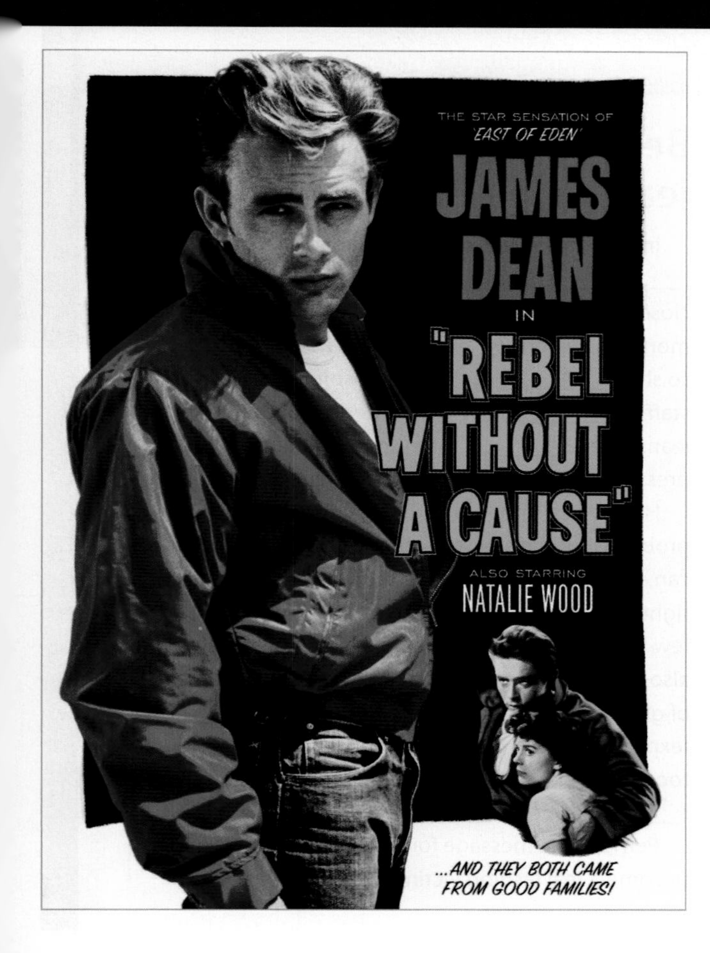

In 1986, *Life* magazine reported that 13 pairs of jeans were bought every second. Since its small beginnings, the jeans industry has grown to now be worth more than $700 billion, with almost all production happening at low cost in countries like India and Brazil. Levi Strauss, the young man who made it all happen, would be amazed to see how his practical, unfashionable working pants have become a global trend in fashion.

Glossary:

canvas: a strong heavy material for making tents and for painting on
tailor: a person whose job is to make clothes for individual customers
rivet: a metal pin used to put two pieces of strong material together

—adapted from *Oxford Encyclopedia of the Modern World*, edited by P. Stearns

5 INTEGRATE Review this information from the text. Write the question for each answer.

1 What have jeans helped to spread ________?
ideas about America
2 ________?
in San Francisco
3 ________?
so that the dirt didn't show
4 ________?
to make the pockets stronger
5 ________?
movies in the 1950s
6 ________?
all over the world
7 ________?
in countries like India and Brazil

6 EXPAND Work with a partner. Write three more questions about the text. Then exchange questions with another pair and answer them.

7 VOCABULARY Match the adjectives to their opposites.

casual	classic	unfashionable	tight
stylish	loose	formal	trendy

Oxford 3000™

8 IDENTIFY Which adjectives from Exercise 7 are used to describe wearable items in the article? Scan paragraphs 4 and 5 to check.

9 INTEGRATE Label the pictures with the words. Then discuss the questions with a partner.

collar heel leg pants sleeve top

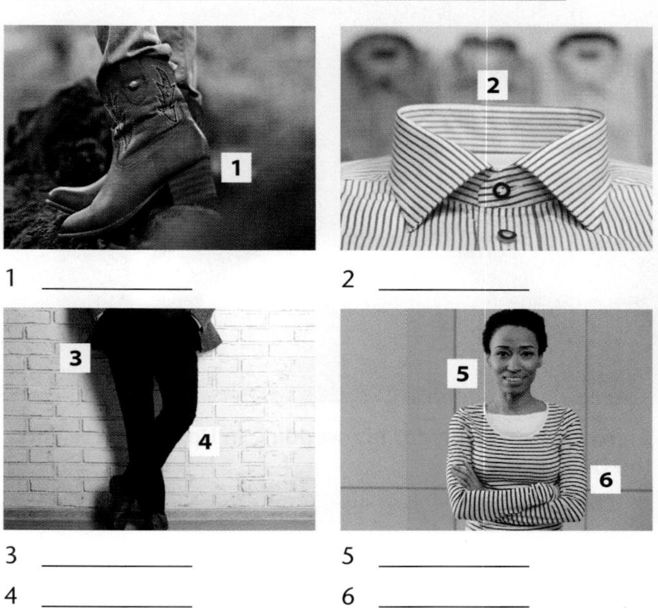

1 ________
2 ________
3 ________
4 ________
5 ________
6 ________

1 Which of the words from Exercise 7 can be used to describe each picture?
2 What type of each item do you prefer?

GRAMMAR IN CONTEXT Time expressions with the present perfect and simple past

We usually use the present perfect with time expressions that indicate unfinished time periods.

Jeans have been fashionable ***for more than 50 years****.*

Over the past few years*, jeans have become more popular.*

We usually use the simple past with time expressions that indicate finished time periods.

The story of jeans began ***about 170 years ago****.*

Movies ***in the 1950s*** *led to jeans becoming fashionable.*

Note that some time expressions can refer to either unfinished or finished periods.

Have you talked *to the tailor* ***this morning****? (It is still morning.)*

Did you talk *to the tailor* ***this morning****? (It is now afternoon or evening.)*

See Grammar focus on page 164.

10 IDENTIFY Identify the sentences in the text that help you decide if these sentences are true or false. Then discuss your answers with a partner.

1 Jeans are not fashionable now.
2 Jeans are usually made from canvas now.
3 Parents of teenagers have worn loose pants for the past 70 years.
4 More than 30 years ago, *Life* magazine reported on the number of jeans bought.
5 The jeans industry makes more money now than at the start.

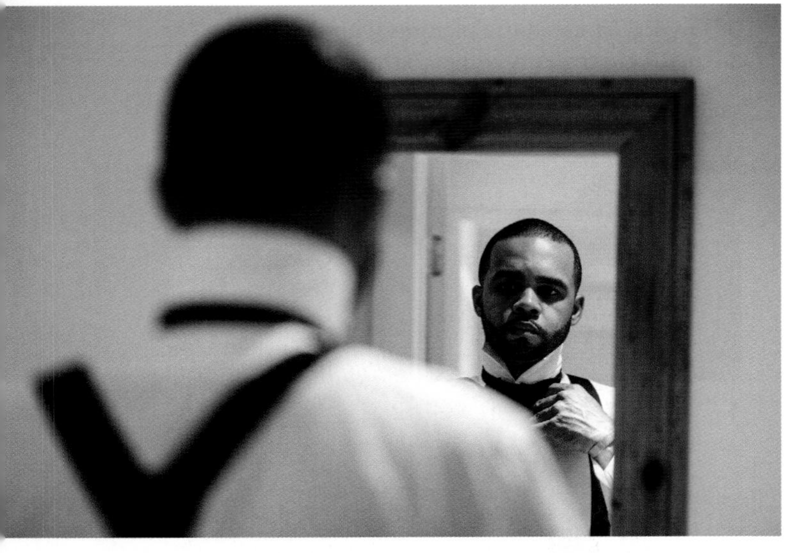

A groom gets ready for his wedding in Upstate New York, the United States

11 APPLY Read the blog post, and complete it with the best form, present perfect or past simple, of the verbs in parentheses.

Search

Dangerous trends

Home | About | Articles | News

Beware! Doctors give skinny jeans a "health warning."

In 2015, a 35-year-old Australian woman [1] __________ (spend) the morning cleaning out her closets while wearing tight jeans. By the end of the morning, her legs [2] __________ (be) as big as balloons, so she [3] __________ (go) to the hospital. The medical staff [4] __________ (have to) cut her out of the skinny jeans. They [5] __________ (be) so tight that they were pressing on the main nerves in her legs!

However, it's not only skinny jeans that cause problems for the stylish—other fashionable clothes can also be dangerous. Over the years, many men with tight collars [6] __________ (complain) of neck pain, but few [7] __________ (be) aware that those collars might also increase the pressure to their eyeballs and the risk of glaucoma. Similarly, millions of women [8] __________ (experience) pain in their feet and legs after spending too long in shoes with very high heels, and some [9] __________ (develop) serious back problems too.

Perhaps the message for the super-stylish is don't become a real fashion victim…

12 WHAT'S YOUR ANGLE? Discuss the questions in a group.

1 What kind of jeans do you have?
2 How long have you had them?
3 When do you wear them?
4 What kind of jeans did you wear ten years ago?
5 What kind of jeans would you never buy?
6 Have you ever been a "fashion victim"?

6.2 Working Trends

1 ACTIVATE Discuss the questions in a group.

1 Do you feel busier now than you did in the past? Why or why not?
2 Do you or people you know work more hours than in the past? Why or why not?

2 IDENTIFY Watch the start of a lecture, and answer the questions.

1 What question is the lecture about?
2 What is the lecturer going to discuss?

WRITING SKILL Note-taking while listening

Making notes when you listen will help you use the information later.

Use the speaker's signpost phrases to help organize your notes.

...now let's move on to discuss...

To make your notes short, simple, and clear:

- use key words, abbreviations, numerals, and symbols to keep them short.
- use bullets to keep them organized.
- underline or circle the main ideas to keep them clear.

This will help you follow the speaker and understand your notes later.

Include:

- main points and examples.
- questions, names, and references to research later.

Review your notes when you finish listening to revise and reorganize them as needed. A diagram could be helpful with this revision.

3 IDENTIFY Look at the notes a student made on the first part of the lecture. (Some words are missing.) Identify the following.

1 features that make the notes short and clear
2 main points
3 examples
4 a question for later research

U.S. changing work patterns

Big research questions:

1 People working more now?

OR

2 [1] ______ helping us work less?

[2] ______ answer from research! e.g., people say/think they work more hours, but [3] ______ show this not true

??? Does this apply to all types of jobs?

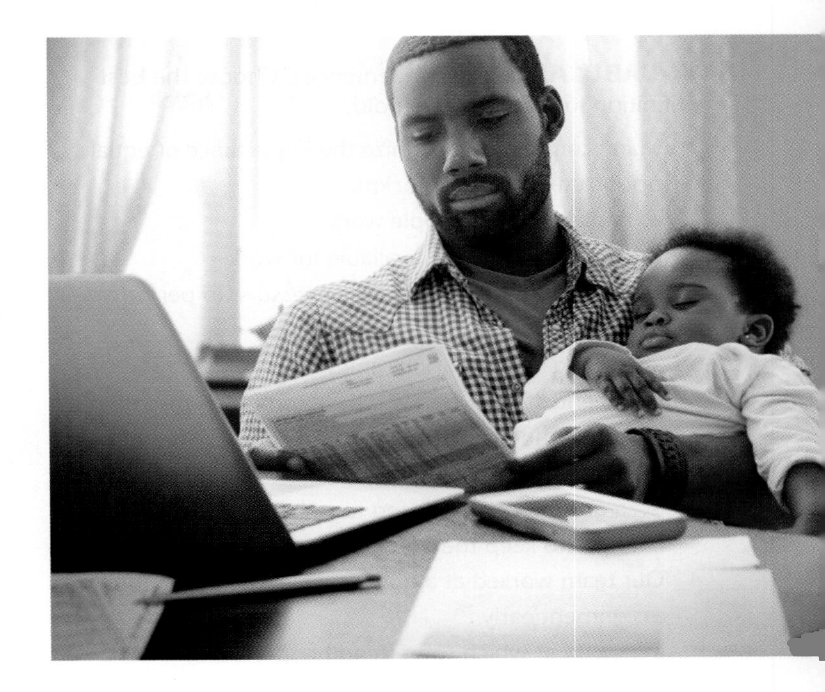

4 INTEGRATE Watch the first part of the lecture, and complete the notes in Exercise 3 with one or two words in each blank.

5 IDENTIFY Match the key ideas from the next part of the lecture to the definitions.

___ roles and responsibilities
___ busyness
___ communication
___ schedule
___ efficiency

a the quality of doing something well with no waste of time or money
b the feeling of always being busy
c a list of things you have to do and the time to do them
d the activity of expressing ideas and giving information
e the position and jobs a person has

6 INTERACT What do you think the lecturer might say about each key idea? Discuss each one with a partner.

7 **IDENTIFY** Watch the next part of the interview. Number the key ideas in Exercise 5 in the order they are mentioned. Did the lecturer include any of your suggestions from Exercise 6?

8 **VOCABULARY** Read the sentences. Choose the best definition for the words in bold.

1 Many companies recognize the importance of equal opportunities in the **workplace**.
   a a place where people work
   b a group of people available for work
2 My sister is worried about the **pressure** to perform well at her new job.
   a feeling sadness about an event
   b feeling stress when you have too much to do
3 Couples who divide **household** responsibilities get a lot more done.
   a a group or family living together in one place
   b work to keep the house clean
4 Our team worked at a good **pace** and finished the assignment early.
   a speed at which something happens
   b the quality of work being done
5 The new conference room was built **for the benefit of** the sales department.
   a to bring something new
   b to be useful for
6 If he quits his job now, he will receive his **pension** right away.
   a payment to someone who no longer works
   b an increase in the amount paid to a person

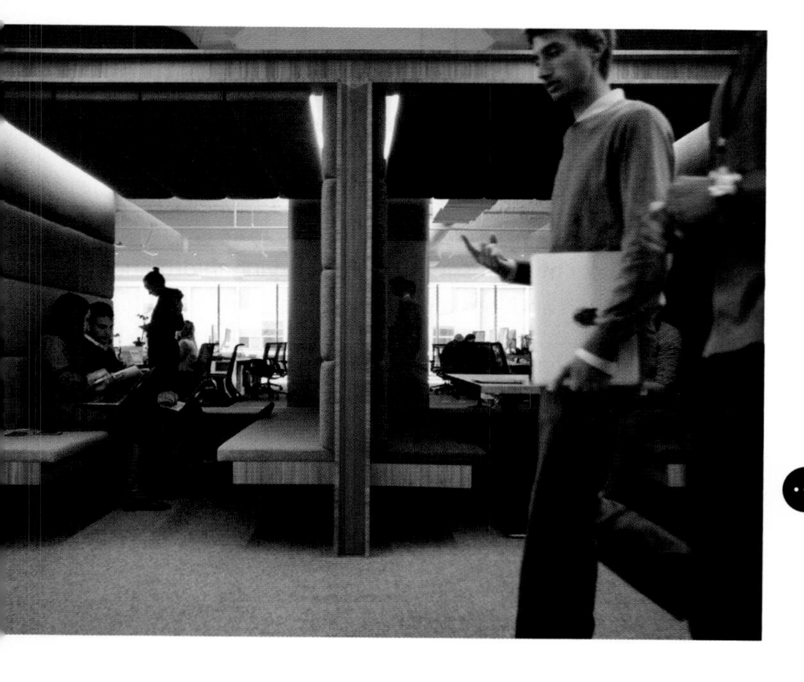

7 I want to **retire** in five years and travel the world.
   a to stop working because of illness
   b to leave a job because you have reached the appropriate age to do so

Oxford 3000™

9 **USE** Complete the sentences with the words from Exercise 8.

1 I don't want to ________________ early. I will be bored at home.
2 If I improve my ________________, I will be able to complete the project by the end of the week.
3 My boss changed the meeting time ________________ the team.
4 One of the best benefits that my company offers is its ________________.
5 He left his job because he didn't like the environment in the ________________.
6 The ________________ chores should be done by the entire family, not just one person.
7 My co-worker was under so much ________________ that he ended up getting sick.

10 **PREPARE** Work with a partner. Plan how to organize your notes for part of the lecture about busyness and people's work schedules.

1 Where are you going to write them?
2 Are you going to use different colors, styles (e.g., underlining)? What for?
3 Will you use a diagram?

11 **WRITE** Watch this part of the lecture again, and take notes. For each key idea, add a question that you could research later.

12 **IMPROVE** Compare your notes with your partner.

1 Do you have the same information?
2 Are your main points and examples clear?

13 **EXPAND** Watch the final part of the lecture, and take notes. Add a question to each key idea.

14 **IMPROVE** Review, revise, and reorganize your notes. Then compare your notes in a group. Discuss the questions you added to the notes on the lecture. Can anyone answer them?

15 **WHAT'S YOUR ANGLE?** Discuss these questions in your group.

1 How do you think work will change in the future?
2 Will these be positive or negative changes?

6.3 Quick Fixes

1 ACTIVATE Preview the images, and complete the ad for the podcast series with the words in the box.

grapefruit	cookie	cabbage	sleeping
vinegar	TV	high-protein	burger

Can you complete the information about these famous diets?

1820
Lord Byron, the English poet, makes drinking [1] ________ and water popular.

1930s
The Hollywood Diet—the low-calorie diet suggests eating a [2] ________ with every meal.

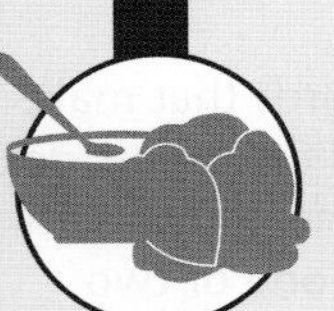

1950s
The [3] ________ Soup Diet—this diet promises you will lose about 11 pounds a week by eating less and having this soup every day.

1970
The [4] ________ Beauty Diet suggests losing weight by taking medication to sleep.

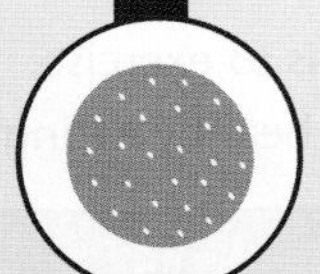

1975
The [5] ________ Diet—a Florida doctor creates a special cookie to help people lose weight.

1991
Low-Fat—with this trend, people started cutting fat from their diet (McDonald's even introduced a low-fat [6] ________).

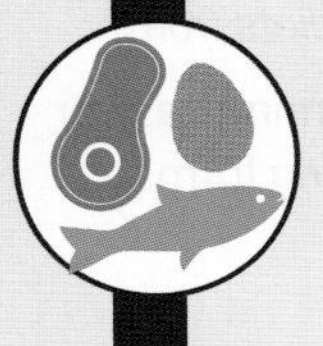

1992
The Atkins Diet—eating only [7] ________, low-carb food is made popular in a new book.

2004
The Biggest Loser first appears on [8] ________, and taking part in reality shows becomes a way to lose weight.

2 WHAT'S YOUR ANGLE? Answer these questions.

1 Which of the diets in the ad had you heard of before?
2 What other diet trends have you heard of?
3 Do you know anyone who has tried any of the diet trends? What was their experience?

LISTENING SKILL Previewing using images

Previewing pictures before listening will help you understand the speakers more easily.

The images will indicate what the topic is. You can then:

- think about what you already know about the topic.
- predict information which might be included
- check key vocabulary before you listen

3 PREPARE You are going to listen to the introduction to a podcast. Review the information below and in Exercise 1, and answer the questions.

1 What points do you think Dr. Costello will make in the podcast?
2 What key words do you think you will hear?

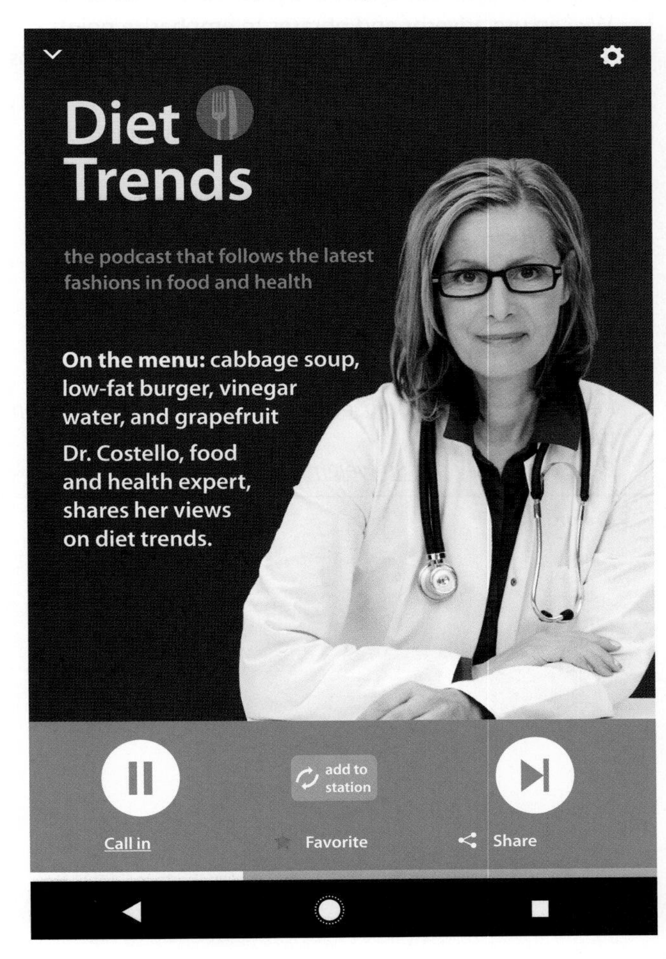

4 **IDENTIFY** Listen to the podcast. Answer the questions.

1 Which familiar information did you hear?
2 Which key words did you hear?

5 **INTEGRATE** Listen again. Choose the main points Dr. Costello makes.

- ☐ a New diets come along frequently.
- ☐ b Men prefer diets that promise fast weight loss to traditional diets.
- ☐ c Studies show that diets that promise fast weight loss don't work.
- ☐ d People don't like making changes forever.
- ☐ e Some doctors support diets that promise fast weight loss.
- ☐ f It is important who gives the diet message.
- ☐ g There is too much information about healthy eating.
- ☐ h The way to lose weight is to control food and exercise.
- ☐ i The important thing is to eat at certain times of day.

6 **INTERACT** Which of Dr. Costello's ideas do you agree with? Discuss them with a partner.

VOCABULARY DEVELOPMENT
Adverbs and phrases for emphasis

We can use adverbs and phrases to emphasize points. This makes our message clearer to other people. Adverbs and phrases are usually stressed in speech.

Some phrases are usually placed at the beginning of the sentences.

In fact,... *More importantly,...* *To tell you the truth,...*
***In fact**, many can have the reverse effect.*
*And, **more importantly**, can they keep the weight off?*

The adverbs are normally placed before the word to be emphasized.

actually *clearly* *honestly* *simply* *just* *(not) even*
*People are **clearly** confused by a lot of the diet information they read.*
*People **actually** put on weight.*

Oxford 3000™

7 **INTEGRATE** Can you remember which adverbs and phrases were used to emphasize each point in the podcast? Complete the sentences.

clearly	even	more importantly	not even	
just	to tell you the truth		simply	honestly

1 And, perhaps ________, why do some people follow one fashionable diet after another, ________ when they know the last one failed?
2 These kinds of fashionable diets are ________ not successful in the long term.
3 Many of us don't want to make long-term changes in our lifestyle, ________ if it makes us overweight.
4 They are connected to people who are ________ beautiful, or charming, or both.
5 It ________ doesn't matter.
6 People ________ don't know what to think.
7 ________, as someone who has to watch her weight, I understand the appeal of these diets.

8 **IDENTIFY** Listen and check. Underline the main point of emphasis in each sentence in Exercise 7.

9 **WHAT'S YOUR ANGLE?** Choose the words that make these points show your opinions. Which of the points do you feel strongly about? Practice making the points with words or phrases to emphasize them. Add one or two more points of your own about diets, food, and health.

1 Diet trends are **bad** / **not bad** for your health.
2 **Most** / **Few** people put on weight when they stop following a fashionable diet.
3 Diet trends are **fine if** / **no good even if** carefully controlled.
4 The **best** / **worst** way to control weight is to exercise.
5 We need **more** / **less** information about healthy eating.

GRAMMAR IN CONTEXT
used to and *be / get used to*

To talk about situations or regular actions in the past that don't happen anymore, we use a form of *used to* + infinitive.

*We **used to eat** low-fat food and lots of carbs.*
*We **didn't use to think** about diets so much.*
*Where **did you use to get** information about diets from?*

To talk about regular activities being or becoming easy or familiar, we use a form of *be / get used to* + *-ing* form.

*We **are used to following** our life choices.*
*We need to **get used to accepting** the fact.*
***I'm not used to exercising** so much.*
*How did you **get used to eating** those types of food?*

See Grammar focus on page 164.

10 **IDENTIFY** Complete the sentences from the podcast with the correct form of *used to* or *be / get used to*. Then listen and check.

1 And just when we ________________ doing all this, food bloggers started telling us something different.
2 And then we can go back to what we ________________ do.
3 Maybe these famous people ________________ be fat, maybe they ________________ be.
4 In comparison, we ________________ getting colder, harder messages from doctors.

11 **IDENTIFY** Correct the errors in the *used to* and *be / get used to* forms.

1 I use to be a vegetarian, but I'm not anymore.
____
2 I'm used to cook for myself now.
____
3 I getting used to being careful about what I eat.
____
4 I used try all sorts of diets when I was younger.
____
5 I'm not really used buying groceries online.
____

PRONUNCIATION SKILL ***used to***

Note the correct pronunciation of *used to* in spoken English:

- *used* has one syllable. The *s* is pronounced /s/ (not /z/); the *-ed* is not pronounced.
- *to* is usually stronger when at the end of a sentence.
  /juːs tu/
  I ***used*** *to.*
- *to* is usually weaker when followed by another word.
  /juːs tə/
  I ***used to*** *do more exercise.*
  I'm ***used to*** *having that.*
- when the next word starts with a vowel sound, a short /w/ sound is often added.
  I ***used to*** *(w)eat meat.*
  I got ***used to*** *(w)exercising more.*

12 **NOTICE** Read the following sentences. Predict the pronunciation of "used to". Then listen and check.

1 A: Liz, do you do yoga in the morning?
B: I used to. Now I do yoga in the afternoon.
2 A: Do you enjoy chocolate as much as your sister does?
B: I used to eat it often. I'm trying to eat healthier now.
3 A: David, do you like to do any water sports?
B: I used to waterski. Now I just like to swim.
4 A: Does it bother you that your husband doesn't eat meat?
B: Not anymore. I'm used to it now.
5 A: What do you do to stay active?
B: I used to bike to work every day. I had to stop after I injured my knee.

13 **APPLY** Practice saying the sentences from Exercise 12 with the correct pronunciation of *used to*.

14 **INTEGRATE** Which sentences in Exercise 11 are true for you? Change the others, so they are true, too.

15 **WHAT'S YOUR ANGLE?** Answer the questions.

1 What quick fixes do people usually want in these areas of life?

exercise	education	fashion/appearance

2 Have you ever tried a quick fix? Did it work? Why or why not?

6.4 Your Honest Opinion

1 ACTIVATE Look at the pictures, and discuss the questions.

1 What do you think Kevin and Max might be talking about?
2 What do you think Andy and Max might be talking about?

2 IDENTIFY Watch the first part of the video. Did you predict correctly?

3 ANALYZE Answer the questions. Then watch the first part of the video again to check.

1 Did Max ask for Kevin's opinion?
2 How happy is Max to hear Kevin's opinion? How can you tell?
3 What could Kevin do better next time?

REAL-WORLD ENGLISH Asking for and giving opinions

When you ask a friend or someone you know well for their opinion, you can use these phrases:

In your honest opinion,...?
What do you think?

When you give your opinion, you need to judge how much information to give and how direct you should be. Think about these questions:

- Has the other person asked for your opinion?
- How honest do you want to be?
- How honest does the other person want you to be?
- How will your opinion affect the other person?

You can use these phrases to give opinions.

In my opinion,...
The way I see it,...
I think...
Don't get me wrong,...

4 ▶ **ANALYZE** Watch the second part of the video. How is it different from the first with regard to asking for and giving opinions?

5 ▶ **IDENTIFY** Watch the second part of the video again. In each pair, choose the phrase used by Max and Andy. Then decide if each phrase is asking for (A) or giving (G) an opinion.

1 ☐ a Give me your honest opinion. Do I look like a clown? ___
☐ b What's your opinion? Do you think I look like a clown? ___

2 ☐ a No, I don't think you look like a clown. ___
☐ b What? No, of course not. ___

3 ☐ a Tell me the truth. ___
☐ b Tell me honestly. ___

4 ☐ a Well, since you're asking… OK, maybe you do look a bit…strange. ___
☐ b Well, since you want to know…maybe there is some truth in what he said.

5 ☐ a Does Kevin actually have a point? ___
☐ b Is Kevin really right? ___

6 ☐ a You're not wrong—you just have your own style.
☐ b Don't get me wrong—you have your own style, but… ___

6 **INTERACT** Work in pairs. Choose situation 1 or 2, and prepare what you will say. Then role-play the situation. Discuss what worked well in your role play. Then swap roles and repeat.

Situation 1: You are not sure about whether to change your college major. You have been taking classes for a semester, and you have enjoyed them. However, you don't like your teachers, and you think they don't like you. You got feedback from them that you don't participate enough. You ask the opinion of your good friend and classmate on your participation and on the teachers. You have known each other for a long time and like each other a lot.

Situation 2: You are unhappy because your boss criticized a report you wrote. You have only had the job for three months, and you have been trying really hard to impress your boss. You tell your colleague about the situation and ask for their opinion on the report. You don't know your colleague very well, but they are a very respected and experienced member of the team.

7 **ANALYZE** Work with another pair who role-played a different situation. Act out your role plays for each other, and then compare how and why the language you used was different.

8 **WHAT'S YOUR ANGLE?** When was the last time you were asked for your opinion? Who asked you, and what was it about? Think about what you said. Did you follow the advice in this lesson?

GO ONLINE
to create your own version of the English For Real video.

6.5 Fashion Victim

1 ACTIVATE Think about the trends in the box. Then discuss the questions.

big eyebrows	big beard	vintage clothes	toe shoes

1. Which of these fashion and beauty trends have you seen?
2. How fashionable are they now?
3. What other trends have there been in the past few years?

2 IDENTIFY Listen to James and Dena talking about fashion trends. Which trends did they used to follow?

SPEAKING Talking about past habits

When talking about past habits:

Use *used to* to talk about a general past habit.

*I **used to** walk to school.*

Use past tenses to talk about specific examples.

*I actually **went** the long way to school that day.*

In a conversation, when talking about past shared experiences, use questions to involve the other person in what you are saying.

Do you remember the day when…?
What was the name of the place where we went?

3 INTEGRATE Listen again and answer the questions.

1. What is James wearing now?
2. Why did he stop wearing them in the past?
3. What does Dena think about them?
4. What kind of jeans did James have?
5. Did he enjoy wearing them?
6. What was the problem with them?
7. What did Dena use to have that she saw in some photos recently?
8. Does Dena have a tattoo?

GRAMMAR IN CONTEXT *do* for emphasis

To emphasize an action, we can add *do / does* or *did* before a simple present or simple past verb. Notice that we use the base form of the verb after the emphatic *do, does*, or *did*.

*I **do** like beards.*
*She **does** like jeans.*

We can show contrast with *do / does* or *did*.

*I **didn't** get a real tattoo, but I **did** have fake ones.*

We can also use *do* before an imperative, especially for offers.

***Do** try the shoes on before you buy them.*

See Grammar focus on page 164.

4 IDENTIFY Listen and add *do, does*, or *did* to the extracts from James and Dena's conversation.

1. I ________ like those jeans.
2. I ________ have those, but I never wore them much.
3. You ________ look trendy with your big beard.
4. I ________ have very big eyebrows for a while.
5. I don't have any, but I ________ think about it…

5 INTEGRATE Add *do, does*, or *did* for emphasis or contrast to the correct place in the sentences below. Make changes to the verb if necessary. Listen and check, and then repeat.

1. I want a new hairstyle.
2. We didn't have dyed hair, but we had very long hair.
3. I don't have any jeans these days, but I used to own five pairs.
4. He doesn't like sports clothes, but he likes sneakers.
5. You wear vintage clothes.
6. They didn't use to buy a lot of clothes, but they used to make them.

6 PREPARE Think of two fashion and beauty trends you have followed and make some notes.

7 INTERACT In a group, share your experiences of following fashion trends.

8 WHAT'S YOUR ANGLE? Discuss your group conversation with a different partner.

1. Who followed similar fashion trends to you in the past?
2. Who would you like to go shopping for clothes with? Why?

Now go to page 152 for the Unit 6 Review.

7 Surroundings

UNIT SNAPSHOT

How do our surroundings affect our behavior?

How do our surroundings affect how we feel?

In what ways do we try to control our surroundings?

BEHIND THE PHOTO

1 Look at the factors below and answer the questions. Think of examples of places you know to support your ideas.

sounds light smell space temperature nature beauty people

1 How important are these factors in influencing our perception of our surroundings?
2 How can these factors influence our perception of surroundings positively and negatively?

2 Compare your answers with a partner. How similar are your views?

REAL-WORLD GOAL

Visit a new place and post a photo of it on social media

7.1 Cluttered Spaces

1 ACTIVATE Look at the photo. Discuss the questions in pairs.

1 What kind of clutter can you see in the room?
2 Would you like to work or study in this room? Why or why not?
3 How would you improve this room?

VOCABULARY DEVELOPMENT Quantifiers

We use quantifiers to talk about the number or amount of something.

all (of)	*most (of)*	*lots of*
plenty of	*some*	*none of*

There are ***lots of*** *things on the floor.*
I want to keep ***most of*** *my stuff.*

Some quantifiers can only be followed by count nouns.

(a) few *several* *a number of* *(not) many*

I have ***several*** *pillows on my bed.*

Some quantifiers can only be followed by noncount nouns.

(a) little *(not) much*

*There is****n't much*** *space in the room.*

Note that *a few* and *a little* mean "some," but *few* and *little* mean "not as many/much as wanted/expected."

They had ***a few*** *things in the closet, like clothes and shoes.*
They had ***few*** *things in the closet. Most of their stuff was on the floor.*

Oxford 3000™

2 IDENTIFY Choose the correct quantifier to complete each sentence. Sometimes both are possible.

1 There are *several* / *a little* books on the floor.
2 I have *a little of* / *lots* of clothes in my closet.
3 There is *some* / *a number of* stuff under my bed.
4 *None of* / *All of* my socks are in pairs.
5 There's *several* / *not much* light in the room.
6 I have *a number of* / *a few* things to throw away.
7 There is *plenty of* / *most of* space for everything in my room.
8 I am happy I still have *little* / *a little* space in my closet.

3 INTEGRATE Which of the sentences in Exercise 2 are true for your bedroom? Tell your partner.

4 WHAT'S YOUR ANGLE? Work in pairs. Describe your favorite and least favorite rooms in your home.

1 What is in the rooms?
2 Why are they your favorite and least favorite rooms?

5 IDENTIFY You are going to listen to a podcast about decluttering. First, listen to extracts with three people from the podcast. What key words related to the topic do you hear?

LISTENING SKILL Recognizing levels of formality

Recognizing the level of formality of English will help you understand the relationship between speakers or between a speaker and an audience.

In addition to vocabulary, formal and informal English often use different grammar. For example, less formal English tends to use more contractions and parts of sentences rather than full forms and complete sentences.

Most of my clients report that life is much easier. (formal)
Me and you loved the ideas…the kids weren't so happy. (informal)

Sometimes English is more formal or official, e.g., in announcements or speeches.

The time now is 10:30.

A lot of English is semiformal. You hear this frequently in more informal TV shows or interviews, between bosses and employees at work, or among professors and students in college.

Several writers suggest that our stress levels and happiness will improve when we declutter.

In closer relationships, e.g., between friends and family, you hear much more informal language.

Yeah, honey, but only 'cause they wanna buy more stuff.

6 IDENTIFY Listen again and identify the level of formality of each extract. Write *1*, *2*, or *3*. Compare your answers with a partner, and explain how you decided.

___ Informal
___ Semi-formal
___ Official / formal

7 **APPLY** Listen again and write the words and sentences each speaker used to express these ideas.

Speaker 1:

1 It's 10:30. ______________

2 talks about ______________

Speaker 2:

3 The children accepted the idea. ______________

4 possessions / things ______________

Speaker 3:

5 removing ______________

6 It is difficult. ______________

8 **ASSESS** Listen to the complete podcast, and choose the correct answers.

1 Liza thinks it is not good for our health to
  a throw away things.
  b give away everything.
  c have too many things.
2 Some authors say that giving away things makes us
  a less stressed.
  b less happy.
  c less rich.
3 When you manage to keep to a plan for giving things away,
  a you must tell other people.
  b you should reward yourself.
  c you are allowed to go shopping.
4 One of Liza's suggestions is to put things in boxes to find out
  a what you really need.
  b how many things you have.
  c where to store things.
5 The children of the people interviewed
  a loved the idea of decluttering from the start.
  b were already very neat and tidy.
  c changed their mind about decluttering.

9 **INTEGRATE** Work in groups of three, Students A, B, and C. Listen to the two strategies and to Ed and Sarah's experience again. After you listen, do the following:

Student A: Summarize the first strategy.

Student B: Describe the second strategy.

Student C: Describe what happened in Ed and Sarah's family.

10 **WHAT'S YOUR ANGLE?** Which strategy would work best for you? Why? Tell your group.

GRAMMAR IN CONTEXT
Present perfect continuous

We use the present perfect continuous to talk about an activity or situation that started in the past and continues now or has only just stopped.

*You **have been bringing** more and more things into your home.*

We can use the present perfect continuous with *for* and a period of time.

*Many of your things **have been sitting** in your home **for** years.*

We can use the present perfect continuous with *since* and a date, day, time, or event.

*I**'ve been working** with people with too much stuff **since** 2009.*

We often use the present perfect continuous to give reasons for a present situation.

*The house looks great. He**'s been cleaning** it all morning.*

See Grammar focus on page 165.

11 **APPLY** Rewrite the sentences using the present perfect continuous and *for* or *since*.

1 I moved to my current home four years ago.
  I've been living in my current home for four years.
2 I started using my storage system six months ago.
3 I began planning to clean up my place last month.
4 I started hiding things under the bed years ago.
5 I began selling my old stuff online in January.

12 **INTERACT** Write questions with *How long* for each sentence in Exercise 11. Interview your partner. Use your imagination to answer the questions if necessary.

13 **WHAT'S YOUR ANGLE?** Follow the steps.

1 Look at the photos, and choose the surroundings you consider the best.
2 Find three other students you could share this home with.
3 Tell the class why you would all choose that kind of place.

7.2 Beauty All Around

1 ACTIVATE Which of these images is the most beautiful to you? Tell your partner why.

2 WHAT'S YOUR ANGLE? What is the most beautiful place you have visited? Why do you consider it so beautiful?

3 ASSESS Skim the article. Then add the paragraph letter next to its main idea.

___ The meanings of the words environment and aesthetics have changed.
___ It is now possible to study environmental aesthetics.
___ In the past, studying beauty in the environment meant studying beauty in nature.
___ Studying the beauty of the environment is a new idea.
___ The aesthetics of environment is a very broad and important subject.

4 IDENTIFY Read the article and check your answers to Exercise 3.

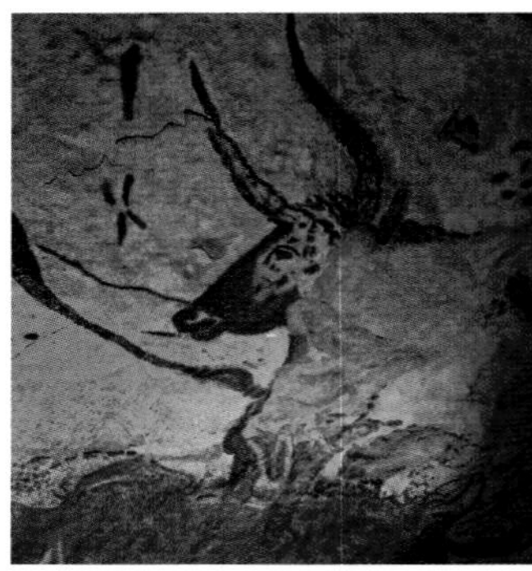

Studying the beauty of our surroundings

A Looking at the clouds out of an airplane window, standing in a Japanese garden, looking at the stones on the ground and how they have been carefully arranged, and sitting in an elegantly decorated room—all of these activities can show us the beauty of our surroundings. But did you know that you can now attend college courses on **this**? That is correct; students can now specialize in *environmental *aesthetics*, involving the study of arts, philosophy, social sciences, architecture, and the environment.

B Seeing a new subject being born in education is quite unusual, as **most** are considerably old. For centuries, we have studied art, trying to understand what makes things beautiful to us. However, it is only in the past 30 years that researchers have decided to do the same with our surroundings, and **they** have been asking questions such as what is "environment," why do we find **it** beautiful, and how does it affect us?

C Before the 20th century, the history of environmental aesthetics is the history of the aesthetics of nature. People have been observing nature and using it as a model for art for a very long time. The earliest paintings that we know about are cave paintings from 30,000 years ago, and **these** already show that our ancestors were looking carefully at nature back then. The Greek philosopher Aristotle wrote about the beauty and order of nature 2,400 years ago, and poets have been writing about **the same thing** ever since.

D Over the past two centuries, however, the concept of "environment" has become broader. Depending on how we approach it, the **idea of "environment"** may now include not only the natural world but also the interior of a building, the commercial and industrial landscape of a city, or even the other people around us. Similarly, the concept of "aesthetics" has also changed and continues to do so—from older **views** related to taste and judgment of what is beautiful to more recent ones involving how we perceive and experience "beauty."

E **The aesthetics of environment** is, then, a rich and varied field, and its importance is equally broad. It **has increased the range of traditional aesthetics** to include the **many different settings** in which we participate, from rooms to neighborhoods, from villages to the countryside, from the experience of a single person to the relationships in a social group, from magnificent natural landscapes to our ordinary daily life. And in doing so, it reminds us that we are not independent from **our environment** and that we should care for it.

***aesthetics:** the study of beauty

—adapted from *Encyclopedia of Aesthetics*, edited by Michael Kelly

READING SKILL Recognizing and understanding forward and backward references

Writers use pronouns such as *it*, *them*, *those*, *which*, *many*, *one*, and *so* to refer to something mentioned in the text so they can avoid repetition. The references can refer to things earlier in the text.

*...looking at the stones on the ground and how **they** have been carefully arranged...*

They can also refer to things later in the text.

*We used to see **it** as strong, a "mother nature," protecting us, but our view of nature has changed in recent times.*

The thing referred to might be a word, a phrase, or an idea that has been expressed in a sentence or paragraph. For example, *which* and *so* often refer to a clause, sentence, or idea.

*There are different interpretations of the word environment, **which** makes things more complicated.*

*The concept of "aesthetics" has also changed and continues to do **so**.*

To understand a reference, consider if the pronoun is singular or plural; if it refers to a person or a thing; if it could refer to something mentioned before or after; and if it can refer to a word, phrase, clause, or idea. Then read the sentence and try to use the context to identify what the pronoun refers to.

5 IDENTIFY Read paragraphs A to C. Decide what these words in bold refer to.

1 this (A) _________
2 most (B) _________
3 they (B) _________
4 it (B) _________
5 these (C) _________
6 the same thing (C) _________

6 EXPAND Read paragraphs D to E. Find the words that refer to these underlined phrases.

1 the idea of "environment" (D) _________
2 views (D) _________
3 the aesthetics of environment (E) _________
4 has increased the range of traditional aesthetics (E) _________
5 many different settings (E) _________
6 our environment (E) _________

GRAMMAR IN CONTEXT Present perfect and present perfect continuous

We use the present perfect for actions that started and finished in the past with a result now.

*Our view of nature **has changed** in recent times.*

We use the present perfect continuous for actions that started in the past and continue now.

*Poets **have been writing** about the same thing ever since then.*
*How long **have** people **been observing** nature?*

There is sometimes little difference between the present perfect and the present perfect continuous. It depends on how we see the action. Do we see it as something finished or something in process?

*For centuries, we **have studied** / **been studying** art.*

See Grammar focus on page 165.

7 APPLY Put the words in the correct order to make questions.

1 What / researchers / have / to do / decided / ?
2 What / they / doing / have / since then / been / ?
3 How long / poets / been / have / about nature / writing / ?
4 What / become / broader / has / over the past two centuries / ?
5 Which / changing / has also / concept / been / ?
6 What / of traditional aesthetics / the range / increased / has / ?

8 IDENTIFY Read the article again, and answer the questions in Exercise 7 using complete sentences.

9 APPLY Complete the sentences with either the present perfect or the present perfect continuous forms of the verbs in parentheses. Then compare your answers with a partner, and explain your choices.

1 A: What are you doing?
B: Painting. I _________________ (work) on this picture all morning.
2 A: _________ you _________ (read) this book about the environment?
B: Yes, I finished it last week. I _________________ (read) this one about nature and art since then.
3 A: I _________________ (research) this subject all morning but still don't really understand it.
B: _________ you _________ (try) this website?
4 A: We _________________ (know) about environmental problems for years now.
B: And we still _________________ (not do) much about them.

10 VOCABULARY Complete the phrases with the words in the box.

education	specialize	attend	do well
research	review	philosophy	results

1 _________ for your exams
2 _________ in a particular subject
3 _________ class
4 ancient and modern _________
5 _________ in college
6 get good _________
7 _________ something online
8 get an all-around _________

Oxford 3000™

11 INTEGRATE Complete the sentences with the words from the box in Exercise 10. Which sentences do you agree with? Compare your ideas with a partner.

1 Everyone needs to _________ college to _________ in life.
2 A good _________ is more important than a good job.
3 _________ always show how much someone has _________ the material before taking the test.
4 Learning how to _________ is more useful in today's world than studying a subject like _________.
5 Students shouldn't _________ too early in their education.

12 WHAT'S YOUR ANGLE? Imagine you are going to study one of the subjects below. Number them in order of preference. Then explain your order to your partner.

___ Architecture
___ Environmental aesthetics
___ Art
___ Environmental science
___ Philosophy

The Chay River flows through a valley in Lao Cai Province, northern Vietnam

7.3 Travel Lessons

1 ACTIVATE How does a change of surroundings make you feel? Choose the top three feelings and explain your choices to your partner.

relaxed	excited	tired	happy	nervous	bored

2 IDENTIFY Read the start of a travel blog. How did the writer use to feel on vacation?

Home | About | Search

Three travel tips

I've learned a lot in my life. I've been lucky enough to go to college, and I have all kinds of qualifications, but this isn't how I learned my most important lessons. I learned those from traveling.

I've always been a busy person, and, to be honest, me and vacations haven't always had a good relationship. At times, I've been too bored to enjoy my surroundings. Yes, you read that right. I was too bored. I missed my friends, I missed my exciting life in a big city, I missed Wi-Fi, I missed social media, and, most of all, I missed being busy. I just didn't know how to be somewhere different. Vacations were a waste of time because I simply wasn't open enough to appreciate new surroundings or the people I met.

But I've learned my lessons, and here are the three important ones traveling has taught me.

Read more...

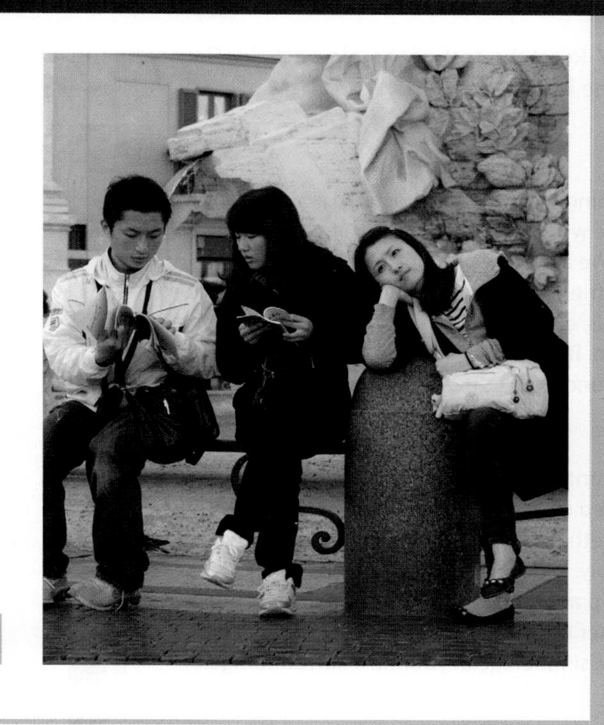

GRAMMAR IN CONTEXT
Too and *enough* with the *to* infinitive

We often use *too* + adjective + *to* infinitive for explaining or giving a reason.

*I've been **too bored to enjoy** my surroundings.*
*The hotel is **too expensive to stay** in.*

We can also use (*not* +) adjective + *enough* + *to* infinitive for the same purpose.

*I've been **lucky enough to go** to college.*
*The water was**n't warm enough to go** swimming.*

See Grammar focus on page 165.

3 IDENTIFY Find examples of *too* and *enough* with the *to* infinitive in the article.

4 APPLY Complete the sentences with *too* or (*not*) *enough* and the adjective in parentheses.

1 I can't take that jacket on vacation. It's ________________ (small) to fit in my suitcase.
2 Air travel is ________________ (expensive) to fit many people's budget, though it is getting cheaper because of competition.
3 Most travelers are ________________ (brave) to travel on their own. Many still prefer to travel in groups.
4 A one-week vacation is often ________________ (short) to be relaxing. Two weeks minimum is better.
5 Travel websites and apps are usually ________________ (detailed) to provide reliable and up-to-date information about travel destinations. We don't need travel books anymore.

5 WHAT'S YOUR ANGLE? Complete the sentences, so they are true for you. Then compare your answers with a partner.

On vacation…

1 I'm usually too ________________ to ________________.

2 I'm never ________________ enough to ________________.

3 I'm always too ________________ to ________________.

4 I'm often ________________ enough to ________________.

6 IDENTIFY Read the rest of the blog article. Complete the notes on the lessons learned in the chart below.

Lesson 1

The first thing to do on vacation is to slow down. Most of the time we go too fast through life to experience it properly. We are busy with our lives, our problems, our work, our friends, our family, our studies, and we don't change this, even when on vacation. So, I'll say it again. Slow down. Breathe. Relax. Look around, and enjoy the new surroundings.

Lesson 2

An important lesson from travel is learning to see how complicated our lives have become and then deciding to do something about it. What can we do? We can live more simply. Leave your phone in your bag and leave your laptop at home; take one small bag, not two large ones. Rather than bringing your usual life with you, find a new, simpler life in your new surroundings.

Lesson 3

The last of my top three is that we should learn to be more open and to make new friends in the new place. Don't be afraid. Smile and speak. Strangers are friends we haven't met yet, and on vacation, we can meet so many new people. They could be other travelers or local people, and, yes, they might be very different from us and our usual friends. But we shouldn't be too shy to speak or not interested enough to listen. We need to be open to the world and everyone in it.

	What	How
Lesson 1	*Slow down*	*Breathe, relax, look around you, and enjoy the new place*
Lesson 2		
Lesson 3		

WRITING SKILL
Using a variety of sentence lengths

Use a mixture of long and short sentences to make your writing interesting.

Longer sentences can give several details, which works well for exploring ideas more fully.

I missed my friends, I missed my exciting life in a big city, I missed Wi-Fi, I missed social media, and, most of all, I missed being busy.

Make longer sentences by joining shorter ones with conjunctions *such as*, *and*, *but*, *so*, and *because*. Use commas to break the sentence into groups of ideas. You can use a semicolon instead of a comma + a conjunction to join two long sentences that are more closely connected.

I've been lucky enough to go to college, and I have all kinds of qualifications, but this isn't how I learned my most important lessons.

Leave your phone in your bag and leave your laptop at home; take one small bag, not two large ones.

Short sentences make a point more clearly and are usually more emphatic.

I've learned a lot in my life.

I was too bored.

7 IDENTIFY Read Lesson 3 in the blog article again. Identify two examples of short sentences and two examples of longer sentences.

8 APPLY Rewrite these groups of shorter sentences as one longer sentence. Add conjunctions and change the punctuation as necessary.

1 Read about the area. Talk to local people. Learn more.

____

2 Don't hurry. Take your time. However, remember that vacations are for doing new things, too.

____

3 I like to be alone. I enjoy it. I'm happy enough by myself.

____

9 INTEGRATE Rewrite the longer sentence as one or two regular sentences and one short sentence.

1 We're used to doing the same old thing every day, but we should try new things to wake us up and show us the world in a new way.

____

____

2 You don't need to be nervous when things go wrong because you can always find a different way to do things. For example, if there is no Wi-Fi to check directions, you can always ask someone.

____

____

3 Many of us think we are too smart to learn anything new, but this obviously isn't true; and, also, what is the point of going somewhere new if you don't want to learn?

____

____

10 PREPARE Think about three lessons you have learned while traveling. Write your notes in the chart.

	What	How
Lesson 1		
Lesson 2		
Lesson 3		

11 WRITE Use your notes in Exercise 10 to write a blog article about the three lessons you have learned while traveling.

- Include a variety of sentence lengths
- Use too + adjective + to infinitive and (not +) adjective + enough + to infinitive
- Write up to 300 words

12 SHARE Work with a partner. Review your partner's blog article.

What do you like most about the article?

Does it include a variety of sentence lengths?

What could be improved?

13 IMPROVE Use your partner's feedback to rewrite your article.

14 WHAT'S YOUR ANGLE? Read other classmates' blog articles. Answer the questions

1 Who has learned similar lessons to yours?

2 Who has learned the most interesting lesson?

7.4 I'm Sorry to Say This

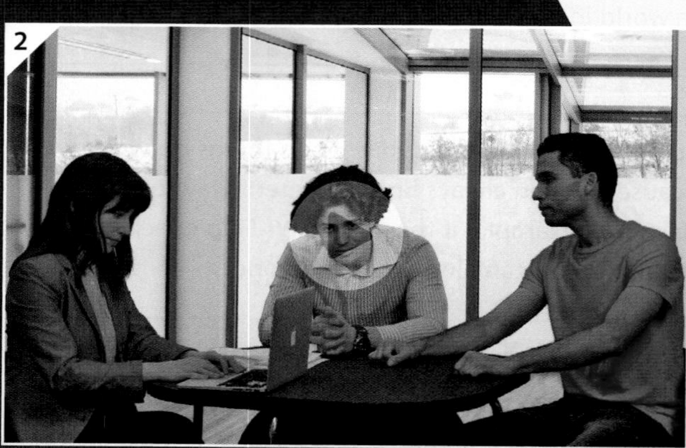

1 ACTIVATE Discuss the questions with a partner.

1 What can go wrong when making vacation plans?
2 Has anything ever gone wrong with your vacation plans?

2 IDENTIFY Watch the first part of the video about Max and Andy's vacation plans. What's the problem? What do they decide to do?

3 ASSESS Read the summary. Then watch the second part of the video and fill in the missing information.

Max and Andy visit the travel agent, Lisa, to ask about their [1] __________. They haven't heard from her in [2] __________ days. She tells them there are no flights on [3] __________, only on [4] __________. They are angry because it means they will [5] ____________________ of vacation. She tells them she has booked them [6] ____________________, but they're [7] __________. Andy says she shouldn't have made the reservations, and Lisa [8] __________. Max asks what she's going to do about the problem. Lisa says she'll call them [9] __________ with a solution. Afterward, Max and Andy agree to travel by [10] __________ instead.

REAL-WORLD ENGLISH Making a complaint

To make a successful complaint, it helps to think about how strong, direct, and polite the complaint needs to be for the situation.

There seems to be some sort of problem. (softer and more indirect)
This is not good enough. (stronger and more direct)

When you make a complaint, the problem should be explained very clearly.

We've been waiting to hear from you. It's been five days already.
I placed an order last week, but it never arrived.

It is also useful to stay focused on the result we want.

We were wondering what solutions you can offer.
We need to know what you're going to do about it.
How can this be resolved?

ENGLISH FOR REAL

4 INTEGRATE Which sentences did Max, Andy, and Lisa say? Watch the scene in the travel agency again, and check your answers.

1 Andy:
- ☐ a I'm sorry, but that's not good enough.
- ☐ b What? That's not good enough.

2 Andy:
- ☐ a I'm sorry to say this, but you shouldn't have gone ahead with those hotel reservations.
- ☐ b Perhaps it wasn't really a very good idea to make those reservations.

3 Lisa:
- ☐ a I'm terribly sorry about this problem.
- ☐ b You're right. I apologize.

4 Max:
- ☐ a We need to know what you're going to do about it…
- ☐ b We would be very grateful if you could let us know how this is going to be solved.

5 Lisa:
- ☐ a I'll see what can be done.
- ☐ b I'll get you a solution as soon as possible.

6 Andy:
- ☐ a We'd appreciate it. Thanks.
- ☐ b That's really great. Thanks for all your help.

5 ANALYZE Discuss the questions in pairs.

1 Which of each pair of sentences in Exercise 4 is more direct? How did you decide?
2 Would the other sentence in each pair get a different response? In what way?

6 INTERACT Work in a group of three (A, B, and C) to do a role play. Prepare what you will say, and role-play the situation. Then swap roles and repeat.

Student A: You are eating on your own in a restaurant. You were given a very small, very noisy table; the food took a long time to arrive and was cold; and now you are waiting for the check. (You have asked for it three times.) You call over a server and complain. You also ask for some sort of action and compensation.

Student B: You are a server. Two other servers in the team of four are out sick today. You are very busy, and now a customer has just called you over to make a complaint.

Student C: Observe the role play, and make notes so you can give feedback.

7 ANALYZE Discuss the role play in your groups.

1 Was the complaint successful in each role play?
2 Was the language direct or indirect?
3 How did Student A's language affect Student B's response?

8 WHAT'S YOUR ANGLE? Think of a complaint you made that had a successful outcome and a complaint that wasn't successful. What were the situations? Why do you think one was successful and one wasn't?

GO ONLINE
to create your own version of the English For Real video.

7.5 A Place to Study

1 ACTIVATE List the different places where you have studied (e.g., home, library, coffee shop). Where exactly do you study in each place? Why?

2 WHAT'S YOUR ANGLE? Which features and conditions are important for a good study environment for you?

3 INTERACT Compare your answers to Exercise 2 with a partner, and add your own ideas. Then agree on the three features and conditions you both consider the most important.

4 IDENTIFY Listen to a student talking about two places to study—one she likes and one she doesn't like so much. What are the two places? Complete the diagram.

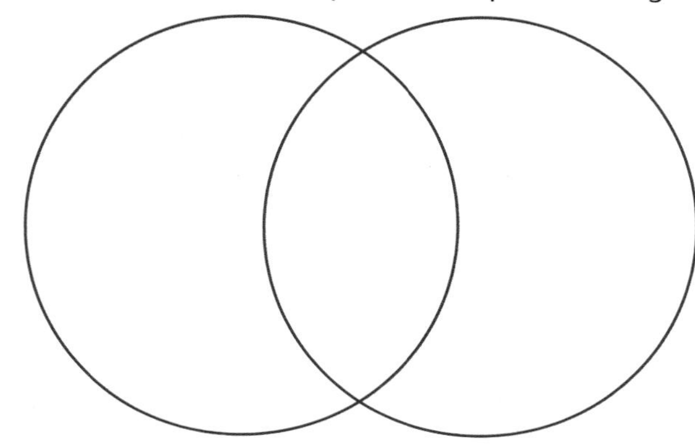

5 ASSESS Listen again. Make notes on the diagram about the things that are different and the same about the two places.

SPEAKING Talking about similarities and differences

When we compare two things, we can organize our ideas by talking about similarities and differences. This helps our audience follow the comparison.

Use signpost words and phrases to show when things are similar.

alike *in common* *similar to* *both*

***Both** places have really good Wi-Fi.*

Highlight when things are different with words and phrases for contrast.

differs from *in contrast* *while*

***In contrast**, the library has never been a good place for me to study.*

6 IDENTIFY Listen to the student's description again. Complete the extracts with a signpost phrase.

1 It has big tables _________ the college library.
2 The atmosphere of the coffee shop _________ the library so much.
3 The coffee shop is so peaceful _________ the college library is always so noisy.
4 The two places are _________ in that I have to actually get out of my pajamas to get to them.

PRONUNCIATION SKILL Sentence stress

In English, we don't stress all the words in a sentence but only those that communicate important information. The types of words usually stressed are nouns, verbs, adjectives, adverbs, negatives, and long conjunctions. Words such as auxiliary verbs, modals, articles, and prepositions are usually shorter and quieter.

When speaking, it is important to use the correct sentence stress in order to make your message clear.

7 NOTICE Listen to the sentences in Exercise 6, and identify the stressed words. Compare your answers with a partner. Listen again and check. Practice the sentences.

8 IDENTIFY Complete the sentences with a signpost word or phrase. Then identify the words that should be stressed. Listen and check.

both	in common	while	in contrast

1 The library closes at eight, _________ the coffee shop is open until ten.
2 _________ study areas have big windows and lots of natural light.
3 It's always too cold in there. _________, this room is too hot.
4 The two places have absolutely nothing _________.

9 PREPARE Identify your favorite study environment and one that you don't like so much. Create a diagram like in Exercise 4.

10 IMPROVE Practice your description with a partner and give feedback. Was it clear which study environment was better and why?

11 INTERACT Work in a group. Describe your two study environments. When you listen to the other students' descriptions, ask questions to find out more.

Now go to page 153 for the Unit 7 Review

8 Change

UNIT SNAPSHOT

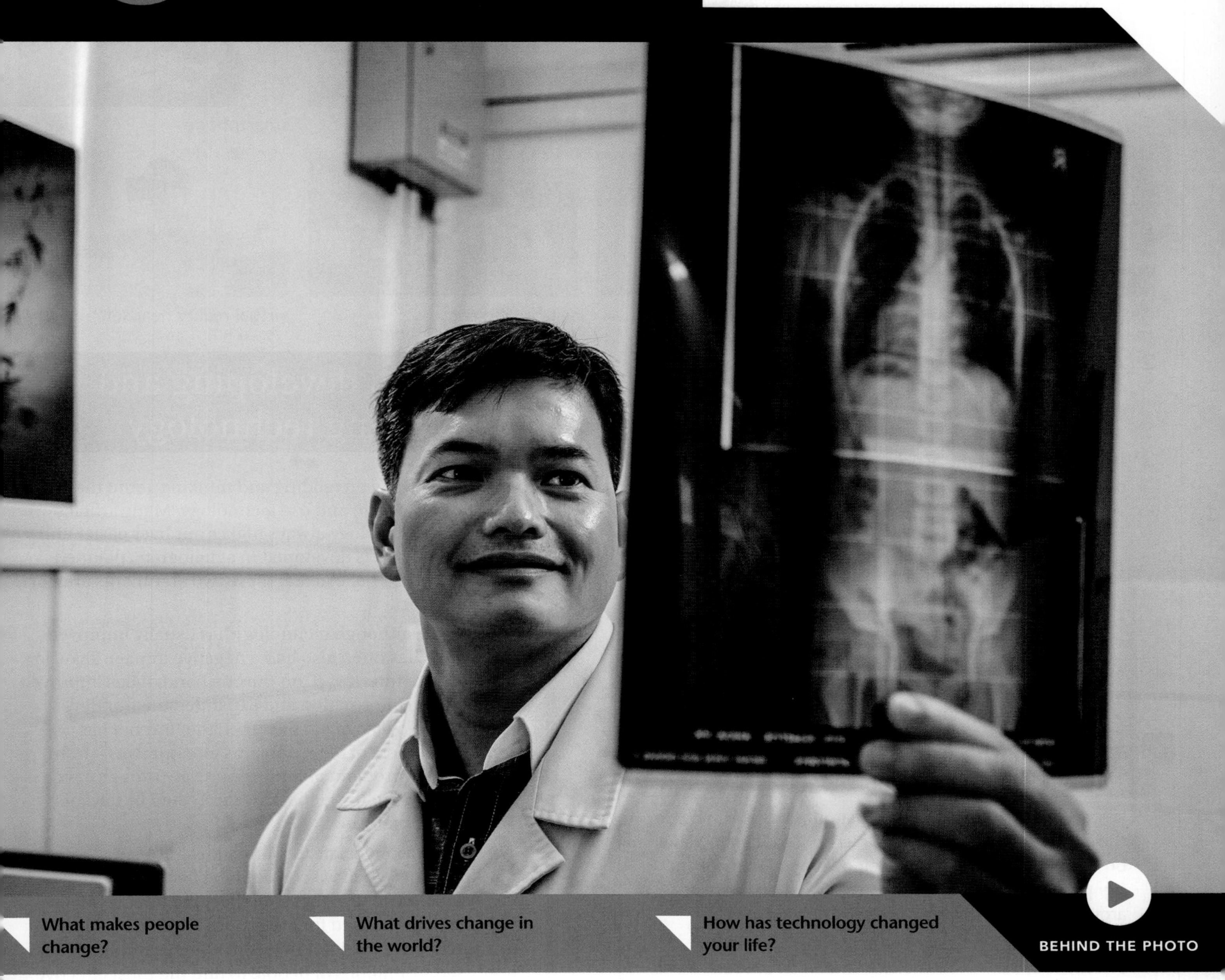

What makes people change?

What drives change in the world?

How has technology changed your life?

BEHIND THE PHOTO

1 How has technology changed the way we do these things? Discuss your ideas with a partner.

cooking	driving	looking after our health
paying for things	learning	watching movies
listening to music	exercising	organizing our time

2 Which of these activities will change the most because of technology in the future? Discuss the question, and choose your top three.

REAL-WORLD GOAL

For a week, change something you do every day

8.1 What Next?

1 ACTIVATE Look at the pictures and answer the questions.

1 Which of these things have you never used?
2 Which are you going to use this week?
3 Which will you use more often in the future?

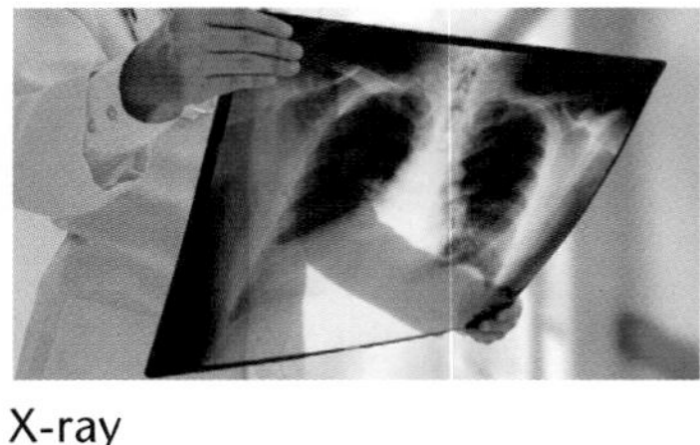
X-ray

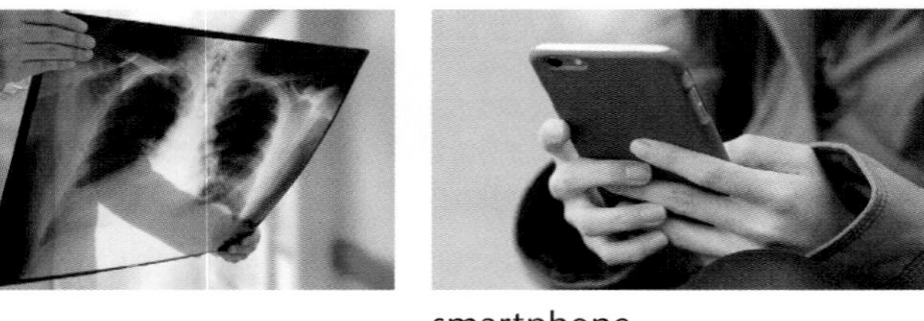
smartphone

GPS

drone

self-driving car

virtual reality headset

2 ASSESS You are going to read an article that features GPS and X-rays. What do you think you might learn about these items?

3 IDENTIFY Read the article, and number the topics in the order they are discussed.

___ Art is an example of how people can use technology in new and different ways.
___ People generally believe that the technology we use was made to help us.
___ We don't know how we will use technology in the future.
___ Some technology is used for things it wasn't designed for.

READING SKILL
Understanding contrasting points

Writers often include contrasting arguments and views in their articles. This allows the reader to see different views on the topic and decide on their own opinion. Look for signpost words and phrases that show when the next argument will be different from the one just given.

although *however* *unlike* *in contrast* *instead*
actually *while* *on the one hand,… on the other (hand)*

If, ***on the one hand****, it has expanded the frontiers of human knowledge and interactions,* ***on the other****, the Internet has brought a variety of new problems into our lives.*
While *we now think of X-rays as medical tools, they were not immediately used for serious purposes.*

On developing and using technology

Lately, I have been reading and thinking about the ways in which we design and use technology. Many articles claim that technology always makes our lives easier and better and that it is developed in a deliberate, planned way. However, I believe that these two arguments are not always correct.

First of all, although technology has usually improved our lives, it has often also had a negative impact. Take, for instance, the Internet. If, on the one hand, it has improved the access to information and expanded the frontiers of human knowledge, on the other, the Internet has brought a variety of new problems into our lives—from the everyday problem of finding our way through a web of information to the global threats created by hackers, viruses, and malwares.

My next reasons relate to planned technology development. When we consider the history of some inventions, we realize that some very useful technology was actually designed for other purposes rather than the function we use it for nowadays. For example, GPS is now used by millions of people to find the most effective route to a target location. However, GPS was not originally developed with civilians in mind. It was, in fact, designed for the military.

Moreover, some technology that we think of as having a particular purpose was not "designed" at all. X-rays, for example, were actually discovered by German physicist Wilhelm Roentgen in 1895 completely by accident. Also, while we now think of X-rays as medical tools, they were not immediately used for serious purposes. Instead, they were generally considered to be just another type of "photography." For a period of time, it was even fashionable for young ladies to send X-rays of their hands as gifts.

4 IDENTIFY Review the two examples of contrasting arguments in the Reading Skill box. Match the statements in the box to the items.

It has made some things better.
It didn't have a serious use when discovered.
It is used for medical purposes nowadays.
It has caused problems as well.

	The Internet	X-rays
Argument		
Contrasting argument		

The good thing is that, by acknowledging that technology can have positive and negative effects and that it can usually go beyond its original purpose, we are free to think of new and better uses for it. Consider, for example, the way some artists now use their GPS tracking to draw beautiful pictures over large geographical areas.

This brings us to an interesting question: What will we use today's technology for in the future? We might not be able to control whether it is used for good or bad purposes. However, we can be certain of one thing: with the speed of technological development increasing all the time—in recent years we have had the arrival of drones, driverless cars, and virtual reality—it is going to be exciting to see the new and unexpected ways people find to use it.

—adapted from *Science, Technology, and Society*, edited by Sal Restivo

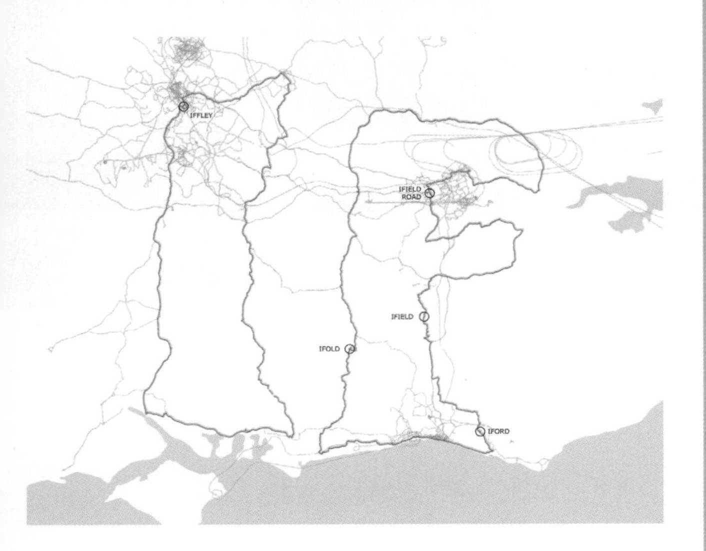

5 INTEGRATE Read the text in detail. Then match the contrasting arguments, and identify which signpost word or phrased is used.

however   actually   although

1 Technology has usually improved our lives.
2 Technology development is always planned.
3 GPS is used by civilians.

a Some technology was designed for other purposes. ________________

b It was not originally developed for them. ________________

c It has often had a negative impact. ________________

GRAMMAR IN CONTEXT Talking about the future

There are several different ways of talking about the future. In different situations, we use the present continuous, *be going to*, *will*, *might*, and the simple present.

Predictions

We use *will* for predictions based on our personal feelings. We often use the expression *I think* + *will*.

*What **will** we use today's technology for in the future?*
***I think** people **will** use technology to create art.*

We can use *might* for predictions when we are less certain about them.

*We **might** not be able to control whether it is used for good or bad purposes.*

We can use *be going to* for predictions, especially when there is some evidence for them.

*Looking at how prices have already changed, technology **is going to** get a lot cheaper.*

Plans

We can also use *be going to* for plans and intentions when we don't know or don't say the time or place.

*I'**m going to** buy a new phone.*

We use the present continuous for fixed plans when we know the time or place.

*They'**re repairing** the X-ray machine tomorrow morning.*

We use the simple present for future schedules.

*He **has** a meeting with the IT team on Monday.*

See Grammar focus on page 166.

6 IDENTIFY Read part of another article. Choose the best verb forms to complete it.

> The way we carry technology [1] *is going to / won't* change. As materials get lighter and stronger, new ways of making and using items [2] *might / are going to* appear. This is very positive according to supporters of technology since it will make our lives much easier. They claim that, for example, handheld devices like cell phones [3] *won't / are going to* be necessary anymore—either we [4] *will / won't* wear all our technology, or it [5] *is going to / might* be put inside our bodies. For others, however, this is not a happy thought since it [6] *will / isn't going to* be even more difficult to escape technology than it is now. Activities such as reading, socializing face-to-face, and even thinking [7] *are going to / might* disappear forever.

7 INTEGRATE Identify the contrasting arguments about technology in the future in the extract in Exercise 6.

8 INTERACT Which side of the argument in the text in Exercise 6 do you agree with? Discuss your ideas with a partner. Use the phrases below to help.

Look at what's happening already. People are going to...
I don't know. We might...
It won't happen because...
I think people will...

9 APPLY Which of these are you planning to do at some point soon? Do you know when? Write sentences using *be going to* or the present continuous + time/place.

1 (buy a new phone)
____

2 (have an x-ray)
____

3 (try out a wearable device)
____

4 (use GPS)
____

5 (have a day without technology)
____

10 WHAT'S YOUR ANGLE? Tell your partner about your technology plans from Exercise 9. How similar are your plans?

11 VOCABULARY Work in pairs. Discuss and write definitions for the technology words in the box.

handheld	**access** (v)	upload (v)	**browse** (v)
virtual	**applications**	download (v)	

Oxford 3000™

12 INTEGRATE Complete the questions with a word from the box in Exercise 11. Use each word only once.

1 How will we ________ information?
2 What ________ will we not be able to live without?
3 What will happen to ________ devices?
4 How will we ________ and ________ data?
5 What will we use ________ reality for?
6 How will we ________ the Internet?

13 WHAT'S YOUR ANGLE? What do you think will happen in the future? Discuss the questions from Exercise 12 in a group.

8.2 New Ways

1 ACTIVATE How do you get your music and movies? Why?

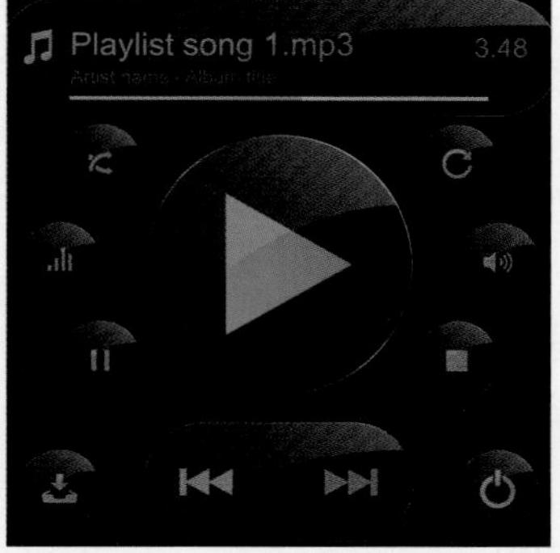

2 IDENTIFY Skim the essay. Answer the questions.

1 What type of media does it mention?
2 Which ways of accessing media are discussed?

Nowadays, many people seem to think that it is preferable to stream or download movies, TV shows, and music instead of buying DVDs, Blu-ray discs, or CDs. There are certainly positive points about streaming and downloading, but there are also some drawbacks. In this essay, I will discuss the advantages and disadvantages of accessing music and movies this way.

The main advantage of streaming or downloading is that it is quicker and easier since you don't have to go to a store. If you have a credit card and access to the Internet, you have access to movies and music anytime. There is almost no limit to choice—unlike in a store—as you can usually stream and download things from anywhere in the world. Another great advantage is storage. If you have hundreds of DVDs, for example, they take up a lot of space, but if you download, you only need virtual storage. Of course, when you stream a movie, you don't need storage at all.

However, there are also good arguments to support those people who prefer the physical media. Firstly, it is nice to feel that you actually own the Blu-ray or CD. A download can easily be deleted, and if your device is lost or stolen and you haven't stored anything in the cloud, you will lose all your music and movies. Another advantage is that the boxes CDs and DVDs come in can have useful information. Therefore, while you listen, you can read about the songs, for example. The musicians and movie companies also benefit more from this due to difficulty with sharing. Downloads can sometimes be illegal, so the musicians and movie companies don't get any money from them.

In conclusion, although streaming and downloading have many advantages, I personally still prefer to buy the DVD or CD—or even the vinyl record. This may be because of my hobby, which is playing the guitar. If I were a professional musician, I wouldn't want people to illegally download or stream my music. Moreover, I also love having a shelf full of music and movies I own.

3 **INTEGRATE** Read the essay in detail, and complete the notes on the plan.

Introduction:

streaming / downloading music and movies is better than

____

For / advantages:	Against / disadvantages:
quick + easy	______________
______________	______________
______________	______________
______________	______________

Conclusion:

streaming / downloading has positive points, but prefer ______________ because ______________

WRITING SKILL
Using cause and effect linking words

Readers are more likely to agree with your ideas if you include information about causes and their effects. Use cause and effect linking words to present the facts and your opinions more clearly.

Downloads are cheaper ***because*** *you do not pay for packaging.*

Cause = you do not pay for packaging

Effect = downloads are cheaper

You only need an Internet connection. ***As a result****, streaming is easier.*

Cause = only need an Internet connection

Effect = streaming is easier

Cause

because *since* *as* *because of* *due to*

Effect

so *therefore* *consequently* *as a result*

4 **INTERACT** Work in pairs (A and B). Find your group of linking words in the essay in Exercise 2. Explain the cause and the effect linked by these words to your partner.

Student A	Student B
since	*due to*
as	*so*
therefore	*because of*

GRAMMAR IN CONTEXT
Zero, first, and second conditional

The zero and first conditional talk about something that is real or possible.

To talk about a possible general situation and the usual result, we use the zero conditional.

If you ***have*** *a credit card and access to the Internet, you* ***have*** *access to movies and music anytime.*

To talk about a particular situation in the future and its likely result, we use the first conditional.

If you ***forget*** *the Wi-Fi password, you* ***won't be*** *able to watch the movie.*

We use the second conditional to talk about something that is not real. The *if* clause talks about an unreal situation, and the result clause talks about the imaginary result.

If *I* ***recorded*** *a song, I* ***would want*** *people to pay to download it.*

See Grammar focus on page 166.

5 **ASSESS** Identify the two verb forms in each conditional sentence in the Grammar in Context box.

6 **IDENTIFY** Find one more example of each type of conditional in the essay in Exercise 2.

7 **APPLY** Complete the sentences with the verbs in parentheses in the correct form.

1. It's a fact that if people ______________ (want) to watch a movie online, they ______________ (need) to have a good Internet connection.
2. We're lucky. If our Wi-Fi ______________ (not be) so good, we ______________ (have to) find a different way to access movies.
3. It's a great series. You ______________ (stay up) to watch the whole thing if you ______________ (start) watching it now.
4. If I ______________ (be) an actor, I ______________ (be) happy for people to watch my movies anytime and anywhere.
5. If you ______________ (access) music and movies online, you ______________ (have to) be prepared to pay for them.

8 WHAT'S YOUR ANGLE? Discuss the questions with a partner.

1 What do you do if you want to listen to music?
2 What will you do if there is a problem with your Wi-Fi tomorrow?
3 What kinds of movies would you be in if you were an actor?

9 PREPARE Work in pairs. Choose one of the topics to write about. Make notes in a table.

- What are the advantages and disadvantages of technology in the workplace?
- What benefits to learning does the Internet give students? Are there any drawbacks?
- Some people think that social media is good for us, while others disagree. What advantages and disadvantages does social media bring to our social lives?

For / advantages	Against / disadvantages

10 WRITE Write a for-and-against essay.

- ☐ Include four paragraphs.
- ☐ Introduce the topic you are going to argue.
- ☐ Write one paragraph with arguments for and one with arguments against.
- ☐ State your position in a final conclusion.
- ☐ Include cause and effect linking words.
- ☐ Include conditional sentences.
- ☐ Write up to 300 words.

11 SHARE Review your partner's essay. Does it include clear "for" and "against" paragraphs? What other feedback can you give them to help them improve their essays?

12 IMPROVE Use your partner's feedback to rewrite your essay.

13 WHAT'S YOUR ANGLE? Read another classmate's essay, and discuss if you agree with their arguments and position.

A web design office in New York City, the United States

8.3 A Working Future

1 ACTIVATE Discuss the questions with a partner.

1 What jobs have you and your family done?
2 Could machines do any of these jobs now?

2 ASSESS Which of these jobs do you think machines will do in the future? What would be the positive and negative consequences of this?

firefighter

lecturer

mail carrier

office worker

trash collector

LISTENING SKILL Predicting while listening

Good listeners predict before they listen and while they are listening. Predicting helps the listener stay engaged and connect information they already know to the topic of the listening.

While listening, listeners check the predictions made earlier. These predictions are then confirmed or rejected and replaced with new predictions.

Use questions to help your predictions:

- What is the speaker's point of view?
- What conclusion will the speaker give?

Use information you already know:

- What do I know about this topic?
- What has the speaker already talked about?

Use pauses in the listening to reflect on what you have heard and make further predictions.

3 IDENTIFY Read the information about a podcast, and answer the questions.

1 What and which period will be the main focus of the podcast?
2 Do you think the expert's views will be positive or negative? Why?

The Workplace ACD RADIO PODCAST

This week's work expert explores the working lives we can look forward to.

4 ASSESS Listen to the first part of the podcast and check your answers to Exercise 3.

5 IDENTIFY Which information do you think Dr. Kelly will give next? Choose two and explain your choices to a partner.

- [ ] a A number of problems created by technology
- [ ] b Examples of jobs technology will do in the future
- [ ] c The history of technology for the past 100 years
- [ ] d A reason why we will be happier in the future

6 **ASSESS** Listen to the conclusion of Dr. Kelly's response and check your predictions.

7 **IDENTIFY** Discuss these questions with a partner. Then listen to the next part and check your predictions.

1 What do you think is Dr. Kelly's overall point of view about the changing workplace? Why?
2 What do you think she will say about the following?
a People changing jobs
b Learning new skills
c Job titles

8 **INTEGRATE** The host will ask these questions. Discuss them with a partner and predict Dr. Kelly's answers. Then listen and check.

1 How will mobile technology affect the workplace in the future?
2 Will technology take all our jobs in the end?

GRAMMAR IN CONTEXT
Will and the future continuous

We use *will* + infinitive without *to* to make predictions about future events.

That number ***will get*** *higher.*

We use the future continuous to make predictions about future situations. We often use time phrases to say when we are talking about.

In a few years, machines ***will be delivering*** *all our mail.*

We also use the future continuous to make predictions about future events that we expect to be happening at a specific time.

This time tomorrow, I ***will be attending*** *a conference on the future of the workplace.*

We don't use the future continuous with state verbs like *know* and *have.*

Americans ***will have*** *12 to 14 careers in their lifetime.*

See Grammar focus on page 166.

9 **IDENTIFY** Choose the best form of the verb to complete each prediction. Then listen to the complete podcast and check.

1 We will *have / be having* to learn to do different things.
2 In a few years,…we will *use / be using* our higher skills in different jobs.
3 In a few years,…we will *live / be living* happier lives.
4 A job change every year will *be / be being* normal.
5 We will *learn / be learning* new skills throughout the whole of our working life.
6 We won't *be / be being* lecturers, bank clerks, or delivery people.
7 Employers will *have / be having* to be more flexible with their workers.
8 Technology will not *take / be taking* all our jobs.

10 **INTERACT** Which of Dr. Kelly's predictions in Exercise 9 do you agree with? Discuss them with a partner.

VOCABULARY DEVELOPMENT
Future time phrases

We use time phrases to say when we are talking about.

In five years...	*= five years from now*
This time tomorrow...	*= at the same time tomorrow*
By 2050...	*= no later than 2050*
The year after next...	*= in two years*
The day after tomorrow...	*= in two days*
Twenty years from now...	*= in 20 years*

Oxford 3000™

11 **IDENTIFY** Listen and complete the predictions with time phrases.

1 ________________, all delivery vehicles will be driverless.
2 ________________, machines will be doing many more jobs.
3 ________________, people will be working only two days a week.
4 ________________ of the next decade, most people will be working from home.
5 ________________, no one will work ________________.

12 **INTEGRATE** Ask questions to find out which statements from Exercise 11 your partner agrees with.

Do you agree that all delivery vehicles will be driverless by 2030?

13 **WHAT'S YOUR ANGLE?** Make predictions for the short- and longer-term future of your work or education. Compare them in a group.

This time next month,...
In December,...
At the start of next year,...
By 2025,...
In 20 years,...

8.4 Promises, Promises

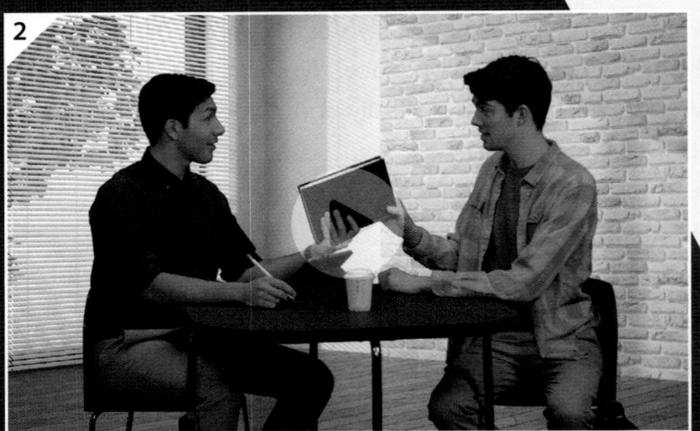

1 ACTIVATE What promises have you made or people made to you this week?

2 IDENTIFY Look at the pictures, and answer the questions.

1 Who do you think makes a promise?
2 What do you think the promise is about?

3 ASSESS Watch the video, and check your answers in Exercise 2.

4 IDENTIFY Watch the first part of the video again, and then complete the sentences with the correct name, *Kevin* or *Sam*.

1 _________ asks to borrow something.
2 _________ asks for reassurance.
3 _________ makes a promise.
4 _________ asks for a reason.
5 _________ gives a deadline.
6 _________ accepts a request.

5 ANALYZE Watch the second half of the video. Which other promise does Kevin make?

REAL-WORLD ENGLISH Promising

We often make promises when we are requesting something. A promise can make it more likely that the request is accepted.

We often use *will* to make promises.

I promise I'll...
I will, I promise. I won't forget.
I'll definitely...

Sometimes the other person demands a promise or asks for further reassurance after the promise.

Promise me you'll...
Will you? Are you sure?

ENGLISH FOR REAL

6 **INTEGRATE** Read and complete the lines from the video with an appropriate form of the verbs in parentheses. Then listen and check your answers.

KEVIN: By the way, could [1] ________________ (I / borrow) your forensic technology book?

SAM: Uh, OK.

KEVIN: I promise [2] ________________ (I / take care) of it.

SAM: [3] ________________ (you / will)? [4] ________________ (I / need) it back by tomorrow. Why do you need it?

KEVIN: I want to get a job at the forensic tech company!

7 **PREPARE** Practice the dialogue in Exercise 6 with a partner.

8 **INTERACT** Work in pairs (A and B). Choose a situation and do a role play.

Situation 1

Student A: You need somewhere to stay for two nights. You know Student B (a classmate and a friend) is going away, so their apartment is free. Ask to stay there, and promise to take care of the place when your classmate/friend initially says no.

Student B: You are not happy with Student A's request, and need some guarantees from your classmate/friend.

Situation 2

Student A: You want to borrow $150 to pay a bill. You ask a very good friend to lend you the money. You are sure that you can pay it back next week.

Student B: Your close friend asks you if you can lend them money. You have lent your friend money before, and it took a long time to be returned. You wonder when they can return the money.

Situation 3

Student A: You haven't finished your assignment. Ask Student B (your teacher/professor) for an extra two days to complete it. When your teacher/professor reminds you that this is the second time you have asked for an extension, promise to meet the new deadline.

Student B: You don't like any of your students to hand in work late, but you understand if there are special circumstances. You need to know how the student will meet the new deadline.

9 **ANALYZE** Discuss the promise made in your role play. Did Student B feel confident in the promise? Why or why not? Change roles, choose another situation, and do another role play.

10 **WHAT'S YOUR ANGLE?** Have you ever broken a promise? What happened?

GO ONLINE
to create your own version of the English For Real video.

8.5 The Next Big Thing

1 ACTIVATE Complete the sentences. Then discuss your answers with a partner.

1 Two of my favorite apps are ________________.
2 I agree that technology is ________________.
3 I often ________________ social media ________________.
4 There should be a law about cell phones and ________________.

PRONUNCIATION SKILL
Linking vowels with vowels

In connected speech, you sometimes hear extra sounds between certain words. These can come between words ending and starting with vowel sounds.

/w/	*two (w) of*	*e.g., after words ending with /u/, /oʊ/, and /aʊ/*
	go (w) away	*now (w) open*
/j/	*I (j) agree*	*e.g., after words ending with /aɪ/ and /eɪ/*
	day (j) and night	

2 IDENTIFY Review the sentence parts in Exercise 1. Identify where the linking sounds will go. (There may be more than one in each sentence.) Then listen to people giving their answers. Check yours and practice the sentences.

3 INTEGRATE Discuss your answers for Exercise 1 with a different partner. Notice other examples of linking sounds you and your partner use.

4 IDENTIFY Listen to people speculating about the next big thing in technology. Number the things in the order they are mentioned.

___ virtual reality ___ robots
___ flying cars ___ cell phones

SPEAKING Speculating about the future

When we speculate about the future, we make predictions about what it might be like. When we do this, we often use modal verbs such as *will*, *might*, *may*, and *could*. We can also use some adverbs and phrases to show how sure or unsure we are about our ideas.

- *That probably won't…*
- *I imagine that…*
- *I bet…*
- *It's unlikely that…*
- *I suppose…*
- *There's no chance of…*

We can respond to other people's views by saying how likely we think they are.

- *Well, maybe, but…*
- *You might be right.*
- *It's a possibility, but…*
- *That definitely won't happen.*

5 INTEGRATE Listen to the discussion again. Check the phrases in the Speaking box as you hear them.

6 IDENTIFY Read and listen to four sentences from the discussion. Identify the speculating phrase and also one linking sound in each sentence.

1 My guess is it won't be anything to do with cell phones.
2 I'm pretty sure they are at the end of the line now.
3 I wonder if it will be something to do with virtual reality.
4 I wouldn't be surprised if they go on sale and nobody buys them.

7 PREPARE Work with a partner. Decide what will be the next big thing in technology, and write a list of reasons to support your idea.

8 INTERACT Work in a group with different students. Have a discussion speculating about the next big thing in technology.

9 WHAT'S YOUR ANGLE? Have you changed your mind on the next big thing in technology? If so, what arguments convinced you? If not, what arguments made you more certain about your prediction?

Now go to page 154 for the Unit 8 Review.

9 Reviews

UNIT SNAPSHOT

How does sharing an experience change it?

What's the difference between a review and an opinion?

Why do people like to read about other people's experiences or views?

BEHIND THE PHOTO

1 Discuss the questions in a group. Think of examples to support your ideas.

1 In which ways do people share their views about things they watch, listen to, read, or eat?
2 Are other people's views useful? Why or why not?
3 Are there any disadvantages to sharing views?

2 Change groups. Share your answers and try to agree on three disadvantages to sharing views.

REAL-WORLD GOAL

Read an online review for something you see, read, eat, or listen to this week

9.1 Box-office Success

1 ACTIVATE What's your favorite movie of all time? Make a list of things that are really good about it. Discuss your list with a partner.

2 INTERACT Work with a partner. Decide on the three most important things that make a good movie.

3 IDENTIFY Read the headings from a blog article about what makes a good movie. Then skim the article, and number the headings in the correct order. Did you notice any of your ideas from Exercise 2?

___ a People we love
___ b It's all in the details
___ c Part 1, part 2, part 3
___ d Clear messages

MOVIEBLOG

Search

Home | About | Articles | News

Sign in

Key rules for a good movie

What makes a good movie? This cannot be an easy question to answer since thousands of movies fail at the box office every year, but there seem to be some general rules that give a movie a chance of success. Many of the directors and writers who made the classic movies knew and applied these rules, and we still see the same rules in action today.

1___

A good movie has characters that the audience likes and identifies with. However, they are rarely perfect people and often find this out about themselves in the movie. For example, a director may include a scene where a character **finally** recognizes that they are being **childish**. This helps make the characters seem more **real** to us as well as more interesting to watch. Of course, this depends not only on the script but also on the performances of the cast. The actors who are chosen for the roles must be able to play them in a way that makes us believe in them.

2___

One part of a movie that is not always noticed by viewers is the theme—for example, the idea that good people always win or that lying is bad. There can be more than one theme in a good movie, but it is usually strong and clear enough to make the audience think about it. After all, the theme is the message a director wants viewers to take with them once the movie is over—and the message of a good movie can affect an audience's views in a **deeper** and **richer** way.

3___

A successful movie also has a clear beginning, middle, and end. The part that is probably most important is the beginning. The scenes when we are introduced to the plot, the themes, and the main characters of a movie are essential for its success since the rest of the movie gradually develops them. A good movie also has an ending that follows well from the previous parts and that leaves audience members feeling they have learned something about the world. Between the beginning and the end, there will be a good story, simple enough to be summarized in one or two minutes—most audiences do not want to feel confused about the plot, except in a mystery or detective movie.

4___

All great movies have convincing details all the way through. These help the audience understand the time and place where the story happens. If the details are not correct, it is **impossible** to believe in the movie.

These are certainly not all the factors that a director must consider when making a movie. However, they are essential points. If one or more is not present, the movie will probably not be a great one.

READING SKILL
Recognizing and understanding connotation

Some words in English have a connotation in addition to their dictionary definition. The connotation refers to an idea suggested by a word in addition to its main meaning. It can be positive or negative.

*a **classic** movie from the 1950s* (positive—high quality and still good to watch)

*an **old-fashioned** movie from the 1950s* (negative—not interesting or relevant now)

When looking up the meaning of a word, check if the definition contains information that shows the word can be used to express a positive or negative idea.

By understanding the connotation of the words chosen by a writer, we can better understand the writer's views and attitude.

4 ASSESS Find the words in bold in the article. Then complete the connotation of the phrases with the correct option. Is the connotation positive or negative?

1 **finally** recognize (positive / negative): understanding something very late, when you *might* / *don't* expect someone to recognize it earlier
2 being **childish** (positive / negative): acting in a way that people think is like a child, which is *wrong* / *amusing* for an adult
3 characters seem more **real** (positive / negative): more like people we know in life and, therefore, *not so interesting* / *more believable*
4 in a **deeper** and **richer** way (positive / negative): providing a *more expensive* / *more significant* experience
5 **impossible** to believe (positive / negative): even if you really want to think something is *true* / *not true*, you can't

5 INTEGRATE Read the text again, and answer the questions.

1 What must actors be able to do?
2 What part of the movie do people not always notice?
3 Which part of the movie does the author think is the most important?
4 What kind of ending does a good movie have?

6 WHAT'S YOUR ANGLE? Which of the answers in Exercise 5 do you agree with? Discuss your views with a partner.

7 VOCABULARY Find these words in the text, and match them to the definitions. Then complete the definitions with *who*, *where*, *when*, or *that*.

script	plot	theme	scene
character	performance	cast	director

1 ________: a person ________ appears in a movie or book
2 ________: the series of events ________ make the story of a movie, book, etc.
3 ________: the subject or main idea ________ runs through the whole movie, book, etc.
4 ________: all the people ________ act in a movie
5 ________: a part of a movie or book ________ the action happens in one place
6 ________: the way the people ________ are in the movie act
7 ________: a person in charge of a movie ________ tells the actors what to do
8 ________: the written text ________ contains all the words from the movie

8 INTEGRATE Complete the sentences with the correct word from Exercise 7. Change the form if necessary.

1 The final ___ of the movie was very moving.
2 Many people have praised the ___ of the film's incredible ___.
3 The ___ of the movie is well developed and reflects our world today.
4 The leading actress fell in love with the ___ as soon as she read it.
5 I think the ___ of this film did an amazing job telling the story!
6 Children's movies often have serious ___ to teach them about the world.
7 Some actors stay in ___ even when they aren't filming. Apparently, it improves their performance.

GRAMMAR IN CONTEXT
Defining relative clauses

Defining relative clauses tell us which person or thing we are talking about. We cannot understand what the sentence is talking about without this information.

We use the relative pronouns *who* or *that* to talk about people.

Many of the directors and writers ***who*** *made the classic movies knew and applied these rules.*

We use *which* or *that* to talk about things.

The part of a movie ***which*** *is probably most important is the beginning.*

A good movie also has an ending ***that*** *follows well from the previous parts.*

We use *whose* to talk about things or people that belong to someone.

Actors ***whose*** *movies do well usually get the best roles in future works.*

We can leave the relative pronouns out if they are the object of the verb.

*A good movie has characters (**who**) people **like**.*

We can also use the relative adverbs *when* and *where*.

The scenes ***when*** *we are introduced to the plot, the themes, and the main characters of a movie are essential for its success.*

The place ***where*** *the action of a movie happens might be crucial for the plot.*

See Grammar focus on page 167.

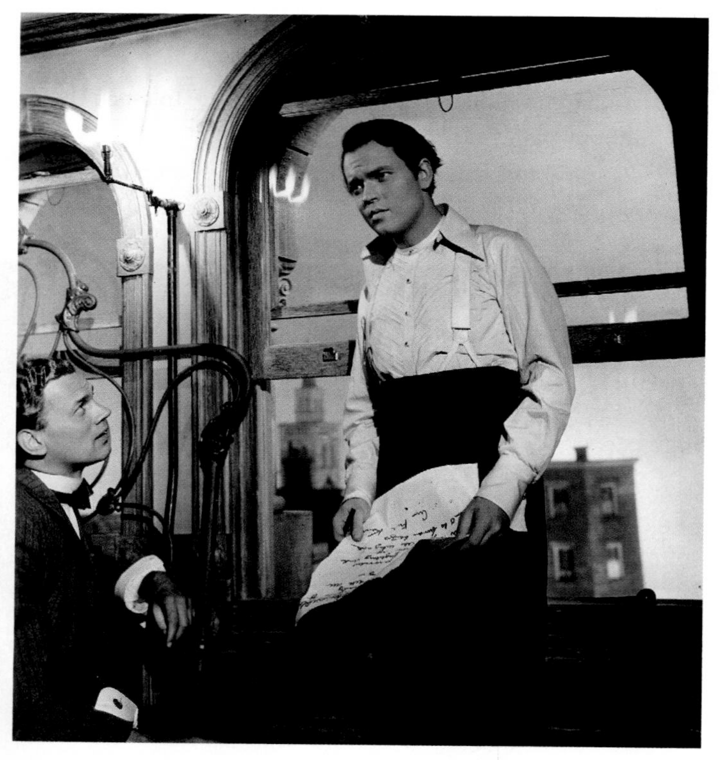

9 APPLY Complete the sentences with the information in parentheses. Use a defining relative clause with *who, which, that, whose, when,* or *where.* Leave the relative pronoun out if possible

1 The movie ______________________ was good. (We saw the movie yesterday.)
2 The actor ______________________ won an award. (The actor played the main character.)
3 The scene ______________________ was too long. (The main character was injured in this scene.)
4 The script ______________________ won an award. (This script was written by a teenager.)
5 I don't like directors ______________________ ____________. (These directors' movies are very long.)
6 The movie is showing in the new theater ____________ ______________________. (We went to the new movie theater last week.)

10 INTEGRATE Complete the summary about the movie *Citizen Kane* with the appropriate relative pronoun.

Citizen Kane is a 1941 American film [1]___ was directed by Orson Welles. Not only did Welles direct and co-write the film, but he was also the actor [2]___ starred in the leading role. There are many critics [3]___ say that this is one of the best films ever made. It relates the life story of Charles Foster Kane, a wealthy newspaper magnate [4]___ success defines him despite his poor background. He rises to prominence only to see the life and relationships [5]___ he built throughout his life fall apart. A reporter must decipher Kane's dying words at the Xanadu mansion [6]___ he spent his final years, living alone and isolated.

11 WHAT'S YOUR ANGLE? Choose four items from the box. Describe an example of each to your partner. Does your partner agree?

a great plot	a convincing character
a famous director	a scary scene
a strong cast	a boring script
a common theme	an award-winning performance

For me, a great plot is one that has lots of action and surprises, like the plot in the movie...

9.2 Good Reads, Good Eats

1 ACTIVATE Choose two of the places in the box. What's the best one of these you have ever been to? Why? Tell your partner what was special about it.

bookstore	restaurant	shopping mall
park	movie theater	

2 IDENTIFY You are going to watch a video reviewing the place in the picture. Which of the places in Exercise 1 do you think it is?

LISTENING SKILL
Listening for specific information

When you listen for specific information, it helps to identify the type of information. For example, are you listening for a place name, a number, a date, a description, or something else?

How much *U.S. consumer spending is online?* (listening for a percentage or an amount)

Listen for key words connected to the information you want, and then listen carefully for the details.

Online shopping *is becoming more and more popular.* ***More than half of all consumer spending in the United States*** *is now done this way, and Internet sales are increasing year after year.*

3 ASSESS Read the questions, and decide what type of information you need to listen for in order to answer them.

1 Who needs to think of different ways to attract customers?
2 How can shopping feel more personal?
3 How many branches of the bookstore are there?
4 When was the bookstore building first constructed?
5 What used to be stored in the building before it was a bookstore?
6 Who voted it the best bookstore in the world?
7 Where can you go when you have finished looking at books?
8 What can you buy in the store in addition to books?

4 INTEGRATE Watch the video and answer the questions in Exercise 3. Compare your answers with a partner.

PRONUNCIATION SKILL Assimilation

When we speak at a natural speed, some consonant sounds at the end of individual words change. These sounds are affected by the sound at the start of the next word.

nonfiction books → *nonfictio**m** books*
best bookstore → *bes**p** bookstore*

5 NOTICE Read the sentences. Predict where assimilation will occur. Then listen and check.

1 I ordered the split pea soup, but I didn't like it.
2 When I get home, I just want to sit back and read my new book.
3 Mario is such a good cook. He could open his own restaurant.
4 The bistro around the corner offers first-class service.
5 Don't worry about the bill. Dinner is on me!

6 NOTICE Listen and write the first word in each phrase. Then listen again and repeat.

1 ________ branches		4 ________ people	
2 ________ prizes		5 ________ boy	
3 ________ book		6 ________ be	

7 INTERACT Work with a partner. Repeat the sentences from Exercise 5. Give each other feedback on the assimilated sounds.

GRAMMAR IN CONTEXT
Non-defining relative clauses

A non-defining relative clause can give extra information about a person or thing. It does not tell us which person or thing we are talking about since we already know that. Therefore, the sentence makes sense without the extra information in the clause.

*Touching and smelling the food, **which** is an important part of food shopping, is possible in these places.*

*The church was closed by Napoleon, **whose** army took it in 1794.*

The non-defining relative clause goes after the noun it refers to and has commas around it (or a comma and a period if it is at the end of the sentence).

*Customers, **who** love browsing the bookshelves and looking at the beautiful painted ceiling, can also spend time in the store's comfortable and stylish café.*

See Grammar focus on page 167.

8 APPLY Add the information in the second sentence to the first sentence as a non-defining relative clause.

1 I went to the bookstore. The bookstore was very busy.

____

2 The bookstore didn't have a copy of the novel. The bookstore was quiet at that time of day.

____

3 I got most of these books online. These books are for college.

____

4 The bookstore serves coffee upstairs. The coffee is great.

____

5 A special discount card is available to regular customers. The discount card is very good.

____

9 EXPAND Read the article, and choose the best places to add the non-defining relative clauses.

1 who were lawyers
2 where they were sent by their law firm to work for two years
3 where they now lived again
4 which has been a useful guide to restaurants in New York for many years

Zagat: The Restaurant Guide for New York

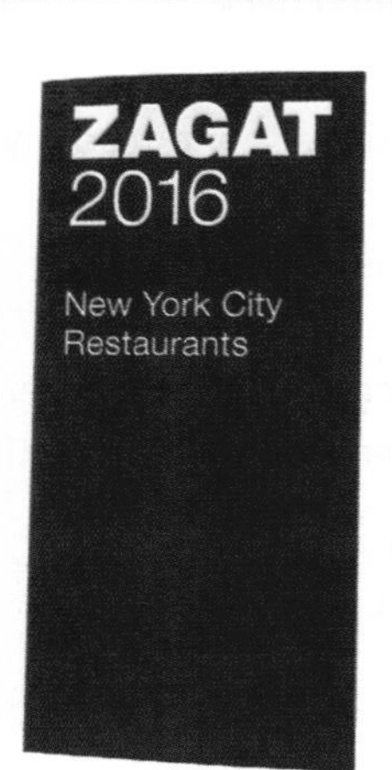

The little red Zagat book about restaurants is now an international bestseller, and the company that publishes it is now also a successful online industry worth millions of dollars.

The book was started by the Americans Tim and Nina Zagat. They were a couple who had an active social life and enjoyed eating out. The first version of their guide was made for Paris, and it just rated their favorite restaurants. The Zagats wanted to make the eating-out experience more enjoyable for their friends and anyone else who wanted to read their book. It was a hobby and not a business at that point.

Then, in 1979, the Zagats were at a dinner party with friends who complained that some of the reviews of restaurants in New York were **hopeless**—you could not trust the opinions given. So the Zagats started a guide for New York. They still did it as a hobby, but now the guide also included reviews based on their friends' experiences, taken from a survey questionnaire evaluating the food, decoration, and service at each restaurant they visited.

In order to cover costs, in 1983, the Zagats decided to sell copies of their guide. In a short time, the guide became very popular, and in 1985, it was featured in a cover story in *New York* magazine. The book sold 75,000 copies a month the following year.

The business continued to grow, and the books become an important cultural guide. In 2011, the Zagats sold the company to Google for a reported $125 million. However, the couple continued to operate the business from Google's New York office since it is a job they love.

—adapted from *Savoring Gotham: A Food Lover's Companion to New York City*, edited by Andrew F. Smith

Oxford 3000™

10 WHAT'S YOUR ANGLE? Answer the questions.

1 Have you or anyone you know ever used the Zagat restaurant guide?

2 Where do people get restaurant information where you live?

VOCABULARY DEVELOPMENT
Adjective suffixes (*-able, -ful, -ive, -less, -al*)

You can add suffixes to nouns and verbs to make adjectives. Recognizing these endings can help you identify these words in a sentence and understand their meaning.

*Many people believe that fighting this is **useless**—after all, how can stores survive when the Internet is so **powerful**?*

Adding suffixes to nouns and verbs also helps you increase the number and variety of words you can use.

***creative** store owners*	***traditional** markets*	***comfortable** and stylish café*
-ful	*power—**powerful***	[1] ________
-less	*use—**useless***	[2] ________
-al	*tradition—**traditional***	[3] ________
-ive	*create—creative*	[4] ________
-able	*comfort—**comfortable***	[5] ________

Oxford 3000™

11 IDENTIFY Review the article about the Zagat guide. Complete the Vocabulary Development box with another example of each type of adjective from the text.

12 INTEGRATE Complete the adjective in each phrase with the correct suffix from the Vocabulary Development box. (Use a dictionary to check if you need to change the spelling at the end of the main word.)

1 enjoy________ atmosphere

2 bottom________ drinks

3 help________ waiters

4 internation________ food

5 extend________ menu

13 BUILD Complete the sentence with the appropriate noun or verb using the suffix given.

1 David is very ________ful. He owns several businesses in the city.

2 My favorite restaurant uses local produce and specializes in ________al cuisine.

3 The architect was very ________ive with the building design.

4 The owner of this store is very ________able. She has great style.

5 This phone app doesn't work. It is ________less!

14 WHAT'S YOUR ANGLE? In your opinion, how important is each of the things in Exercise 12 for a restaurant? Tell your partner.

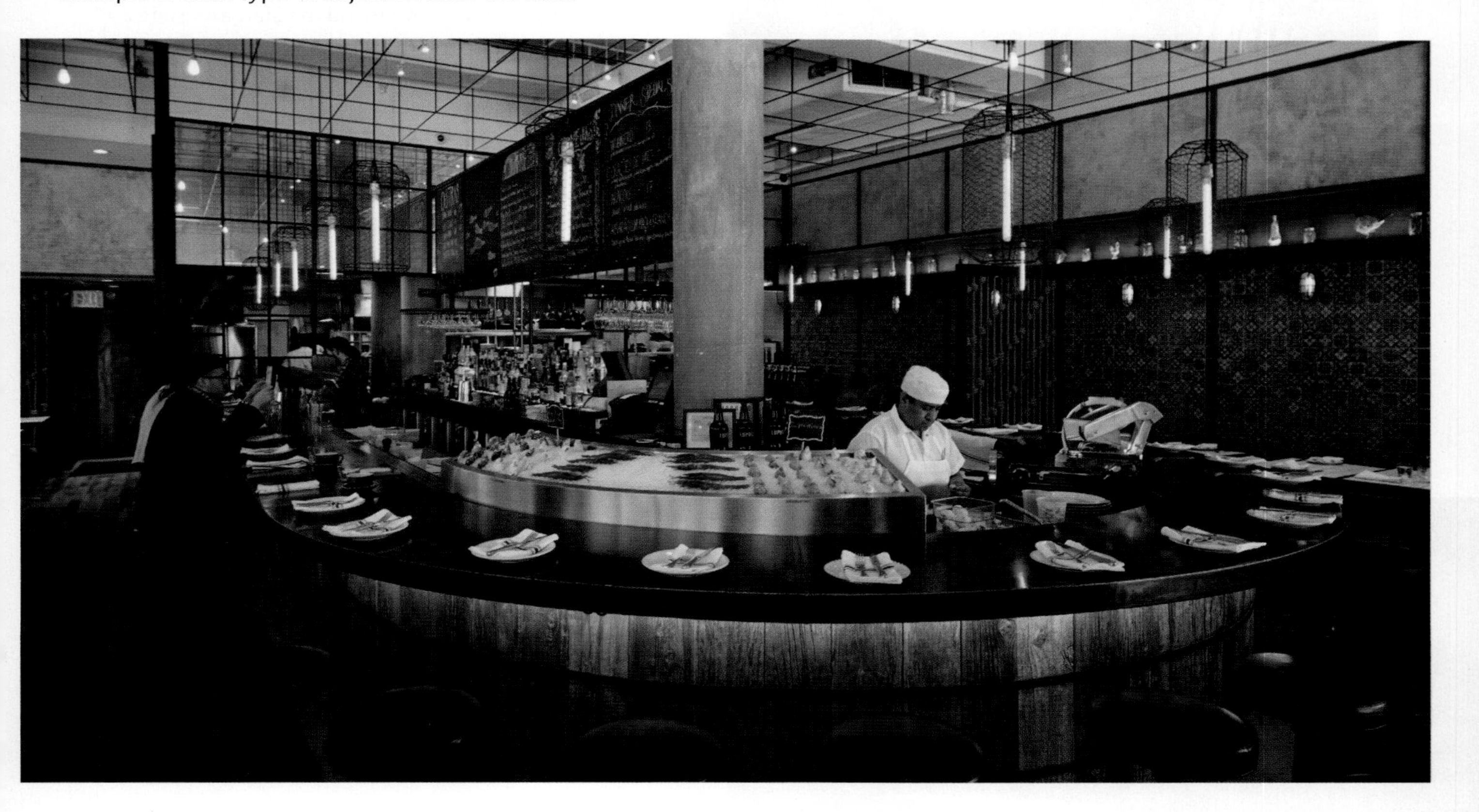

9.3 Star Rating

1 ACTIVATE Discuss the questions with a partner.

How do you decide which...

restaurant to go to? book to read? phone to buy?
place to stay? movie to see?

2 IDENTIFY Read the start of the online review. What is it reviewing? What is the reviewer's overall opinion?

Find 

Newby Place ◎◎◎◎◎ *362 reviews*

Many reviews say this hotel is the best in the area, and it is easy to see why. It was a real five-star experience.

3 INTEGRATE Read the rest of the review and complete the information about the hotel.

Hotel: Newby ______________________

Rooms: ______________________

Restaurants: ______________________

____

Facilities and services: ______________________

____

When we arrived, the first thing we saw was the famous aquarium, and it was full of neon tetras (small blue-and-red freshwater fish), which entertained our four-year-old while we checked in. We had booked a Dream Standard room, and we got an early check-in. This room is a large double room with a view of the sea, although there was no outdoor seating area, which was the only disappointing thing about our stay. Next time, we would book a Dream Special suite, a more expensive option that comes with a second bedroom and a small terrace. For those of you with lots of money, I would recommend the Stargazer suites: three-room suites on the top floor that also come with free access to the executive lounge. However, they are less child-friendly.

There are three restaurants in the hotel: French, Italian, and Euro-Thai fusion. This last one served an interesting mix of Asian and European food. Though we seemed to spend a lot of time eating and sleeping, we did at least use some of the hotel's facilities. The pool was a good size and a lovely place to spend afternoons. There was also a well-equipped gym, which, I have to admit, we didn't use at all. The ocean was clean and great for swimming and snorkeling. The hotel also has sailing boats and sculls (small, light rowboats) available to rent by the day.

The staff was extremely friendly, and the service was excellent. When we had a problem with our daughter's bed, it was fixed immediately. Room service was quick, and the buffet breakfast exceptional with everything you could want: fruit, cheese, eggs, yogurt, bread, and much more. We really do recommend this hotel, but perhaps we will try to spend a little more time using the gym or boats and a little less in the restaurants next time.

4 ASSESS Read the review again, and write the writer's opinion about these things.

the swimming pool: ______

the staff: ______

the gym: ______

the service: ______

WRITING SKILL
Using definitions and relative clauses

At times, we need to define words and phrases we use in our writing. Using a variety of ways of doing this can make your writing more engaging.

Relative clauses

...a Dream Special suite, a more expensive option that comes with a second bedroom and a small terrace.

Information in parentheses

...it was full of neon tetras (small blue-and-red freshwater fish)...

Colon

...with everything you could want: fruit, cheese, eggs, yogurt, bread, and much more.

An additional sentence

This last one served an interesting mix of Asian and European food.

5 IDENTIFY Find the examples from the Writing Skill box in the review.

6 EXPAND Find other examples of definitions in the review.

7 APPLY Use a dictionary to check the words in bold, and then add information to the sentences to define these words. Use the method from the Writing Skill box in parentheses.

1. The book has an interesting **epilogue**. (additional sentence)
2. The **mezze** at this restaurant is fantastic. (colon)
3. They're actually going to make a **prequel** to this movie. (information in parentheses)
4. The **mosaic floors** are beautiful. (additional sentence)
5. I loved the **live cooking stations** in the main restaurant. (relative clause)

8 PREPARE Make notes on the following. Include your opinion and any interesting details.

a restaurant you ate at: ______

a place you stayed at: ______

a book you read: ______

a movie you saw: ______

9 INTERACT Tell your partner briefly about each thing on your list in Exercise 8. Give some details and your opinion. Answer your partner's questions.

10 DEVELOP Choose one thing from the list in Exercise 8. Make notes of important details and your overall opinion. Add any relevant information your partner asked about.

11 WRITE Write a review of the place or thing you chose.

- Include definitions of less common words
- Include relative clauses
- Include a star rating
- Include your opinion and recommendations
- Write up to 300 words

12 IMPROVE Read your partner's review. Is there any more information you need before deciding whether to visit, read, or see the reviewed item?

13 WHAT'S YOUR ANGLE? Read other classmates' reviews. Choose a place to eat, a place to stay, a book, or a movie you definitely want to experience and one you definitely don't want to experience. Explain your choices.

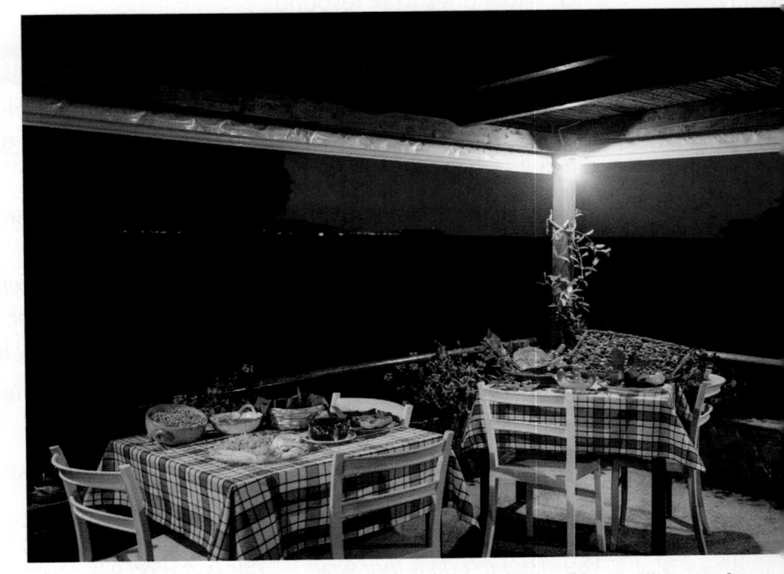

A Mediterranean dining experience in Pollica, Italy

9.4 It's Interesting, But…

1 ACTIVATE Discuss the questions with a partner.

1. Who is it most difficult to receive criticism from (e.g., friends, family, classmates, teacher, boss, etc.)? Why?
2. Who is it most difficult to give criticism to? Why?
3. Does the mode of communication (e.g., phone, face-to-face, email) change how easy or difficult it is? Why?

2 ANALYZE Emma, the teaching assistant for Max's class, is talking to Max about his artwork. Look at the picture, and discuss the questions with a partner.

1. What do you think Emma thinks of the artwork? How can you tell?
2. How do you think Max feels? How can you tell?

3 IDENTIFY Watch the video and answer the questions.

1. What does Emma like about Max's work?
2. What does she think he has done wrong?
3. How does Max respond?

REAL-WORLD ENGLISH Giving and receiving criticism

In some relationships, criticism is more usual, particularly in a power relationship (e.g., teacher to student, boss to employee). However, the criticism needs to be given well to be effective. In general, it can be difficult to hear negative views.

When giving criticism, we often start with a positive comment and then use some phrases and words to "soften" the negative part.

It's very well done…but it seems you didn't understand what you were supposed to do here.
I like this part, but I'm not sure the purpose of this is clear.
It's interesting. However, I don't think this is the best way to…

We usually avoid being direct as such language might unnecessarily upset the person receiving the criticism.

This is wrong. *You did a bad job.* *Terrible.*

Also, when giving criticism, it helps to end with suggestions on how to improve. (It's good to avoid negative language here.)

~~Don't do that~~. *Why don't you try doing this?*
~~You shouldn't do it that way~~. *This is a good way to do it.*

When receiving criticism, thank the person for the comments.

Thanks for your feedback. It's really helpful.
I appreciate your taking the time to look at my work. Your comments are really useful.

4 **IDENTIFY** Listen to extracts from the video and complete the phrases Emma uses.

1 Well, ________________, and your brush strokes are ________________. But I'm ________________ the purpose of this piece is clear.

2 ________________ you didn't understand what you ________________ to do.

3 I mean, ________________, but the theme of the competition is symbolism of nature—and ________________…symbolic.

4 ________________ at the environment in a way that everyone can relate to.

5 ________________ you could work on some other pieces?

6 ________________ symbols in nature that are more… universal. OK?

7 ________________, Max. ________________ next week. Same time?

5 **PREPARE** Work with a partner. Use the chart below or your own ideas to create a situation for a role play. Decide on the details of the situation, including:

- the relationship and social distance between the two people
- the goal of the person giving the criticism and how to reach this goal (e.g., language to use and action to take)
- how the person criticized will respond

Teacher Student Friend Family member Worker Boss Colleague	criticizes	student friend family member worker boss colleague	for	being late. not working enough. being rude. doing bad work. not helping enough. talking too loudly. wearing the wrong clothes. (other).

6 **INTERACT** Now use the situation you created in Exercise 5 to do a role play. Decide who is giving the criticism.

7 **ANALYZE** Discuss the role play. Was the goal of the person giving the criticism achieved? How?

8 **INTERACT** Work with the same partner. Choose another situation, change roles, and do the role play.

9 **WHAT'S YOUR ANGLE?** Do you think receiving criticism is always helpful? Why or why not?

GO ONLINE
to create your own version of the English For Real video.

9.5 Spoiler Alert

1 ACTIVATE Look at the themes below. Discuss the questions with a partner.

1 What movies or books have themes that match these?
2 Can you think of any other basic themes?

human vs. nature human vs. human human vs. technology

2 WHAT'S YOUR ANGLE? Which is your favorite theme? Why? Tell your partner.

3 IDENTIFY Listen to a description of a book and its plot.

1 What theme from Exercise 1 is in it?
2 Have you read the book or seen the movies?

SPEAKING Describing the plot of a book or movie

When you describe the plot of a book or movie, to keep everyone interested, you need to organize your ideas and plan the amount of detail to give.

Before you describe the plot, you can provide information such as the **title**, the **author**/**lead actor** + **director**, the year it came out, and the **type** of story (comedy, horror, etc.).

The movie I'm going to talk about is…
It was directed by…and came out in…
The novel was published in…
It's a comedy starring…

Then you can describe the **setting** (the place and time at which the action happens), the **theme**, the **main characters**, and the **plot**. We usually use the simple present to do this.

It's set in…
It's mainly about the theme of…
The main character is… / She's a…

But be careful not to give a spoiler. Don't tell people how the story ends (unless they ask)!

4 INTEGRATE Complete the headings of the summary with the correct words in bold from the Speaking box. Then listen again and check.

1 Title	*The Old Man and the Sea*
2	Ernest Hemingway
3	1952
4	Santiago Manolin
5	Cuba in the 1940s
6	man and nature, age and youth

GRAMMAR IN CONTEXT Tag questions

We use tag questions to check information or to ask someone if they agree with us.

We use a positive tag question after a negative statement and a negative tag question after a positive statement.

*You hadn't seen the movie, **had you?***
*He was helping Santiago, **wasn't he?***

We can reply to a tag question with a short answer.

She's directed two other movies, hasn't she?
Yes, she has.
There aren't only two characters, are there?
No, there aren't.

See Grammar focus on page 167.

5 APPLY Read the extracts from the discussion, and complete the question tags. Then listen and check.

1 You've read it, ________________, Jo?
2 He hadn't published anything before that, ________________?
3 That's his name, ________________, Jo?
4 …he had helped Santiago with the boat before he went, ________________?
5 It's pretty sad, ________________?

6 IDENTIFY Can you remember the short answers to the tag questions in Exercise 5? Write positive and negative short answers for each. Then listen and check which one the speakers used.

7 INTERACT Add tag questions to the sentences. Then ask and answer the questions with your partner. Give short answers.

1 You watch movies in English.
2 There aren't any good movies on right now.
3 People don't read very much anymore.
4 You've never written a book.
5 Movies were better in the past.

8 PREPARE You are going to describe the plot of a movie or book to your group. Decide what to talk about. Make notes of additional details (title, author, etc.) and list the events of the plot.

9 IMPROVE Describe the plot to a partner. Then listen to your partner's feedback.

10 SHARE Work in a group. Describe the plot again using the feedback from Exercise 9 to improve your description.

Now go to page 155 for the Unit 9 Review.

10 Mysteries

UNIT SNAPSHOT

What makes something mysterious?

Why are mysteries interesting?

How do people solve mysteries?

BEHIND THE PHOTO

REAL-WORLD GOAL

Find out about a local mystery

1 Read the text. Why does the man behave in such a strange way?

A man lives on the top floor of a very tall building. He takes the elevator to the ground floor every day to go to work. When he returns, he takes the elevator halfway up the building and then walks up the stairs for the rest of the way. If it is raining, he goes all the way to the top.

2 Work in groups to discuss your ideas and solve the mystery.

10.1 It's a Mystery

1 ACTIVATE Choose a verb to complete the sentence with your view. Then compare and discuss your views in a group.

I must / like to / don't need to / hate to have an explanation for everything in life.

2 VOCABULARY Complete the phrases with the words in the boxes. Use each word only once.

atmosphere	disappear	mysterious	mystery

1 strange ________
2 ________ circumstances
3 remain a ________
4 ________ forever

evidence	prove	puzzled	reveal

5 little ________
6 difficult to ________
7 ________ to discover
8 ________ the truth

3 BUILD Complete the sentences with the phrases from Exercise 2.

1 One day, they will ________________.
2 The person disappeared in ________________.
3 The reason will ________________ forever.
4 It's ________________ what actually happened.
5 Not many people manage to ________________.
6 The place had a very ________________.
7 There was ________________ to show what happened.
8 People were ________________ the reality.

4 USE Work in a group to tell a mystery story using one or more of the sentences from Exercise 3. Use movie or book plots for ideas.

5 IDENTIFY You are going to listen to the first part of a podcast about mysteries. Two people who think mysteries are important will be mentioned. Which of the jobs in the box do you think they have? Listen and check.

teacher	artist	salesperson	philosopher	scientist

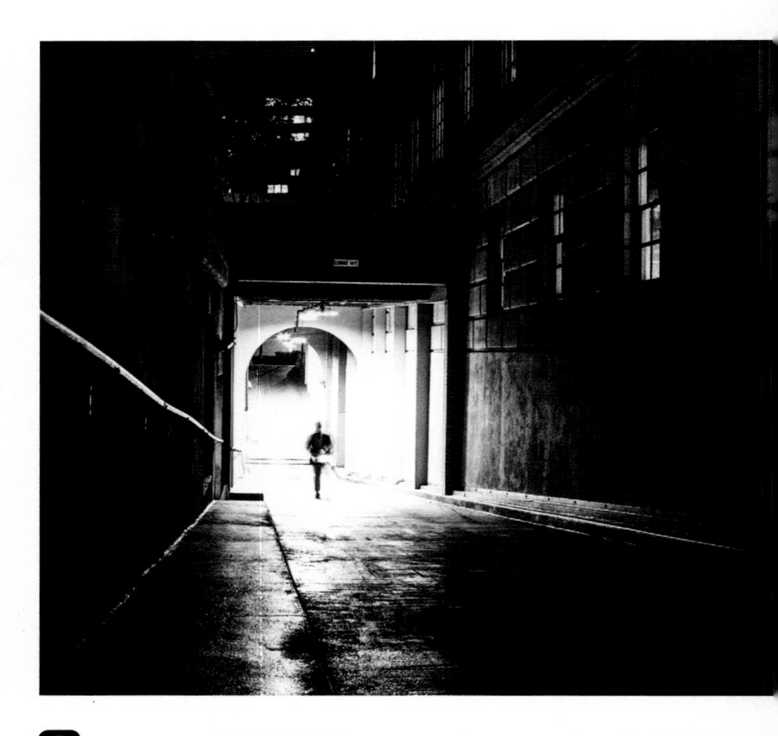

LISTENING SKILL Recognizing chunks of language

Speakers use chunks of language rather than a long line of words with no breaks.

A chunk is a group of a few words—some stressed, some unstressed—with a small pause at the start and end. Chunks are logical: the words are grouped together to show meaning.

That's according to John Newling, ¦ an artist who decided to...

...because without it ¦ we feel ¦ that something important is missing.

Recognizing chunks can help us understand a speaker more easily and the message more clearly.

6 APPLY Listen to extracts from the first part of the podcast, and mark the chunks.

1 We all need mystery in our lives.
2 The insurance company agreed to pay him if he didn't have any.
3 He is not the first to think that mystery is important.
4 Life is not a problem to be solved—it is a mystery to be lived.

7 **INTEGRATE** Listen to the next part of the podcast. Are these sentences true (T) or false (F), according to the speaker?

1 There will be fewer mysteries in the future. ___
2 The woman remembered something from before she went into a coma. ___
3 The majority of people have experienced a mysterious event. ___
4 In the story of the mystery figure, people usually go crazy when they disappear. ___
5 The world is a better place with mystery in it. ___

Glossary:
coma (n)—an unconscious state, deeper than sleep, lasting a long time, and caused by illness or injury
crossword (n)—a game in which you solve clues to find words, then fit the words across and downwards into a square.

8 **APPLY** Listen and complete the chunks in the extracts from the podcast.

1 It is difficult ________________ without mystery.
2 Newling asked people ________________...
3 After all, ________________ a mysterious coincidence?
4 You know it wasn't there yesterday, ________________...
5 At the very least, ________________, mystery makes the world a more exciting place to live in.

9 **INTEGRATE** Listen to part of the podcast again, and complete the notes with words you hear.

Life without mystery—difficult to imagine since [1] _________ can prove or explain nearly everything

However, mysteries still exist...

Examples:

- Artist John Newling asked people to share [2] _________ (in one year, examples from [3] _________ people)

Proved that almost everyone [4] _________ a mystery

e.g., woman waking from coma, answering a crossword clue from when she was asleep

- Personal observations, not scientific [5] _________:
- mysterious coincidence, calling at the same time someone [6] _________ you
- an [7] _________ reappearing in a place you looked before
- a mystery figure leading you from a [8] _________ situation

Mysteries make life more [9] _________ and may also keep us [10] _________.

10 **INTERACT** Has something happened to you or someone you know for which you have no explanation? Tell your partner.

GRAMMAR IN CONTEXT *could, may,* and *might*: Possibility and deductions

We can use *could, may,* and *might* to talk about possibility in the present and to make deductions. They are similar in meaning, though *might* and *could* can suggest more uncertainty than *may*.

*Mystery **could** be simply a normal part of human life.*
*They **might** be going crazy.*
*This **may** be just a coincidence.*

We can use *may not* and *might not* when we are not sure if something is true.

*We **might not / may not** be responsible. But we can't be sure.*

We use *couldn't* when we are certain something is not true.

*That **couldn't** be the reason. I saw the evidence.*

See Grammar focus on page 168.

11 **IDENTIFY** Listen and complete the sentences. Then decide if the person is absolutely certain, more or less certain, or unsure.

1 Stories we read in newspapers _________ be true.
2 Scientific theories _________ be as correct as they claim to be.
3 There _________ be mysteries we will never solve.
4 Some of the mystery stories on the Internet _________ be true.
5 Simple natural reasons _________ be the cause of some of today's mysteries.
6 Many mysterious images you see online _________ be real—they must be edited.

12 **WHAT'S YOUR ANGLE?** How sure are you about the statements in Exercise 11? Explain your ideas to your partner.

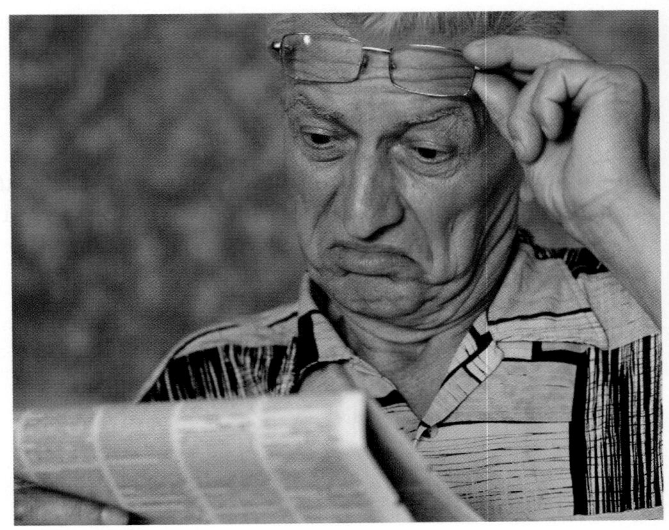

10.2 Mysterious Code

1 ACTIVATE Look at the pictures and answer the questions.

1 Which of these forms of writing can you understand?
2 Which can't be understood by anybody?

hieroglyphics

computer code

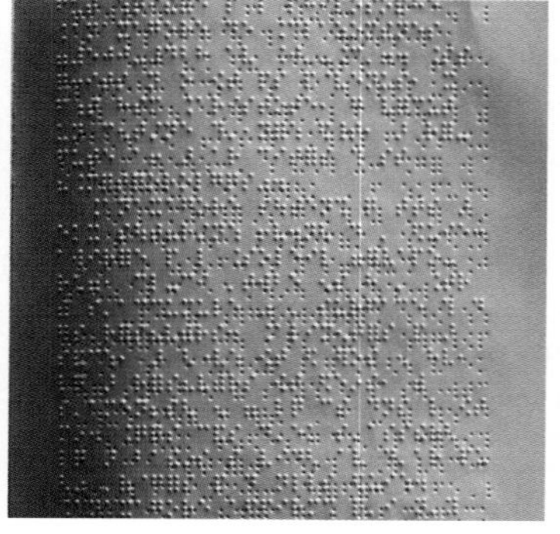
Braille code

Voynich manuscript

2 IDENTIFY Read the title and the first paragraph of the essay quickly. What is the mystery that the writer refers to in the title?

The mystery of the Voynich manuscript: Will it ever be solved?

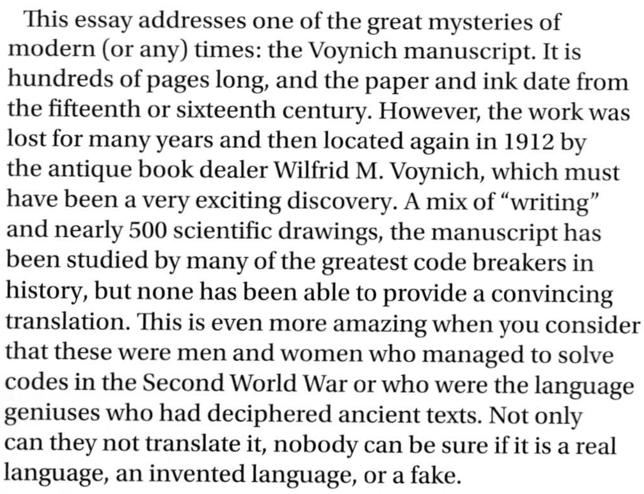

This essay addresses one of the great mysteries of modern (or any) times: the Voynich manuscript. It is hundreds of pages long, and the paper and ink date from the fifteenth or sixteenth century. However, the work was lost for many years and then located again in 1912 by the antique book dealer Wilfrid M. Voynich, which must have been a very exciting discovery. A mix of "writing" and nearly 500 scientific drawings, the manuscript has been studied by many of the greatest code breakers in history, but none has been able to provide a convincing translation. This is even more amazing when you consider that these were men and women who managed to solve codes in the Second World War or who were the language geniuses who had deciphered ancient texts. Not only can they not translate it, nobody can be sure if it is a real language, an invented language, or a fake.

There are two basic theories about the manuscript. On the one hand, it might have been written by a great scholar (many people, including the philosopher William Romain Newbold, who studied it for many years, suspect that it was written by Roger Bacon, a thirteenth-century English philosopher and scientist who some people claim wrote the works attributed to Shakespeare). On the other hand (and it seems that at least as many people believe this as believe the first theory), it could have been a hoax—a clever plan to fool the world. If this is the case, it has succeeded; generations of scholars have given decades of their lives trying to decipher it, getting no closer.

However, a breakthrough may finally have been made. Marcelo Montemurro, a scientist at the University of Manchester in the United Kingdom, has looked for patterns of language using modern computer techniques, and he believes he might have found evidence that it is a language. He says that the language patterns he found couldn't have been inserted into a fake document on purpose. This would have required understanding ideas about language that hadn't been discovered by the time the manuscript was created.

If this is the first step in finding out the meaning of the text, there are many scholars around the world who will be delighted. However, it would be the end of one of the world's great mysteries, and on account of that, I personally hope that it is not the actual solution.

—adapted from *The Oxford Companion to the Book*, edited by Michael F. Suarez S. J. and H. R. Woudhuysen

READING SKILL
Distinguishing between fact and speculation

A fact gives information that is true. It is often supported by evidence or a reference that can be checked.

It was located again in 1912 by the antique book dealer Wilfrid M. Voynich.

Speculation gives opinion and ideas about what might be true. It sometimes is supported by reasons and theories, but these cannot be proved. Some modal verbs such as *may*, *might*, *could*, *must*, and *can't* are often used with speculation.

*It **might** have been written by a great scholar.*

Identifying points as either fact or speculation can help you understand and follow the arguments in a text more clearly.

3 INTEGRATE Read the essay. Complete the table of facts and speculation about the Voynich manuscript. Include at least three examples of each.

Fact	Speculation
Found in 1912 by Wilfrid M. Voynich	

4 ASSESS Compare your table with your partner's. Have you identified the same facts and speculation? Discuss and make changes if necessary.

5 EXPAND Choose three facts from the list on Exercise 3. Then write a statement speculating about each fact.

Fact: No one has been able to translate a single word of it.
Speculation: The words might not mean anything at all.

GRAMMAR IN CONTEXT
Deductions about the past

We use *must have* to make deductions about the past when we are very sure that something was true.

It must have been a very exciting discovery.

We use *can't have* or *couldn't have* when we are very sure that something wasn't true.

*It **couldn't have** been inserted into a fake document.*

When we are not sure about what happened in the past, we can speculate using *could have*, *might have*, *may have*, and *might not have*.

*It **could have** been a hoax.*

See Grammar focus on page 168.

6 APPLY Rewrite the sentence in three different ways using modals from the Grammar in Context box to show different degrees of certainty. Compare with a partner. Which sentence do you agree with the most?

The discovery of the Voynich manuscript was very exciting.

7 IDENTIFY Read the statements from the essay. Choose the sentence that has the same meaning.

1 The discovery of the manuscript must have been very exciting.
   a It's pretty certain that the discovery was exciting.
   b There is a possibility the discovery was exciting.
2 A breakthrough may finally have been made.
   a It's certain a breakthrough was made.
   b It's possible a breakthrough was made.
3 It might have been written by a great scholar.
   a There is a possibility it was written by a great scholar.
   b There is strong evidence it was written by a great scholar.
4 Montemurro might have found evidence that it is a language.
   a Possibly he found evidence that it is a language.
   b It's almost certain he found evidence that it is a language.

8 INTEGRATE Rewrite the sentences with a modal verb to express the same degree of certainty.

1 The Voynich manuscript definitely wasn't written by children.
____
2 Maybe Wilfrid Voynich created the manuscript himself.
____
3 Perhaps other ancient people introduced hieroglyphics to the Egyptians.
____
4 Louis Braille (the inventor of Braille code) was definitely very clever.
____
5 Computer code wasn't easier to learn in the past.
____

9 WHAT'S YOUR ANGLE? Where do you think the Voynich manuscript came from? Speculate with a partner.

VOCABULARY DEVELOPMENT Phrases with *on*

A useful way to organize and build vocabulary is to group together phrases that have a common word—for example, *on*. When you find new phrases that share the same word, add them to the group.

on** the one **hand
on** the other **hand
***on** **account** of*
on** **purpose

Oxford 3000™

10 IDENTIFY Find the four phrases from the Vocabulary Development box in the essay. Then match them to three of the definitions below.

1 not by accident, deliberately ________

2 used to say that you have changed your opinion ________

3 because of ________

4 in general ________

5 at the correct time ________

6 put in a place where people can look at it ________

7 used to introduce the first point of view ________

8 used to introduce a second point of view ________

11 BUILD Match these phrases with *on* to the correct definitions in Exercise 10.

on display on the **whole** **on second thought** on **time**

Oxford 3000™

12 APPLY Choose four of the phrases with *on*. Write a sentence about the past for each phrase. Include two true sentences and two false.

I've seen the Voynich manuscript on display in a museum.

13 WHAT'S YOUR ANGLE? Work with a partner. Guess which sentences your partner wrote in Exercise 11 are true.

A: I was on time for class yesterday.

B: You can't have been because I saw you on the street after class had started.

10.3 What Could Have Happened?

1 ACTIVATE What do you think the mystery is behind each of these pictures? Discuss your ideas in a group.

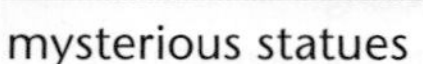

mysterious statues

a strange hole

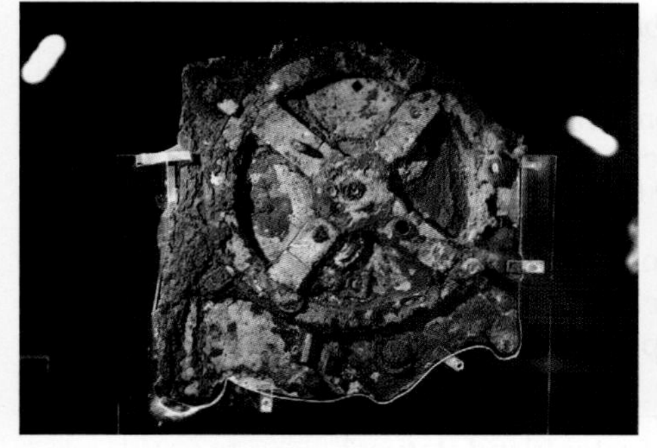

an unexplained object

a puzzling creature

double identity

2 IDENTIFY Read the blog article quickly.

1 Which mystery is the main focus of the blog article?

2 Which of the other mysteries are mentioned?

Home | About | Search

The $2 million mystery challenge!

I've been asking myself a question recently that I wanted to share with you: What is the most puzzling mystery in the world? If enough readers help, perhaps we can solve it!

For this reason, I have been reading about mysteries. There is the Easter Island mystery, where 887 statues that weigh up to 82 tons each were built on the island between 500 and 1,000 years ago. Easter Island is about 2,000 kilometers from the mainland. How were people able to build something so heavy, and why did they want to? Then there is a complex computer-like instrument called the Antikythera Mechanism, which was made more than 2,000 years ago and could calculate the position of the stars. It's a mystery how people could make something so advanced so long ago. However, I have decided that a hole in North America, called the Oak Island Money Pit, is the most mysterious because it should be something we can solve but nobody has.

Let me explain the known facts. Since the hole is on a tiny, rarely visited island off Nova Scotia, Canada, it was not found until 1795, although it is probably much older. The hole is made by humans, and it is very deep. Nobody has been able to climb down it. Consequently, the actual depth of the hole remains unknown. It is a complex structure, and, therefore, we can assume that it was made by very clever people, but nobody can say who. There is some coded writing on a stone in the wall, which apparently says that there are $2 million below. Many people have tried to locate the money, including President Franklin Delano Roosevelt when he was a young man, but nobody has been able to. The hole has a mechanism that automatically fills it with water when someone tries to go down it, and because of this, nobody has found the money (if it is there!).

Therefore, I am writing to ask you, my readers, that if anyone has any theories about it, please share them with us. Together, who knows, maybe we can solve the mystery…and share the $2 million…

3 WHAT'S YOUR ANGLE? Answer the questions with a partner.

1 Which of the three mysteries do you find most interesting? Why?
2 Who do you think might have made the Money Pit?
3 How would you try to get the money out of the Money Pit?

WRITING SKILL
Using reasons and result linking words

When explaining stories and situations, we often give reasons and results. We use linking words to show the reader what the connection between ideas is.

Reason—*since, as, because, because of, due to, for this reason*

Verb clauses can begin with *since*, *because*, and *as*.

Since / Because / As *there is no other explanation, this theory is the best.*
This theory is the best ***since / because / as*** *there is no other explanation.*

Noun phrases follow *because of* and *due to*. *For this reason* needs no additions.

Because of this issue, / ***Due to this issue***, / ***For this reason***, *nobody knows the truth.*

Result—*therefore, consequently, as a result, so*

These linkers usually go at the beginning of the sentence and are followed by a comma.

Consequently, / ***Therefore***, / ***As a result***, *the actual depth of the hole remains unknown.*

4 IDENTIFY Read the article again.

1 Find three more sentences with reasons. What is each one a reason for? What linker is used?
2 Find two more sentences with a result. What is it a result of? What linker is used?

5 APPLY Decide what the connection is between the ideas. Rewrite the sentences using a linker to show this connection.

1 Many people know about this mystery. There is a lot of information on the Internet about it.
2 People love the idea of a mystery animal in the water. Many tourists visit each year.
3 Nobody knew about the hole until the eighteenth century. Few people went to the island before that.
4 We still have no way to explain what happened. It remains a mystery.
5 A program was made about the mystery last year. More people are interested in the mystery now.

GRAMMAR IN CONTEXT
Ability and possibility: Present, past, and future

We use *can* and *be able to* to talk about abilities and possibilities.

We ***can*** *read about the story on the Internet.*
Computers ***are able to*** *solve the mystery.*

We use *could, couldn't*, and *was / were* (*not*) *able to* to talk about possibilities and general abilities in the past.

People ***could*** *visit the place by boat.*
You ***couldn't*** *find out much about the mystery 50 years ago.*
Even 20 years ago, computers ***weren't able to*** *do what they can do now.*

We also use *was / were* (*not*) *able to* and *couldn't*—but not *could*—to talk about particular possibilities in the past

I ***couldn't*** *understand the story when I was young.*
We ***were able to*** *find out the truth after doing some research.*

We can use *be able to* with other tenses.

No one ***has been able to*** *explain what happened.*
I don't think anyone ***will be able to*** *explain it.*

See Grammar focus on page 168.

6 INTEGRATE Complete the sentences with *can*, *could*, or a form of *be able to*. Then check which verbs were used to make the same point in the article.

1 How _________ people _________ build something as heavy as the Easter Island statues?
2 In the past, the Antikythera Mechanism _________ calculate the position of the stars.
3 The Oak Island Money Pit should be something we _________ solve.
4 Since it was discovered, nobody _________ climb down the hole.
5 The hole was made by clever people, but even now, nobody _________ say by whom.
6 Together, maybe we _________ solve the mystery.

7 APPLY Complete the sentences with *could*, *couldn't*, or *was / were able to*.

1 The scientist couldn't completely explain the cause, but she _________ give some reasons.
2 In the past, you couldn't visit the place independently, but you _________ go in a group.
3 The theory _________ explain everything that happened, but you could get the general idea.
4 Fortunately, I _________ escape, but I couldn't get the experience out of my mind.
5 You _________ read about the history, but you couldn't see video of the place until now.

8 INTEGRATE Complete the sentences with your ideas. Then compare your sentences with a partner.

1 Fifty years ago, people weren't able to…in the way we can now.
2 Nowadays, most people still can't…
3 I couldn't…until recently, but I can nowadays.
4 No one has been able to…and I don't think they ever will.
5 People could…in the past, but not as many people do this now.

9 VOCABULARY Which definition is correct? Choose A or B. Use a dictionary if necessary.

1 **analyze** (verb)
  a examine something in order to understand it
  b imagine why something has happened
2 **assume** (verb)
  a think something is true without having proof
  b think up a reasonable explanation for something
3 **build up** (phrasal verb)
  a be full of something
  b develop sth
4 **complex** (adjective)
  a made up of two parts which work badly together
  b made up of many different parts
5 **concentrate** (verb)
  a pay close attention to a single thing
  b decide against something
6 **definite** (adjective)
  a obviously true
  b not likely to change; certain
7 **puzzling** (adjective)
  a hard to understand and confusing
  b as easy as a puzzle game
8 **rational** (adjective)
  a interesting and informative
  b based on reason, not emotions

Oxford 3000™

10 USE Complete the sentences with the words from Exercise 9. Change the form if necessary.

1 Scientists have used all the research to _______________ a new theory about the disease.
2 Smartphones are too _______________ for most people to fix themselves.
3 The first step in problem-solving is to _______________ all the available data.
4 Despite being asked multiple times, the expert only answered "maybe" and refused to give a _______________ answer.
5 I've been _______________ too long on this math problem, and now I've got a headache.
6 The most _______________ explanation is that very clever people dug the hole a long time ago, not aliens!
7 Always check the evidence—if you _______________ too much, you will make mistakes.
8 The crime was _______________ because there was no motive and no suspects.

11 PREPARE Decide on a mystery to write about.

Choose from:

- one of the pictures in Exercise 1
- another famous mystery you know
- a personal story

12 DEVELOP Make notes on the mystery.

- For what reasons is it a mystery?
- What have been the results of any investigations?
- What speculation and theories are there about the mystery?

13 WRITE Write your article.

- [ ] Include reasons and results.
- [ ] Include modals to describe ability and possibility.
- [ ] Include speculation about what might have happened.
- [ ] Write up to 300 words.

14 IMPROVE Read your partner's article. Check that everything from the checklist is covered.

15 WHAT'S YOUR ANGLE? Read other classmates' articles. Can you solve any of the mysteries? Share your ideas with the writers.

A misty street in the Aspromonte mountain in Calabria, Italy

10.4 I Meant to Tell You...

1 ACTIVATE Discuss the questions with a partner.

1 Which of these things do people borrow from friends or family?

money	food	clothes
books	phone charger	other: ________

2 Which is it OK to take without asking?

2 ANALYZE Watch the conversation between Andy and Max. Answer the questions.

1 What things are missing or gone?
2 Who do Max and Andy think have taken or used up the things?
3 What does Max think Andy should do?

3 WHAT'S YOUR ANGLE? Discuss the questions with a partner.

1 Have you ever been in a similar situation to Andy's?
2 What did/would you do?
3 How would you feel if you were Andy?

4 IDENTIFY Watch Andy talking to Kevin. How successful is the conversation? Explain your answer to a partner.

5 ANALYZE Number the parts of the conversation between Andy and Kevin in the order they happened. Then watch again and check.

___ a Kevin reveals how he has resolved the situation.
___ b Andy introduces the issue.
___ c Kevin notices something is wrong.
___ d Andy outlines what behavior is acceptable.
___ e Andy suggests what Kevin should do in the future.
___ f Kevin explains what happened.

ENGLISH FOR REAL

REAL-WORLD ENGLISH Correcting someone

It can be difficult to tell someone they are wrong about something and to correct them, even if they are a friend or family member.

We often prepare someone for the correction we are going to make.

I need to talk to you about…
I don't know how to say this, but…

Before correcting someone, we can start by saying what is acceptable and then present the correction using phrases that make it "softer."

It's fine to…, but could you…
It's OK to…, but perhaps you could…

Use a friendly tone of voice and reassure the person. Humor can also help along with examples of when we or other people have done something similar.

Don't worry about it.
We all make mistakes sometimes.

6 **IDENTIFY** Listen and complete the phrases Andy uses in his conversation with Kevin.

1 Well, I __________ you about that.
2 I mean, it's __________ borrow things, but…
3 But __________ we're out of something, tell us, or replace it.
4 Yeah, __________. So…

7 **ANALYZE** Match Andy's phrases 1–4 in Exercise 6 to why he uses them.

___ a to say what is acceptable
___ b to introduce the issue
___ c to accept his responsibility in the situation
___ d to say what should happen in the future

8 **PREPARE** Work in groups of three (A, B, and C). Think of something that the first person in each pair might do wrong that might need correcting.

roommate—roommate (e.g., borrow things without asking)
student—teacher/professor (e.g., miss an exam)
son/daughter—parent (e.g., take the car without asking)

9 **EXPAND** In your group. choose one of the situations from Exercise 8, and use your ideas to add more detail.

What is the relationship between the two people?
How well do they know each other?
What was the problem? Why did that happen?
How serious is the situation? Why?
What does the second person want to happen? How are they going to achieve this?

10 **INTERACT** Students A and B, do the role play. Student C, observe and note the phrases for correcting that are used.

11 **ASSESS** Student C, give the other two students feedback.

How successful was the conversation?
Did you see all the stages from Exercise 5?
What phrases were used?

12 **INTERACT** Change roles and situation, and do another role play. After feedback, change again.

GO ONLINE to create your own version of the English For Real video.

10.5 Mystery Objects

1 ACTIVATE Take the "mystery object" quiz. What are or were these objects used for? Discuss your ideas in a group.

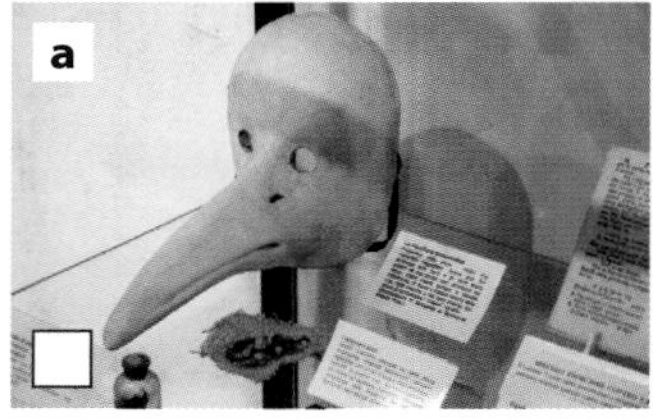

2 IDENTIFY Listen to people talking about the four objects. Number the objects in the order people talk about them.

3 INTEGRATE What are the objects? Tell a partner what you remember from the conversation.

SPEAKING
Speculating about the present and past

We speculate when we are not sure of the facts. Speculating means thinking of different possible explanations for something that happened or might happen.

*It's **probably** something used now.*
***Maybe** it's something firefighters wore.*
*It **could** be something you use in an office.*

When we do this, we try to find evidence to support our ideas.

It looks very old.

4 INTEGRATE Listen again, and match the speculations and the evidence to each object.

Object	Speculation	Evidence
1	firefighters used it	looks like something for an old computer
	used in the office	has a nose cover
	more than 100 years old	has eyeholes
2	used now	looks old
3	used with electronics	has a label
	people wore it	modern design
4	for stylish people	they are fashionable

5 IDENTIFY Listen to the extracts, and complete the phrases used to speculate.

1 It _________ really modern.
2 It's _________ something used now.
3 It _________ over a hundred years old by the look of it.
4 I don't know, _________ it's something firefighters wore?
5 They are _________ a kind of glasses or goggles.
6 They _________ for stylish people walking in polluted cities.
7 I _________ something used with electronics.

PRONUNCIATION SKILL
Unstressed modal verbs in speculating

We don't usually stress modal verbs in a sentence unless they are negative or we want to emphasize or contrast something.

*I might have **seen** one.*
*It must have been something **people wore**.*
*They may have **worn** it to **protect** themselves.*

In sentences speculating about the past, the modal verb usually links to the unstressed *have* that follows it. So, *might have* might sound like *might've*, *must have* like *must've*, *could have* like *could've*, and so on.

6 NOTICE Listen and complete the sentences. Then listen and repeat.

1 The ground is wet. The neighbor _______________ washed her car.
2 My friend isn't answering the phone. He _______________ left it at home.
3 The teacher looks tired. She _______________ corrected a lot of tests yesterday evening.
4 The streets are very quiet. The big football game _______________ started already.

7 APPLY Speculate about the situations in Exercise 6. Practice saying unstressed modals.

The ground is wet. The street cleaner might have come already.

8 INTERACT Review the phrases used for speculating in Exercises 5 and 6. Then speculate about an object for your partner to guess. Change roles.

9 IDENTIFY Which phrases from Exercises 5 and 6 did you and your partner use? Which object was the most interesting to speculate about?

Now go to page 156 for the Unit 10 Review.

11 Wishes

UNIT SNAPSHOT

What kinds of wishes do children make?

How do our wishes change as we get older?

Have any of your wishes ever come true?

BEHIND THE PHOTO

1 Write a wish list for today. Compare your wish list with a partner's. How similar are they?

1 What kind of day do you want?
2 What do you want to happen?
3 Where do you want to go?
4 Who do you want to see/speak to/not see?
5 What do you want to do/eat/buy/read/watch?

2 In the next class, tell your partner which of your wishes came true.

REAL-WORLD GOAL

Write a list of wishes and check which come true by the end of the week

11.1 No Regrets

1 ACTIVATE Look at the activities. Answer the questions with a partner.

1 Which don't you do but would like to?
2 Which do you do but would prefer not to?

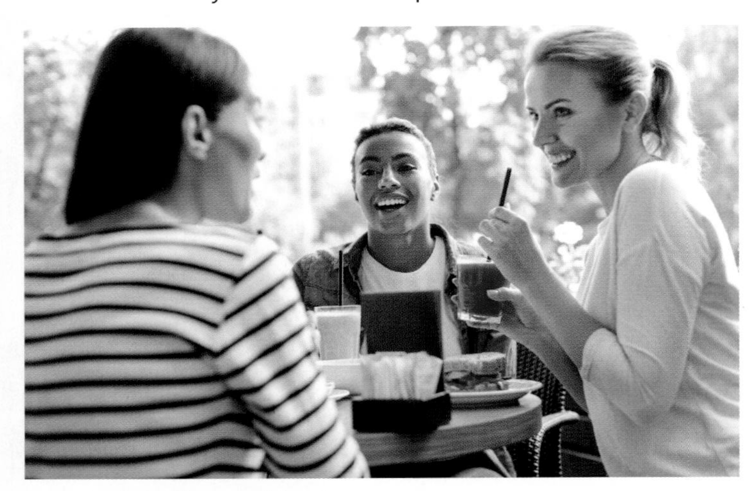
go out a lot with your friends

2 IDENTIFY Read someone's regrets about school. Choose the correct words in the second sentence to explain the meaning of the first sentence.

1 I should have worked harder.
I *worked* / *didn't work* hard.
2 I shouldn't have talked so much in class.
I *talked* / *didn't talk* a lot in class.
3 I should have spent more time in the library.
I *spent* / *didn't spend* a lot of time in the library.
4 I shouldn't have listened to my teachers more.
I *listened* / *didn't listen* to my teachers.

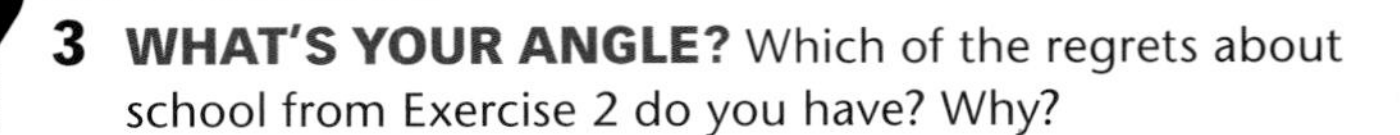

3 WHAT'S YOUR ANGLE? Which of the regrets about school from Exercise 2 do you have? Why?

work very hard

take care of your health

see your family often

use your phone a lot

GRAMMAR IN CONTEXT
Should have: Retrospection and regrets

We use *should have* and *shouldn't have* to criticize things we or other people did or didn't do in the past. The two verb forms say what would have been a better thing to do than what we actually did.

*I **should have** worked harder.*
*I **shouldn't have** talked so much.*

See Grammar focus on page 169.

4 APPLY Complete the sentences with *should have* or *shouldn't have* and the verb in parentheses in the correct form.

1 I ________________ (save) more money. I can't afford to go on vacation.
2 I ________________ (take) more driving lessons. I failed my test again
3 I ________________ (study) art. I really want to be a doctor.
4 He ________________ (listen) to his friends. They never give good advice.
5 They ________________ (be) more friendly. It's no wonder people don't like them.

5 INTEGRATE Choose three of the ideas in the box, and write sentences using *should have* and *shouldn't have* that are true for you. Then compare your sentences with a partner. Do you have any similar regrets?

friends	work	health	family	technology

I should have spent more time with my grandparents when I was younger.

LISTENING SKILL Understanding modals in conditionals and regrets

When we speak at a natural speed, words link together and some sounds disappear or change. When you know how the sound of specific grammar structures change, you are able to recognize them more easily.

I should have sounds like *I should'ev.*

You shouldn't have sounds like *You shoudn'ev.*

She should be sounds like *She shou be.*

They would change sounds like *They wou change.*

He wouldn't eat sounds like *He woudn'eat.*

We could go sounds like *We cou go.*

6 IDENTIFY Listen to the extracts from a podcast, and complete them with the words you hear. Write the words in their full form.

1 ...what people ________________.
2 I ________________ to be cool.
3 It ________________ easy to stop.
4 We ________________ less money today.
5 We ________________ on worrying...

7 INTEGRATE Listen to the podcast, and answer the questions. Compare your answers with a partner. Then listen again and check.

1 What was written on a blackboard in New York?
2 How many people watched the video?
3 What was Bronnie Ware's job?
4 What is the top regret, according to Bronnie Ware?
5 What areas do we often have regrets about?
6 What do men tend to have regrets about?
7 What do women tend to have regrets about?

8 WHAT'S YOUR ANGLE? Read the quote from the interviews. Do you agree that you can learn from regrets? If so, how? Share your views with a partner.

"For me, regrets are great—I can learn from them."

9 VOCABULARY Match the bold verbs in the sentences with their definitions.

1 I **calm down** very quickly after getting angry. ___
2 I don't **regret** anything about my past. ___
3 I learn from things I **get wrong** rather than worry about them. ___
4 I **cope** with life's problems by talking to friends. ___
5 It doesn't take me long to **get over** problems. ___
6 I find it easy to **adapt** to new situations. ___
7 I'm confident I can **deal with** most things in life. ___

a to stop being unhappy about something
b to change to fit a new situation
c to make a mistake
d to stop being angry and to feel normal again
e to feel sorry about something you have/haven't done
f to solve a problem
g to learn to be OK with a problem

Oxford 3000™

10 WHAT'S YOUR ANGLE? Which sentences in Exercise 9 are true for you? Find out how similar you are to your partner.

11.2 Get Over It

1 ACTIVATE Discuss the questions with a partner.

1 Do you reply to posts online? If so, where? How often? Why?
2 Have you or someone you know ever written something online you regretted?
3 What did you do about it?

2 IDENTIFY Work with a partner. Identify the four good pieces of advice, and number them in the best order for writing a reply.

Writing effective replies to online posts

___ Encourage people to reply to your post.
___ State the main idea.
___ Criticize the writer not the ideas.
___ Thank the writer for their post.
___ Provide more detail (e.g., what, why, when).
___ Write about a different topic.

3 ASSESS Read the final paragraph of Sally's blog article and Topreader's reply post. Then answer the questions.

1 What is the topic of Topreader's reply post?
2 Is it an effective reply? Why? Why not?

4 IDENTIFY Read the blog post, and the reply again. Identify the time linkers from the Grammar in Context box.

Next week, my post will continue the topic of regrets, and I'm going to share my biggest regret with you as promised. Meanwhile, I'm asking that you share yours first! This not just because I like to know everything about my followers. Apparently, sharing a regret helps you get over it. I obviously haven't yet, so I'm taking this opportunity to do as the experts say: share it, feel it, get over it. So, I'll share, I promise, but by the time I do, you'll have all shared your regrets—and hopefully gotten over them!

COMMENTS

Topreader—2 days ago

Thanks for your post. I can't believe I'm the first to reply. I love your blog, and I hope your theory works—share it, feel it, get over it. So, here it goes...

My biggest regret is about college—I should have studied art and design, but I didn't. I know it doesn't sound so bad, but when I think about this, I feel terrible. Here's the story.

While I was in the final years of high school, I got really involved in art and even won an art competition. During the last semester, I spent most of my time in the school design studio and wasn't in the library much at all. I loved art, especially photography, and was really good at it. So why didn't I study it in college?

As soon as we left high school, my best friend was given a new car. His parents were rich and his grandparents richer, so this was an amazing car. As soon as I saw it, I was so jealous. I couldn't stop thinking about it, and the following day, I went to the career advisor at school and asked about careers that pay well. Of course, art and design weren't on her list. So I changed my major to business. And until this day, I've regretted it. I hate numbers, I love art, and I can't even drive!

So, now I've shared my regret and felt it; let's hope I can move on from it. It would be great to hear other regrets. Don't leave my story here on its own!

GRAMMAR IN CONTEXT Time linkers

Writers use time linkers to show how one event connects to another event.

We use *as soon as* to show something happens immediately after the other.

As soon as *I saw it, I was so jealous.*

We use *while* and *when* to show things that happen at the same time.

While / When *I was at school, I loved art.*

We can also use *when* (but not *while*) for an action that interrupts another.

I was at home ***when*** *I found out about the car.*

We use *meanwhile* (not *while*) when we use two independent sentences to talk about two things that happen at the same time.

I'm writing the blog. ***Meanwhile****, my friend is editing the photos.*

We use *by the time* when one action is completed before the main action happens.

By the time *he read the message, everyone had left.*

We use *during* when something happens at a point within a period of time.

I visited the advisor ***during*** *the afternoon.*

We use *until* when something happens up to a particular point in time.

He drove the same car ***until*** *he was thirty.*

See Grammar focus on page 169.

5 ASSESS Number the events from Topreader's reply post in the order they happened.

___ He became jealous.
___ He started doing art.
___ He was in the design studio a lot.
___ His friend got a car.
___ He and his friend left high school.
___ He changed his college major.
___ He visited the advisor.

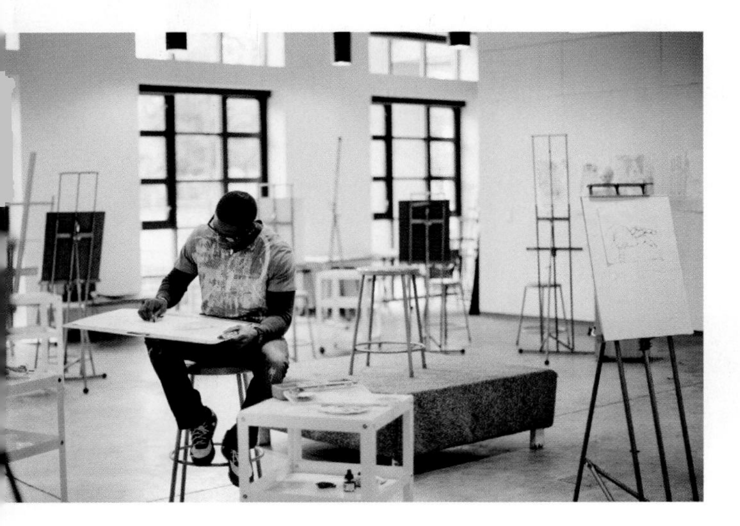

6 APPLY Complete the sentences about the post with the correct time linkers. Check your answers with the text.

1 This coming week, the blog writer is writing her post about her biggest regret. *During / Meanwhile*, her followers are posting theirs.
2 The readers will have posted their regrets *until / by the time* the blog writer does.
3 Topreader feels terrible *when / during* he thinks about what he didn't study.
4 Topreader did a lot of art *during / while* he was in high school.
5 Topreader didn't go to the library much *during / as soon as* his last few months of high school.
6 Topreader felt jealous *as soon as / while* he saw his friend's car.
7 Topreader has regretted his choice from when he made it *during / until* this moment.

WRITING SKILL Using ellipsis

We can leave some words out of sentences when they are not necessary for understanding the text. This is called ellipsis, and it makes the writing more concise and avoids unnecessary repetition.

Verb ellipsis
Sometimes we can leave out a verb form, or we can use only the auxiliary instead.

His parents were rich and his grandparents [were] richer.
I'll share, I promise, but only after you have [shared].

Noun ellipsis
We can leave out nouns, noun phrases, and pronouns sometimes if the meaning stays clear.

I'm going to share my biggest regret with you as [I] promised.

7 IDENTIFY Read the sentences, and identify the words that can be left out. Then find the sentences in the blog text and check.

1 Apparently, sharing a regret helps you get over it. I obviously haven't gotten over it yet.
2 I should have studied art and design, but I didn't study them.
3 I spent most of my time in the school design studio, and I wasn't in the library much at all.
4 I loved art, especially photography, and I was really good at it.
5 I went to the career advisor at school and asked the career advisor about careers that pay well.

8 **APPLY** Rewrite the sentences using ellipsis.

1 My friend has a lot of regrets, but I don't have a lot of regrets.

____

2 School was bad, and college was worse.

____

3 I wasn't interested, and so I didn't try.

____

4 She tried to stop, but she couldn't.

____

5 I love traveling, and I regret that I didn't travel much.

____

9 **PREPARE** You are going to write a reply post to Sally's blog article. Read Topreader's reply again. Answer the questions in pairs.

1 Which sentence did Topreader use to thank Sally for her post?
2 What was his biggest regret?
3 What sentences does he use to ask people to reply to Sally's request?

10 **DEVELOP** Follow the steps.

1 Identify the regret you will write about in your reply post.
2 Make a note of the regret and the events of the background story.
3 Decide which time linkers to use to show the relationship between the events.

11 **WRITE** Write your reply post.

- Respond to the article request.
- Share your own regret.
- Include time linkers.
- Use ellipsis when possible.
- Write up to 200 words.

12 **SHARE** Read your partner's reply post. Does it respond to the article? Is your partner's regret clear? Give each other feedback.

13 **IMPROVE** Rewrite your article using your partner's feedback.

14 **WHAT'S YOUR ANGLE?** Read other replies to the article. Which one did you relate to the most?

11.3 Restarting

1 ACTIVATE Discuss the sentences with a partner. Which do you agree with?

1 The Internet can misinform us.
2 The Internet is a mess, and we need to rebuild the whole web.
3 We overdo the number of hours we spend online.

VOCABULARY DEVELOPMENT Prefixes

We can use prefixes at the start of a word to add to and change the meaning of the word.

mis- = bad or wrongly: ***misinform****, misunderstand*
re- = again or back: ***rebuild****, review*
over- = too much: ***overdo****,* ***overcooked***

By understanding the meaning of a prefix, you can guess the meaning of more advanced words that use a prefix + a word you know.

Oxford 3000™

2 IDENTIFY Work in pairs to write a definition of the three verbs with prefixes in Exercise 1.

3 APPLY Complete the words in these sentences with the ones in the box.

place	load	write	behave	use

1 People sometimes mis_________ the Internet.
2 We have information over_________.
3 The Internet can be used to re_________ history.
4 Children often mis_________ online.
5 The Internet will soon re_________ traditional hobbies.

4 INTERACT Discuss the statements in Exercise 3 in a small group, and choose the top three problems.

5 IDENTIFY Test your knowledge with the questions below. Then read the entry from the *Dictionary of Computing* to check.

1 Who invented the World Wide Web?
2 Who did he work for?
3 When was the first website launched?

Berners-Lee, Sir Timothy John (born 1955), British software developer

Berners-Lee invented the World Wide Web. After graduating in physics from Oxford University, he worked as a computer programmer. While working for CERN (European Organization for Nuclear Research) in Geneva in 1980, he developed a ***hypertext** system for sharing information. In 1989, he suggested a global hypertext system, which he called the "World Wide Web." He created the first Web browser and Web server and, in 1991, launched the first website.

—adapted from *A Dictionary of Computer Science*, 7th ed., edited by Andrew Butterfield and Gerard Ekembe Ngondi

***hypertext:** Text shown on a computer screen with references (hyperlinks) to other text. The reader can immediately access these by clicking on the text.

6 INTEGRATE Read the next article, and answer the questions.

1 What do the three people in the article want to rewrite?
2 What does Berners-Lee want to replace?
3 What did people tell Dong Nguyen they were overdoing?
4 Which invention by Ethan Zuckerman has been greatly misused?
5 What does the writer suggest we should rebuild?

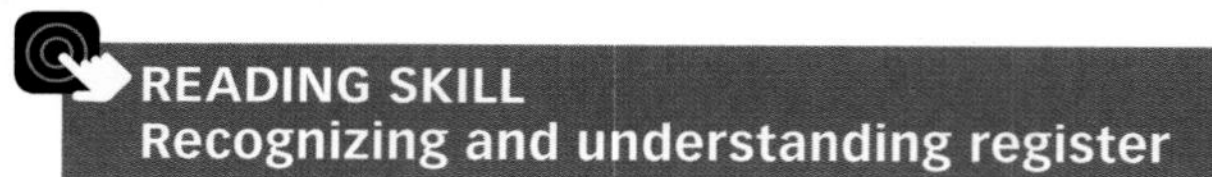

When we talk about how formal, informal, or neutral a text is, we are talking about the register. The register depends on who the writer is writing for, the type of information they are writing, and where people will read the text.

Recognizing the register of the writing will help you understand the text better. For example, an academic register can indicate that the writer is an expert and the source can be trusted, and a humorous register can show that the content should not be taken too seriously. The following features can help you identify the register of a text.

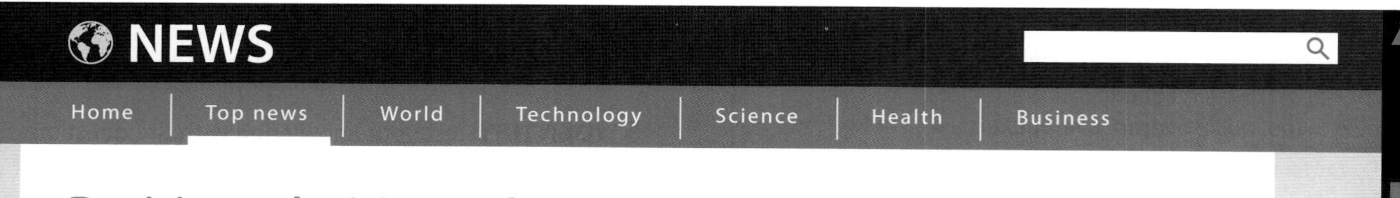

Decisions, decisions—but are they the right ones?

Technology is so integrated into our lives that it sometimes seems as though it has been here forever. It is easy to forget that anything new is the result of ideas, hard work, and design decisions. There may be hundreds of decisions, and once you have made one, it can be difficult to undo. Here, we look at three inventors who wish they could go back and rewrite history.

The first is an Englishman named Tim Berners-Lee, inventor of the World Wide Web. It surprises many people to know that a person actually invented the World Wide Web—it seems so natural to us now despite the fact that it has only been around since 1989. But 20 years after he invented it, Berners-Lee announced in an interview that it would have been better if he hadn't included the famous double slash (//) after http:. The reason? The double slash doesn't have any real function. If he hadn't put it in, it would have saved millions of computer strokes—and quite a lot of paper too.

Another such story is that of a mobile game, Flappy Bird, and its Vietnamese creator Dong Nguyen. Most people would love to do what he did—invent a game that was downloaded 50 million times and that became so popular that in 2013 he was apparently making $50,000 a day from advertising. But what Nguyen hadn't expected was that millions of people would hate him for it. People wrote to him constantly, telling him he had ruined their life: playing for a few minutes a day would be fine, but they were overdoing it, spending hours a day on a rather silly game. He realized that if he hadn't invented it at all, a lot of people could have been happier, so he decided to take it down. And he did.

Finally, there is Ethan Zuckerman, who in the 1990s invented the code that is used in all those annoying pop-up ads. OK, so if he hadn't invented it, someone else might have, but that didn't stop him from saying sorry. In his essay "The Internet's Original Sin," written in 2014, Zuckerman claimed that his intentions had been good. But such is the power of technology—it can go on to have a life of its own that the inventors could never have imagined.

Looking at some of these lessons from the past sometimes makes me wish that we could start again and rebuild the whole technological world. Perhaps if we had planned them better from the start, we would have developed better systems. And we would all be happier now.

Comments:

Topreader—1 hour ago
Love the article! Totally agree with Flappy Bird guy…it took over my life for a while.

BusyBee—2 hours ago
Pop-ups? Hate, hate, hate them. At least I now know the guy's sorry.

	More formal	Less formal
Type of words	longer words, more technical	phrasal verbs, informal words
Word form	full forms	contractions
Style of sentence	longer, passive	shorter, active, questions
Layout style	continuous text	more lists, bullets
Details included	references	personal comments, emoticons

7 APPLY Work in pairs. Compare the texts (1) "Berners-Lee", (2) "Decisions, decisions…", and (3) the two comments.

	Text 1	Text 2	Text 3
Type of words	*longer, technical*		
Word form			
Style of sentence			
Layout style			
Details included			

8 ASSESS Work together with another pair. Discuss the questions.

1 How would you describe each text you analyzed in Exercise 7—more formal, more informal, or neutral?

2 Which would you use to check information, read for fun, or find new ideas or points of view?

GRAMMAR IN CONTEXT Third conditional

We use the third conditional to talk about unreal situations in the past. We use it to talk about imaginary situations or events that are the opposite of what actually happened.

*If the Internet **hadn't been invented**, the past 20 years **would have been** very boring.*

The two clauses can usually go in either order. We can also use the modal verbs *could* and *might* in the main clause.

*I **could / might have done** something useful if I **hadn't spent** so much time playing games.*

See Grammar focus on page 169.

9 IDENTIFY Read the example sentences in the Grammar in Context box, and answer the questions.

1 Was the World Wide Web invented?

2 Has life been boring for the past 20 years?

3 Did the person do something useful?

4 Did the person spend a lot of time playing games?

10 APPLY Put the words in the correct order to form sentences. Then check your answers in the article.

1 if / It would / hadn't included / have been better / he / the famous double slash.

2 it would have / hadn't put it in, / If / saved millions of computer strokes. / he

3 a lot of people / If / could have / he hadn't / been happier. / invented it at all,

4 might have done it. / If / someone else / invented it, / he hadn't

5 developed better systems / If / better from the start, / we would have / we had planned it

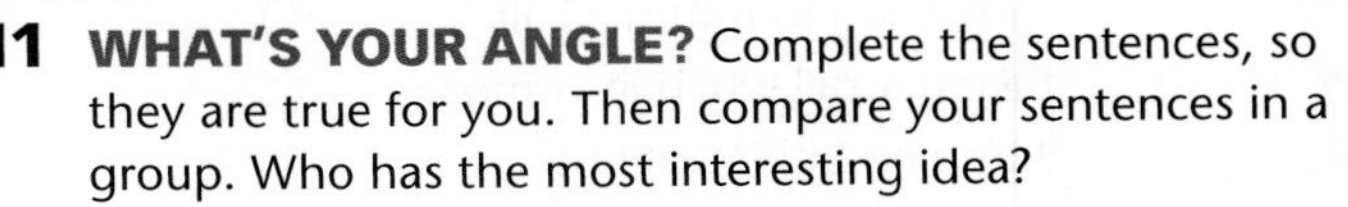

11 WHAT'S YOUR ANGLE? Complete the sentences, so they are true for you. Then compare your sentences in a group. Who has the most interesting idea?

1 I could / couldn't have…if the Internet hadn't been invented.

2 I would / wouldn't have…if cell phones had been cheaper to buy and use.

3 I might / might not have…if mobile games had never existed.

4 I would / wouldn't have…if social media had had a daily time limit of 30 minutes.

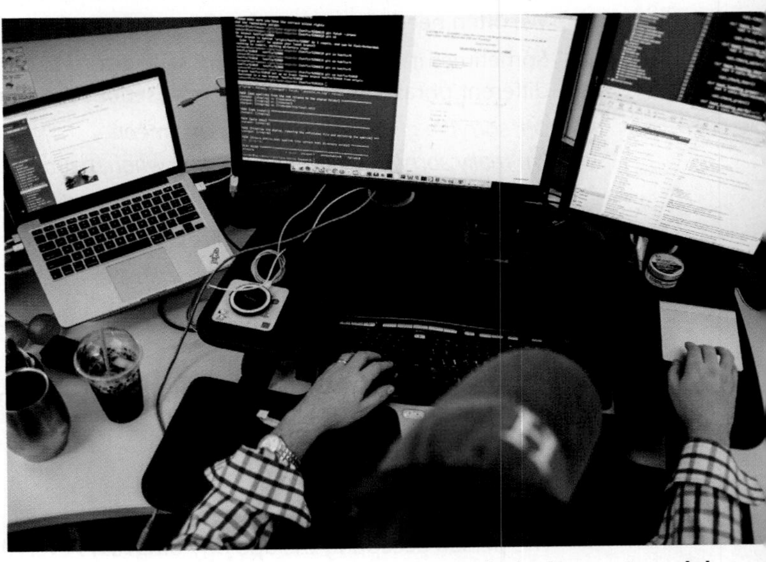

A web designer at work in New York, the United States

11.4 Saying Sorry

ENGLISH FOR REAL

1 ACTIVATE Work in pairs. Which of these would you say sorry for? Think of two more things someone might say sorry for.

Forgetting to return a call
Taking a call when in company
Bumping into someone
Being late for something
Having to leave a meeting early
Saying something in an angry way
Changing plans
Not listening to someone's advice

2 WHAT'S YOUR ANGLE? Have you apologized to anyone this week? What for? Did the person accept your apology?

3 IDENTIFY Watch the video. What five things from Exercise 1 do Kevin and his advisor apologize for?

REAL-WORLD ENGLISH Saying sorry

We often need to say sorry for things we do or say.

Sometimes it is clear what we are saying sorry for, e.g., if we bump into someone. We can use different phrases depending on how serious the situation is.

Oh, sorry! (e.g., after bumping into someone)
I'm really sorry. (e.g., being late again when meeting a friend)
I sincerely apologize. (e.g., after missing the start of a very important meeting)

Other times we need to apologize and say what we are apologizing for.

I'm really sorry for being late this morning.

To make the apology stronger, we sometimes take on the responsibility for what happened.

It's all my fault.

We can also offer to help improve the situation we have caused.

What can I do?
How can I help?

Accepting an apology

The person accepting the apology often says everything is OK.

That's OK. Don't worry about it.

This person can also change the focus from what has happened to more positive things.

The important thing is…

4 **ANALYZE** Watch the video again, and for each of the apologies, answer the questions.

1 Who apologizes to whom? Why?
2 How? Make a note of the phrase.
3 What does the other person say? Make a note of the phrase.

5 **EXPAND** Review the apologies from Exercise 4. Answer the questions.

1 How serious is each situation?
2 Does the relationship between the speakers affect the words they use for making and accepting apologies?
3 Which "apology" isn't really an apology? Why not?

6 **PREPARE** Work in groups of three (A, B, and C). Use the chart to create three different situations for a role play. Look at the example.

What happened?	How serious?	What is the relationship?
bumps into someone	serious	friends
is late		classmates
forgot an appointment	not very serious	teacher + student
was rude		salesperson + customer

Example situation: was rude—not very serious—salesperson + customer

7 **INTERACT** Do a role play using one of the situations you created in Exercise 6. Student A apologizes to Student B while Student C observes.

8 **ASSESS** Share your feedback on the role play. Did everyone think the apologies were effective? Why? Why not?

9 **INTERACT** Change roles and situations, and do another role play. Give feedback and then change roles again.

GO ONLINE
to create your own version of the English For Real video.

11.5 What's on Your Wish List?

1 ACTIVATE Look at the pictures and answer the questions.

1 Are any of these things on your wish list?
2 What other things would you like to do?

2 ASSESS Listen to some friends talking about making a wish list. Which time in their lives should the wishes be from?

3 IDENTIFY Listen to the friends' discussion. Which activities in the pictures in Exercise 1 do the speakers mention?

1 Maggie ___
2 Tammy ___
3 Marcus ___
4 Jack ___

SPEAKING Talking about wishes and regrets

To talk about wishes for the future and now, we can use *would like / love* and *want*. We can also use *hope to* for the future.

*I **would like** to travel the world.*
*I **want** more time to paint.*
*I **hope** to finally finish my degree.*

To talk about past wishes and regrets, we can use *should / shouldn't have* or *would like to have* + past participle.

*I **shouldn't have** changed majors.*
*I **would like to have** bought that car.*

4 APPLY Listen to the discussion again, and identify if these wishes are past, present, or future.

1 Get paintings in a gallery
2 Study art in college
3 Finish master's degree
4 Live somewhere more fun
5 Have more friends
6 Lose some weight
7 Keep in touch with a friend
8 People be nicer to others

5 IDENTIFY Listen to the wishes, and complete the sentences.

1 I __________ get my paintings in a famous gallery sometime.
2 I __________ more time to paint.
3 I __________ have studied art in college.
4 I __________ finally finish my master's.
5 I __________ taken that job in Paris.
6 I __________ lose some weight.
7 I __________ dance better.
8 I __________ really __________ everyone to be nicer to each other.

PRONUNCIATION SKILL *should / shouldn't have*

When we speak at a natural speed, the words *should have* and *shouldn't have* usually get shorter, reduced, and less easy to hear.

I should have listened to him. → *should've /ʃʊdəv/ or should'e /ʃʊdə/*
I shouldn't have moved houses. → *shouldn't've /ʃʊdnəv/ or shoul'n'e /ʃʊnə/*

6 NOTICE Listen to these regrets, and complete the sentences. Then practice saying them.

1 I __________ studied business.
2 I __________ said yes.
3 I __________ stayed in contact.
4 I __________ left earlier.
5 I __________ told them.
6 I __________ asked her.

7 APPLY Work in pairs. Imagine you are in these situations. Express regret about what has happened. Use *should have* or *shouldn't have*.

1 You have just bumped into the car in front of you.
2 You got soaked in the rain.
3 You have a stomachache.
4 You have no money in your wallet.

8 PREPARE Write your own wish list, with one wish each for the present, future, and past.

9 IMPROVE Share your wish list with a partner. When you listen to your partner's wishes, note if they are past, present, or future.

10 SHARE Work in a group. Share your wish lists. After hearing about other students' wishes, are there any wishes for the future that you want to add to or remove from your list?

Now go to page 157 for the Unit 11 Review

12 Wisdom

UNIT SNAPSHOT

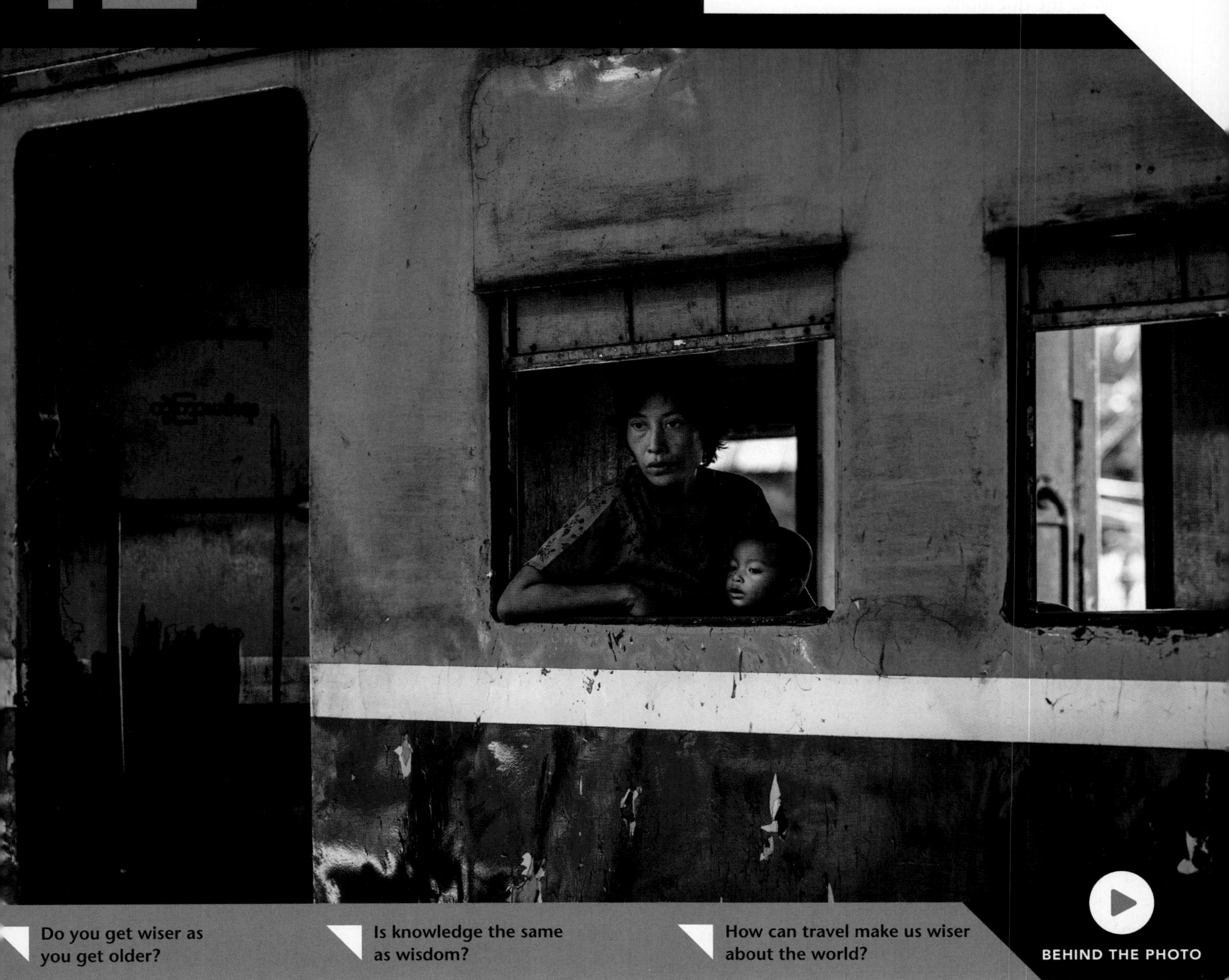

Do you get wiser as you get older?

Is knowledge the same as wisdom?

How can travel make us wiser about the world?

BEHIND THE PHOTO

REAL-WORLD GOAL

Teach someone to do something

1 **Do you know anyone who is wise? Describe them to your partner, and explain why you think they are wise.**

I think my great-grandmother is very wise. She is 91 years old, and she has had many difficult experiences in her life. But she is still a kind and optimistic person and always gives me good advice.

2 **Tell a partner about an experience that has brought you wisdom. Then discuss the question: Does experience always give us wisdom?**

12.1 As the Saying Goes...

1 ACTIVATE Work with a partner. Read the proverb and answer the questions.

"You can't judge a book by its cover."

1 What do you think the proverb means?
2 Discuss with your partner. Do you agree on the meaning?

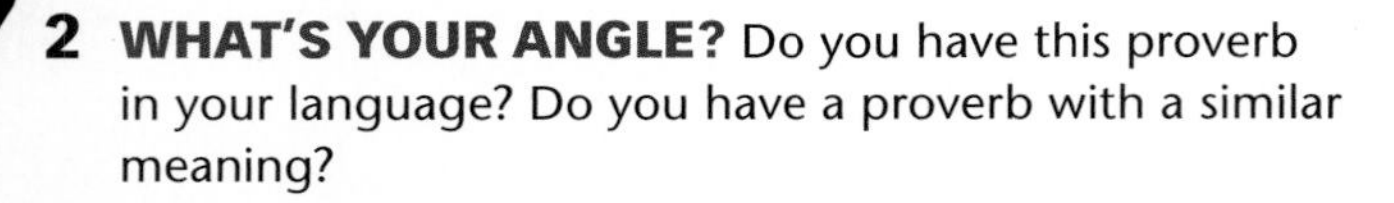

2 WHAT'S YOUR ANGLE? Do you have this proverb in your language? Do you have a proverb with a similar meaning?

GRAMMAR IN CONTEXT Reported speech

We use reported speech to talk about what someone said. When we use reported speech, the verb usually moves back one tense. This helps to show that the words were spoken in the past. The pronouns in the reported sentence might need to change, too.

*"It **is** my favorite saying."*	*He said it **was** his favorite saying.*
*"Grandma **taught** me."*	*He told me that his grandma had **taught** him.*

Sometimes we do not change the tense. This usually happens when something is still or generally true.

*"You **can't judge** a book by its cover."*
*He said you **can't judge** a book by its cover.*

We often use the reporting verbs *say* and *tell*. We use a personal object with *tell* but not with *say*. We can use both verbs with or without *that*.

He told me that... (~~*NOT He told that...*~~)
She said... (~~*NOT She said me...*~~)

See Grammar focus on page 170.

3 IDENTIFY Rewrite the reported sentences in direct speech.

1 He said he knew a lot of proverbs.
"I know a lot of proverbs. "
2 He told me that he had read a lot when he was a child.
"_______________________________"
3 He told me that proverbs were not used by smart people.
"_______________________________"
4 He said that many proverbs were disappearing from modern speech.
"_______________________________"
5 He told me that using proverbs was a good way to impress people.
"_______________________________"

4 APPLY Rewrite these sentences in reported speech.

1 "We use a lot of proverbs in my culture."
He told me that _______________________________.
2 "When I was younger, I asked my family the meaning of many proverbs."
She said _______________________________.
3 "We have learned the meaning of several proverbs in class."
They said _______________________________.
4 "I have always loved learning proverbs."
She told me that _______________________________.
5 "Proverbs are an important part of all languages."
He said _______________________________.

5 WHAT'S YOUR ANGLE? Which four direct sentences from Exercises 3 and 4 do you agree with the most? Tell a partner.

6 INTERACT Work with a new partner. Report your discussion from Exercise 5.

Ali said he didn't know a lot of proverbs, but I told him that...

7 IDENTIFY Work in pairs. Read the proverb and answer the questions.

"There's no time like the **present**."

1 What does the bold word mean?
   a a gift
   b to give something formally
   c now
2 Do you agree with the proverb?

READING SKILL
Recognizing and understanding words with more than one meaning

Many words have more than one meaning. The part of speech can be the same or different.

*a **present** (noun) = a gift*
*the **present** (noun) = the time now*
*to **present** (verb) = to give something to someone formally*

When you are not sure of the meaning of a word:

- Check the part of speech of the word in the sentence.
- Read through the dictionary entry to see if the word can mean different things.
- Think about the general meaning of the sentence and the text.
- Decide on the meaning of the word in the text.

8 APPLY Follow the steps from the Reading Skill box to match the bold words in the article to their correct meanings.

1 ________ (n) a person who makes food
(v) to make food
2 ________ (v) to write your name
(n) an object showing the way
3 ________ (adj) not heavy or difficult
(adj) not dark
4 ________ (n) food
(n) plate, pot, etc. used for food
5 ________ (n) the director of a department
(n) where our mind is in our body
6 ________ (v) able to
(n) a metal container for food or drink
7 ________ (v) to take somewhere
(n) a type of metal
8 ________ (v) to shut
(adj) near

Some proverbial advice

I love proverbs. They are a little window into history, showing us how people lived and thought and carrying the wisdom of those who lived before us into the modern world. Proverbs have a special place in many languages, but they are not easy to define. Archer Taylor, an expert on proverbs, famously explained that there was no definition of the word *proverb*. That, however, doesn't stop us from recognizing them and using them. When language students know them, this is often a **sign** of a high-level motivated learner who enjoys the language.

From a personal viewpoint, as a father of three, my favorite proverb is "Many hands make **light** work." I use it very often when I want my children to help with the **dishes** or cleaning up. Another similar proverb, "Two **heads** are better than one," applies the same idea to thinking and finding solutions. However, with regard to the housework, I am aware that one day my children may say "Too many **cooks** spoil the broth"—a proverb with the exact opposite meaning. Yet both proverbs **can** be true. They are called counter proverbs, and according to Paul Hockings, another proverb expert, there is nothing wrong with them; they just apply in different situations.

Proverbs have to be memorable to be successful. That probably explains why many of them rhyme (for example, "Birds of a feather flock together") or are very visual images ("You can **lead** a horse to water, but you can't make it drink"). It is impossible not to imagine the horse at the water when you say this, which leads me to another interesting fact. Nowadays, we often do not actually say proverbs, or not completely. We usually stop after the first part, for example: "You can lead a horse to water..." People from the same culture will instantly understand what we mean.

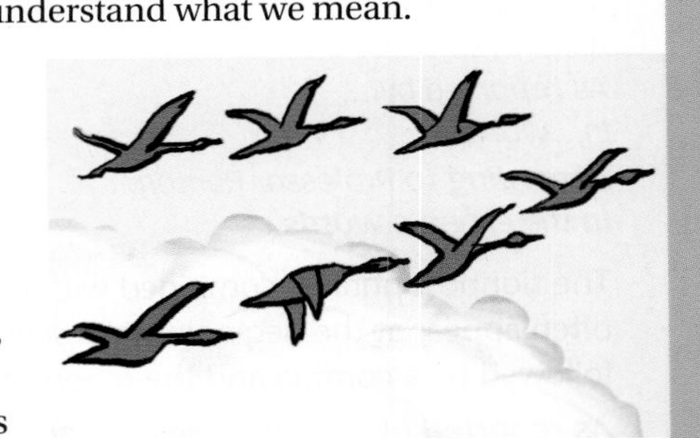

Across cultures, we find many proverbs that are **close** in meaning or even the same. As reported by Thomas Fielding as long ago as 200 years, there is no way to tell where many proverbs come from. Often a country will think of a proverb as its own, and people will be surprised to learn that it exists in other places, too. Some researchers have argued that proverbs show what particular people and cultures are like. However, in his 1989 study, Walter Grauberg suggested that proverbs only show us what people *in general* are like, which would explain why they are shared so widely across cultures.

There are many excellent sites about proverbs online if you are interested in finding out more about them or even learning more of them. So, why don't you spend a few minutes now researching the topic? Remember, there is no time like the present...

Glossary:
broth (noun): a type of meat soup
flock (verb): to come together in a group (the way birds do)

—adapted from *Concise Oxford Companion to the English Language*, edited by Tom McArthur

9 ASSESS Read the article and decide if the sentences are true (T) or false (F) or if the information is not given (NG) in the text.

1 It is difficult to explain the meaning of the word *proverb*. ___
2 Using proverbs can show you are a good language learner. ___
3 The writer does housework every day. ___
4 If two proverbs have the opposite meaning, they are both wrong. ___
5 The image a proverb creates is important. ___
6 We always have to say the complete proverb or people don't understand it. ___
7 Thomas Fielding studied proverbs in Europe and Africa. ___
8 Walter Grauberg said that proverbs tell us about a small group of people. ___

10 IDENTIFY Find the six proverbs in the article. Discuss their meaning with a partner, and choose your favorite.

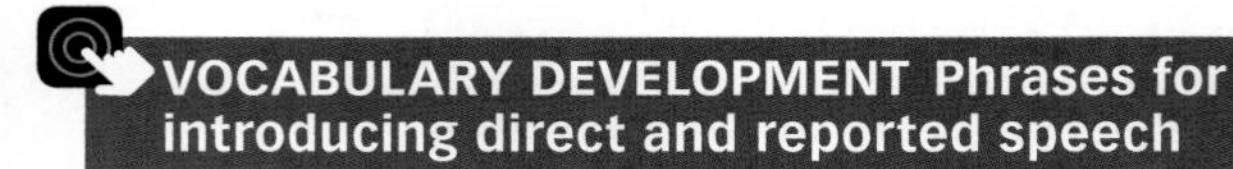

VOCABULARY DEVELOPMENT Phrases for introducing direct and reported speech

When writers include other people's words and ideas, they usually signal this to the reader with signpost phrases combined with the name of the person or source of the information.

According to...,
As...says,...
As reported by...,
In...words,
***According to** Professor Renton,...*
***In** the expert's **words**,...*

The signpost phrases combined with the source name often appear at the beginning of a sentence and are then followed by a comma and the reported information.

***As reported by** The City Times, the proverb is used in both languages.*
***As Archer Taylor says**, there is no definition for the word* proverb.

The phrases can appear in the middle or at the end of a sentence, also separated by commas.

There is no definition for the word proverb, ***as Archer Taylor says**.*

Oxford 3000™

11 IDENTIFY Find two examples of the signal phrases from the Vocabulary Development box in the article.

12 EXPAND Read the article again, and find the person who expressed these ideas. Then complete the sentences with signal phrases different from those used in the text for each person.

1 ________________, there is no definition of the word *proverb*.
2 ________________, there is nothing wrong with counter proverbs.
3 ________________, there is no way to tell where many proverbs come from.
4 ________________, proverbs only show us what people in general are like.

13 INTERACT Work in pairs. Together choose two proverbs from the list. Check the meaning of the bold words, and decide what the proverbs mean.

1 Two wrongs don't make a **right**.
2 Don't count your chickens before they **hatch**.
3 If you want a thing done **well**, do it yourself.
4 All is **fair** in love and war.
5 **Still** waters **run** deep.

14 WHAT'S YOUR ANGLE? Think of two proverbs in your language, one you agree with and one you don't. Write them in English. Then tell a partner your proverbs and explain their meaning.

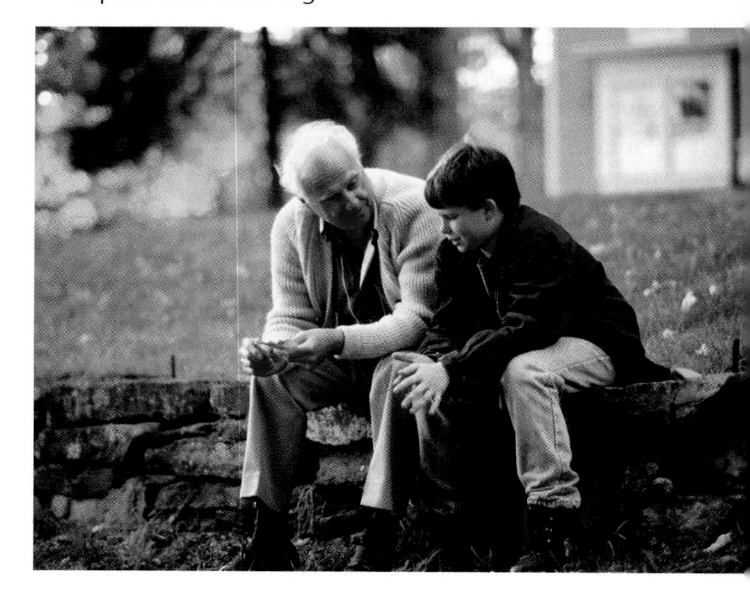

1 ACTIVATE What can you use this for? Make a list of as many uses as you can think of.

2 ASSESS Listen to someone giving some practical advice. What does she suggest using the Post-it for?

GRAMMAR IN CONTEXT Reported questions

We use reported questions to say what someone asked. We usually use the reporting verb *ask*. We can use *ask* with or without a personal object.

"Where do you live?" *She* ***asked*** *(****me****) where I lived.*

We can also use *want to know* (without a personal object).

"When did they arrive?" *He* ***wanted to know*** *when they arrived.*

To report *yes/no* questions, we use *if* or *whether*.

"Do they like it?" *He asked* ***if/whether*** *they liked it.*

Reported questions have statement word order.

*"****Will you*** *be late?"* *She asked if* ***I would*** *be late.*

See Grammar focus on page 170.

3 IDENTIFY Correct the mistakes in the reported questions. Then listen to the extracts and check.

1 He asked me how did I clean my keyboard.
2 Sam wanted to know if had I any more Post-its.
3 He wanted to know me how long I'd known this clever trick.
4 He asked me if did I know any other useful life hacks.

4 APPLY Report these questions.

1 "How do you clean your phone screen?"
She asked me
______________________________.

2 "Do you take care of your laptop?"
She wanted to know
______________________________.

3 "Are you good at looking after your devices?"
She asked me
______________________________.

4 "Why did you replace your last phone?"
She asked me
______________________________.

5 "How often will you clean your keyboard in the future?"
She wanted to know
______________________________.

5 INTERACT Ask your partner the direct questions in Exercise 4. Then report the questions and answers to a new partner. Did you get any of the same answers?

I asked Jasmine if…and she told me that…

6 IDENTIFY Look at the pictures. Discuss these questions with a partner.

Which one of these can you use to…
make your phone alarm louder? ___
get your friends to return your things? ___
identify your different keys? ___
keep your phone and money safe at the beach ___?

a

b

c

d

LISTENING SKILL Distinguishing speakers

When you are listening but not watching a discussion, it helps to be clear about how many speakers there are and who they are. Pay attention to differences between the speakers' voices. This will make comprehension easier.

Listen for differences in the voices.

male / female *fast / slow* *loud / quiet*

Listen for accents.

For example:

	American English	British English
water	/'wɔt̬ər/ *or* /'wɑt̬ər/	/'wɔːtə(r)/
answer	/'ænsər/	/'ɑːnsə(r)/
car	/kɑr/	/kɑː(r)/
on	/ɔn/ *or* /ɑn/	/ɒn/

7 **APPLY** Listen to four speakers. Analyze the differences in their voices, and complete the table.

	Male / female	Speed + volume	UK / U.S.
Speaker 1	male	faster + louder	U.S.
Speaker 2			
Speaker 3			
Speaker 4			

8 **IDENTIFY** Listen to four friends discussing life hacks, and check your answers to Exercise 6.

9 **APPLY** Listen to the conversation again, and complete the table.

	Name	Life hack notes—what, how, and why
Speaker 1		
Speaker 2		
Speaker 3		
Speaker 4		

10 **WHAT'S YOUR ANGLE?** Did you know any of these life hacks? Do you know any other life hacks? Share them with your group.

11 **VOCABULARY** Complete the phrases from the conversation. Then listen and check.

1 figure ___
2 make ___
3 **give** ___
4 notice ___
5 get ___
6 take ___

a use of
b it out
c on with it
d an alternative approach
e an improvement
f **it a try**

Oxford 3000™

12 **EXPAND** Match the phrases in Exercise 11 with the descriptions.

1 To start doing something and make progress with it __________
2 To use something for your own benefit __________
3 To try a different way to do something __________
4 To understand something or someone better __________
5 To be able to tell that something or someone is doing better __________
6 To try to do something you have not done before __________

PRONUNCIATION SKILL Linking

When we speak at a natural speed, the breaks between words and the way the words link can change. This happens when a word ends with a consonant sound and the next word starts with a vowel sound. The consonant sound joins the second word.

an improvement → *a nimprovement*
take advice → *ta kadvice*
alternative approach → *alternati vapproach*

13 **NOTICE** Find the linking in the phrases in Exercise 11. Practice saying the phrases with a partner.

14 **APPLY** Listen and write the sentences. Identify the linking. Then listen and repeat.

1 ____________________
2 ____________________
3 ____________________
4 ____________________
5 ____________________

15 PREPARE Think about the different areas of your life and any things you do that make them easier, better, or more efficient. Complete the sentences with your own life hacks.

1 To manage my time, I...

____

2 To improve my health, I...

____

3 To organize my home, I...

____

4 To stay in touch with friends and family, I...

____

5 To increase my productivity, I...

____

16 INTERACT Choose two or three of the sentences from Exercise 15. Discuss your ideas with a partner.

17 EXPAND Work in groups, and compare your answers. What can you learn from each other? Choose one or more life hacks from the discussion to try out. Share your best life hacks with the class. Which ideas are the most popular? Which are the most unusual?

18 WHAT'S YOUR ANGLE? Which do you value most in daily life: originality, efficiency, creativity or productivity? Why?

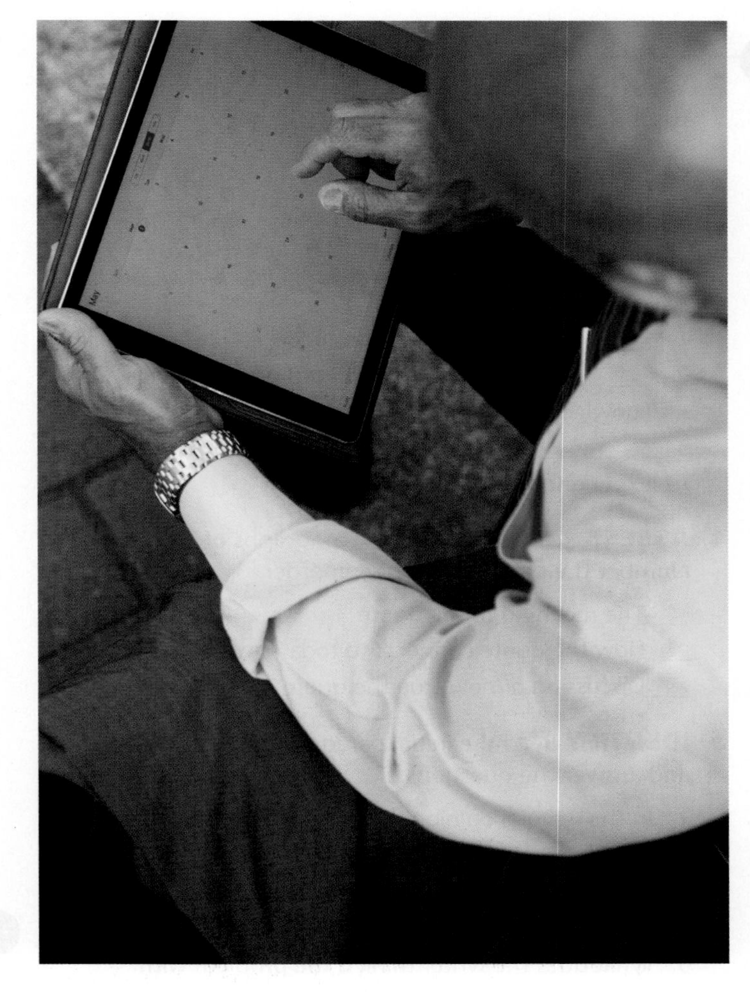

12.3 Wise Words

1 ACTIVATE Match the symbols of wisdom to where they are from. Do you know any more symbols for wisdom from around the world?

Ancient Egypt	Ghana and Cote d'Ivoire	India and Tibet

1 

2 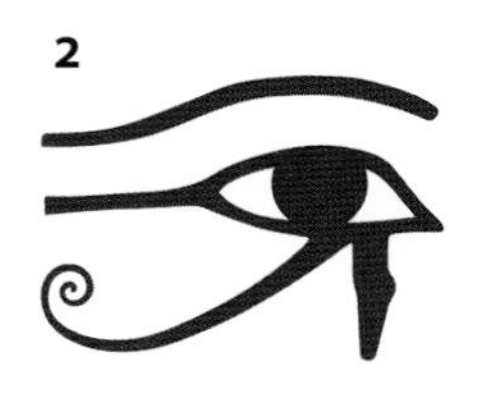

3 

2 WHAT'S YOUR ANGLE? What images represent wisdom to you?

3 IDENTIFY Read the quote. Which three words from the quote match the definitions below?

"Where is the wisdom we have lost in knowledge?
Where is the knowledge we have lost in information?"
—T. S. Eliot

1 _________ facts about something
2 _________ good judgment based on experience and knowledge
3 _________ information and skills you learn from experience and education

4 ASSESS Read the first three paragraphs of an essay. Number the paragraph topics in order.

___ The meaning of the quote
___ How the quote connects to today's world
___ Discussion of how true the quote is

The American poet T. S. Eliot asked this question in his poem "Choruses from 'The Rock'": "Where is the wisdom we have lost in knowledge? Where is the knowledge we have lost in information?" Although written in 1934, it seems very relevant today. In this essay, I will discuss what he might have meant by this and to what extent it is true.

In my opinion, Eliot was suggesting that the three words can be put in order. At the bottom is information, in the middle is knowledge, and the highest is wisdom. Information basically means facts. Knowledge is facts that we know, can make connections with, and can use in other parts of our lives. Wisdom is how we use our knowledge. It involves making good decisions and using our experience in the right way. According to Eliot, in the modern world we are moving from the highest (wisdom) to the lowest (information).

This seems to me to be true. We talk about the "information age," in which computers carry millions of facts, and the "knowledge economy," in which knowledge is the most important thing we can have. However, we do not see an increase in knowledge. For example, many colleges complain that students do not read as much as in the past. This may be because there is less need to learn things when we know we can find answers instantly on our mobile devices. As for wisdom, if we look around the world, we see global warming, hunger, and several other signs that we are not acting in a wise way.

5 IDENTIFY Read the initial paragraphs of the essay again, and answer the questions.

1 In the writer's opinion, what is the order of wisdom, knowledge, and information suggested by the quote?
2 According to the writer, does the quote suggest that the world is getting better or worse?
3 What does the writer think is the problem with information nowadays?
4 What example is given of a problem with modern education?
5 What is a possible cause of the problem, according to the writer?
6 In the writer's opinion, what big world issues show we need more wisdom?

6 WHAT'S YOUR ANGLE? Which answers from Exercise 5 do you agree with? Discuss them with your partner.

WRITING SKILL Writing conclusions

A conclusion signals to the reader that you have finished your essay. A good conclusion can make your text more memorable and the arguments more convincing.

Conclusions should:

- Link the last paragraph to the first.
- Briefly restate the main point.

You can use signpost phrases to indicate the conclusion.

In conclusion,... *To sum up,...*

Effective conclusions often finish in one or more of these ways:

- With a question
- With a call to action
- With a strong final argument
- With a connection to the wider world

7 APPLY Read the essay's conclusion. Identify the features from the Writing Skill box.

> In conclusion, I agree with T. S. Eliot's idea that we have lost wisdom and replaced it with information. The world would be better if we could stop valuing information above everything else and focus more on making wise decisions. The question is how will this happen? Maybe we need to start talking about the "age of wisdom"—and then do something about it.

8 PREPARE Find two quotes you like about wisdom, experience, or learning. Explain their meaning to your partner. Then decide which quote to write about.

9 DEVELOP Plan the introduction and body of your essay by following the steps.

1. Identify the main points and details for the first three paragraphs.
2. Think of reasons and examples.
3. Identify any causes and effects, if relevant.
4. Write your topic sentences.

10 WRITE Write the introduction and body of your essay.

- ☐ Include your quote.
- ☐ Include details and reasons, examples, and, if relevant, causes and effects.
- ☐ Write up to 250 words.

11 IMPROVE Read your partner's essay. Check that everything from the checklist is covered.

12 DEVELOP Review your essay, and make notes on each of the following that could be included in your conclusion.

- A question
- A call to action
- A strong final argument
- A connection to the wider world

13 WRITE Decide which to include, and write the conclusion to your essay.

14 WHAT'S YOUR ANGLE? Read other classmates' essays. Which two quotes do you like the most? Can you think of anything to add to the conclusions of the essays for these quotes?

Students attend a physics lesson at the Gran Sasso Science Institute in L'Aquila, Italy

12.4 Do It Like This

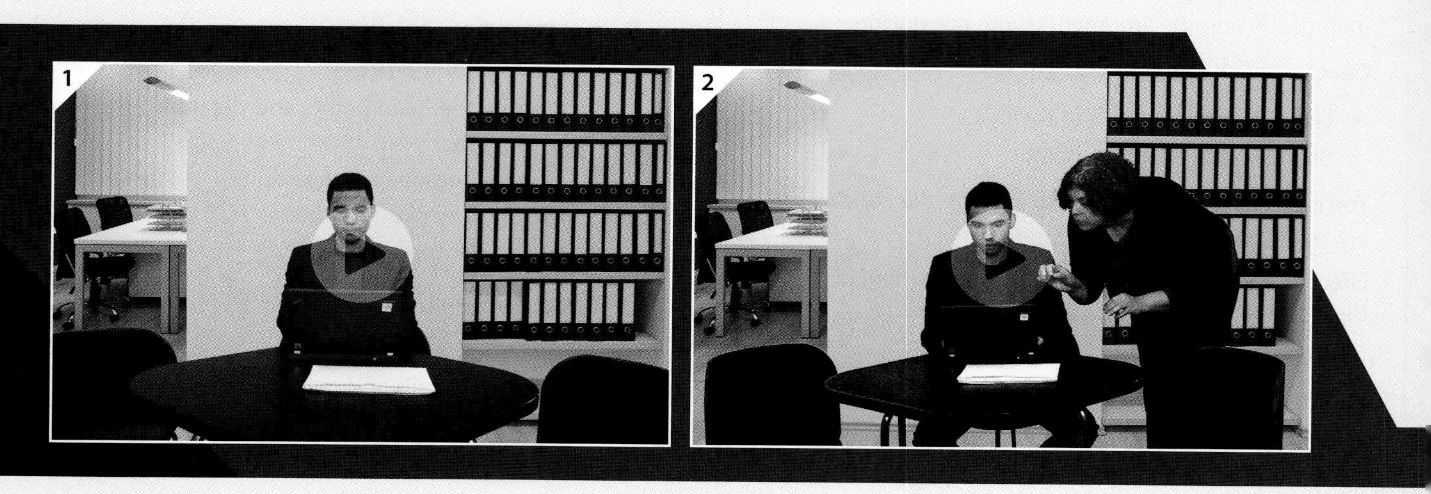

ENGLISH FOR REAL

1 ACTIVATE Discuss the questions.

1 What was the last thing you learned to do?
2 How did you learn it?
3 Have you ever taught someone how to do something?
4 Were you successful? Why or why not?

2 ASSESS Look at the pictures. What do you think Andy is learning to do? Who is teaching him?

3 ANALYZE Watch the video, and answer the questions.

1 What is Andy having a problem with?
2 How does Cathy help?
3 What does Cathy ask Andy to do?
4 What good news does Andy receive?
5 Who does Andy contact to tell his good news?

REAL-WORLD ENGLISH Giving and responding to instructions

Effective instructions should be clear and easy to follow. Use the imperative form of the verb for this along with words such as *first*, *now*, and *then* to indicate the order of the steps in the instructions.

Then *click on the check boxes.*
Now *add the cocoa powder.*

We often include a confirmation check to see if the instruction has been understood.

Click "Move." Is that clear?
Now try it again.

When responding to instructions, we usually let the person know we have understood or ask a question to make sure we have understood.

OK, got it.
Like this, you mean?

If the person has offered to help us, we often end by thanking them.

It worked, thanks!
That was really useful, thanks.

Instructions are different from requests, which usually use question forms or modal verbs.

Could *you come to my office when you're finished?*

4 ▶ **IDENTIFY** Watch the video again, and complete the extracts from the instructions. Compare with a partner.

Cathy: [1] ________________ a folder, and [2] ________________ it "Cathy emails."

Andy: OK, got it.

Cathy: [3] ________________ on the check boxes. [4] ________________ to the toolbar at the top, and click "Move"... [5] ________________?

Andy: Yep, it's clear. [6] ________________.

Cathy: Yes, that's it. [7] ________________ all my messages to the new folder.

Andy: It worked! Thanks! That was a piece of cake!

5 **WHAT'S YOUR ANGLE?** Is giving instructions the same in your language? How can you tell the difference between a request and an instruction in your language?

6 **BUILD** Look at the pictures of someone baking a chocolate cake. Work with a partner to write instructions for each image. Use a dictionary for any vocabulary you don't know.

____

____

____

____

7 **EXPAND** Imagine someone is giving you the instructions to make the cake in Exercise 6. How could you respond? Work with your partner to create a dialogue.

Student A: First, mix butter and sugar together in a bowl.
Student B: Like this, you mean?

8 **PREPARE** Think of one or two interesting things you know how to do (e.g., how to cook something, how to use a computer program, how to fix something). Think about how you could teach someone else to do it. Make notes on what you know. Use the table for your ideas.

What can I do	
Step 1	
Step 2	
Step 3	

9 **INTERACT** Work with a partner. Decide who will give and who will respond to the instructions. Then act out the situation.

10 **ANALYZE** Were your partner's instructions easy to follow? Were they appropriate to the situation? Give feedback.

11 **INTERACT** Swap roles, so the person giving instructions is now responding.

12 **WHAT'S YOUR ANGLE?** Which do you think is easier, learning something new or teaching someone to do something? Why?

GO ONLINE to create your own version of the English For Real video.

12.5 A Glass Half Full

1 ACTIVATE Work in pairs to discuss and complete the advice. Then compare your ideas with another pair.

If you are afraid to do something,...
It's good to see the glass as half full rather than...

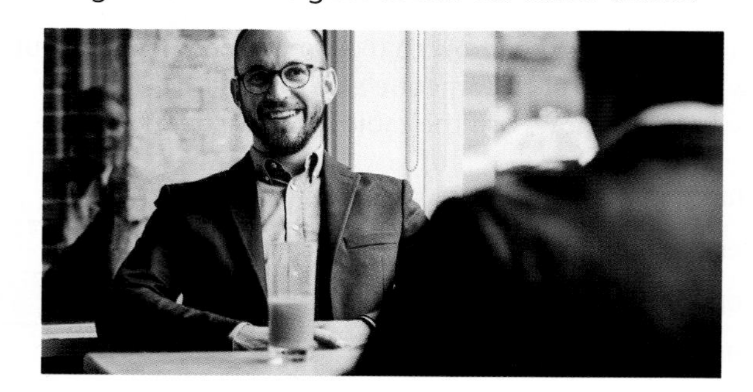

2 ASSESS Listen to people saying the advice. Then answer the questions with your partner.

1 How similar were your ideas?
2 In what situations might someone give this advice?

3 IDENTIFY Watch Kristen talking about some good advice she got. Answer the questions.

1 Who gave her the advice?
2 Which advice did Kristen get?
3 What did the advice help Kristen do?

SPEAKING Reporting a conversation

When you want to report something interesting that someone has said to you, include the following to keep your audience interested:

- Necessary details such as who, when, where, why, and what, e.g., *who—my best friend*
- The main point, e.g., *see the glass as half full*
- Clear connections between ideas, e.g., *cause / effect—that really helps me see things in perspective*
- Appropriate verb tenses, e.g., *I've ever gotten..., she once told me..., see what I can do...*
- Correct pauses and stress, e.g., *...and when things don't go right ¦ I look at things in a positive light*

4 IDENTIFY Watch James talking about the good advice he got. Answer the questions.

1 Who gave him the advice?
2 What advice did she give?
3 How long ago did she give it?
4 What was James trying to do at the time?
5 What did her advice cause him to do?
6 What happened next?
7 What is happening in the future?

5 APPLY Match the sentences to the points in the Speaking box. Some examples match more than one point.

1 Her advice really helped me achieve my dreams. I'm so grateful to her!

____

2 It was actually my Chemistry teacher who told me I should stop studying science and be an artist. I almost burnt the lab down during one of our experiments ...

____

3 I really do think that older people have a lot to teach us.

____

4 I'd been very academic when I was younger, but when I was about 20 I realized I wanted to do something more practical.

____

5 Losing my job made me rethink my ambitions. I'm a lot more independent now, so it's true that what doesn't kill you makes you stronger!

____

6 INTEGRATE Work in pairs. Use the answers to the questions in Exercise 4 to retell James's story.

James got some great advice from his grandmother. She...

7 PREPARE You are going to report a conversation about a good piece of advice you got and that affected something in your life. Use the questions to prepare.

- Who gave you the advice?
- What advice did the person give?
- How long ago did they give it?
- What were you doing at the time?
- What did the advice cause you to do?
- What happened next?
- What is happening now or in the future as a result?

8 INTERACT Listen to your partner's story. Can you answer all the questions from Exercise 7?

9 IMPROVE Work in a group. Share your stories. Does anyone have a similar story to yours?

10 SHARE Work in a new group. Discuss the stories and advice you heard. Which was the best advice in your opinion? Why?

Now go to page 158 for the Unit 12 Review.

Unit Reviews

Unit 1

VOCABULARY

1 Choose the correct word to complete the collocations in the questions.

Which buildings in your country...

1 are *beautifully* / *absolutely* designed?
2 are *differently* / *widely* recognized?
3 do people think *simply* / *highly* of?

What is the best way for people to...

4 *guarantee* / *make* success?
5 *make* / *acquire* knowledge?
6 *take* / *live* simply?

2 Complete the statements with the words in the box.

risks	a difference	
an opportunity	my best	the most

1 I don't like taking _________ and doing new things.
2 I make _________ of my free time.
3 I never miss _________ to see friends.
4 I want to make _________ in the world.
5 I always try to do _________, whatever I am doing.

GO ONLINE to play the vocabulary game.

GRAMMAR

3 Complete the extract with the verbs in the correct tense.

Pyramids of Giza

Of the Seven Wonders of the World, only the pyramids of Giza [1] **remain / are remaining** nearly intact. They [2] **interest / have interested** amateur Egyptologists for many years, and these people [3] **have given / are giving** many explanations for how and why the pyramids exist. Yet, after nearly 200 years of scientific study, it is clear to archaeologists that the pyramids of Giza [4] **are / are being** part of an ancient building tradition and were a very important part of Egyptian culture.

The three pyramid complexes at Giza were built by kings Khufu, Khafre, and Menkare of the Fourth Dynasty (2613 BC–2494 BC) as their tombs and places of eternal worship after their deaths. Significant finds within the pyramids include several coffins of kings from thousands of years ago. One of these [5] **has now resided / is now residing** in the British Museum.

—adapted from *The Oxford Companion to Archaeology*, 2nd ed., edited by Neil Asher Silberman

4 Choose the correct words to complete the sentences.

1 Visitors pay individually to go up *each* / *each of* tower.
2 *Every of* / *Every* window is cleaned three times a year.
3 From the top you can see each *sides* / *side* of the city.
4 Every one of the *buildings* / *building* in the complex is more than 200 meters high.
5 *Each of* / *Each* the towers is home to more than 500 companies.

5 Find the four sentences with verb tense errors and rewrite them.

1 I am knowing lots of very successful people.
2 I don't have the skills I need to be successful.
3 I am not believing good organization is necessary for success.
4 I am agreeing that it's OK to use other people's ideas.
5 I feel that I'm having enough confidence to be successful.

GO ONLINE to play the grammar game.

DISCUSSION POINT

6 Read the quote. What are the positive and negative effects of success? Share your ideas with the class.

"Success makes life easier. It doesn't make living easier."
—Bruce Springsteen, selected from *Oxford Essential Quotations*, 5th ed., edited by Susan Ratcliffe

GO ONLINE and listen to a podcast. Then add your comments to the discussion board.

ZOOM IN

7 What about you?

Task 1 Talk about one goal you want to achieve in the coming year.
Task 2 Write about three of your achievements. Choose a different area of life for each.
Task 3 Find a picture of a great human achievement. Share your opinion on it.

8 Complete the table.

	I did this well	I need more practice
Task 1		
Task 2		
Task 3		

Unit 2

VOCABULARY

1 Complete the statements with the verbs in the boxes.

lead	distract	bring	launch

Newspapers can…

[1] _________ down governments.

[2] _________ people's celebrity careers.

[3] _________ to a more educated society.

[4] _________ readers with sections that don't focus on serious news.

announce	realize	attempt	prevent

People…

sometimes [5] _________ when news is false.

usually [6] _________ to see all sides of a story by reading news from different sources.

often [7] _________ special personal events in newspapers.

especially famous people, sometimes try to [8] _________ stories from getting into the newspapers.

2 Read the statements. Do they represent your view? If not, choose an adverb from the box that more closely shows your opinion.

unfortunately	luckily	naturally	curiously
surprisingly	obviously	fortunately	sadly

1 Curiously, we are more interested in news from closer to where we live.

2 Luckily, we now have TV channels broadcasting news 24/7.

3 Naturally, people prefer to read news on small phone screens.

4 Surprisingly, most major news stories are about bad rather than good news.

GO ONLINE to play the vocabulary game.

GRAMMAR

3 Choose the correct word to complete each sentence.

1 *Either* / *Neither* / *All* of the two reports had much information.

2 I studied *both* / *neither* / *all* subjects, but I enjoyed Journalism more than History.

3 Many online newspapers don't give free access to *all* / *either* / *both* the content.

4 Online news sites and newspapers are popular. I read *either* / *neither* / *all* type since the information is the same.

4 Choose the best verb forms to complete the text.

The first actual radio news program [1] *was* / *had been* broadcast on August 31, 1920 by the 8MK station in Detroit, Michigan. Radio [2] *was being* / *had been* around for a number of years before this but was not widely listened to. At the start of the 1920s, however, this [3] *was changing* / *had changed*. The Scripps family, which owned the newspaper *The Detroit News*, was exploring the idea of expanding into radio, and by this time, it [4] *was hiring* / *had hired* teenage Michael Lyons to get permission from the government to broadcast a news program. Once Lyons had permission, it [5] *was taking* / *took* ten more days to work out how to broadcast the news. There [6] *had been* / *were being* local elections in the area, and the very first broadcast news on the evening of the August 31 [7] *was reporting* / *reported* the results, making history.

5 Think about the past and your plans. What were you never going to do? What were you going to do but then you did something else instead? Write sentences.

GO ONLINE to play the grammar game.

DISCUSSION POINT

6 Read the quote. Was there more good or more bad news today? Do you think everything published as news is news?

"Ever noticed that no matter what happens in one day, it exactly fits in the newspaper?"
—Jerry Seinfeld, selected from *Oxford Essential Quotations*, 5th ed., edited by Susan Ratcliffe

GO ONLINE and listen to a podcast. Then add your comments to the discussion board.

ZOOM IN

7 What about you?

Task 1 Talk about a news story that was important to you.

Task 2 Write a report about some news from your community.

Task 3 Find a powerful photo from a news story. Share the information about what happened.

8 Complete the table.

	I did this well	I need more practice
Task 1		
Task 2		
Task 3		

Unit 3

VOCABULARY

1 Complete the statements with a noun formed by the word in parentheses and one of the suffixes in the box.

-ship	-tion	-ness	-ment	-ence	-ity

1. Most of us want ________ (recognize) for the good things we do.
2. One of the most difficult things to do is make a ________ (commit).
3. ________ (intelligent) is much more important than hard work.
4. Our own ________ (happy) is the most important thing in life.
5. A successful ________ (friend) is more important than a successful professional life.
6. You need the right ________ (personal) to succeed in life.

2 Match the words to the definitions.

keep going	independent	explore
quit	survive	flexible

1. travel through an area you don't know to learn about it: ________
2. ready and able to change in different situations: ________
3. continue to do something despite the difficulties: ________
4. continue to live, especially in a difficult or dangerous situation: ________
5. confident and free to do things without other people's help: ________
6. stop doing something: ________

GO ONLINE to play the vocabulary game

GRAMMAR

3 Complete the sentences with the correct forms of the verbs in parentheses. Which sentences do you agree with?

1. Too many people forget ________ (enjoy) where they are—they are too busy thinking about where they want to go.
2. Governments should stop ________ (spend) money on space exploration and use it for problems in their own countries instead.
3. We need to remember ________ (congratulate) everyone on a team, not only the leader.

4 Choose four items you think are useful for exploration and write sentences using *so* and *such*.

5 Complete the text with the correct form of the verbs in parentheses. (Sometimes two forms are possible.)

World-changing inventions

In the past, most people could not imagine [1] ________ (leave) the earth and going into space. However, after some successful experiments with large rockets, in 1926, scientists began [2] ________ (see) the possibilities. Nowadays several companies have started [3] ________ (plan) for a future of space tourism.

In the past, people attempted [4] ________ (keep) food fresh for longer by salting, smoking, or pickling it. However, in the 1850s, mechanical refrigeration arrived. With this technology, people stopped [5] ________ (get) sick so often from bad food.

Many of us remember [6] ________ (have) our first vaccination—mostly the tears and pain. Vaccinations were first invented in 1796, but it wasn't until 1885 and Louis Pasteur's rabies vaccine that people started [7] ________ (believe) that making people ill could actually help them.

GO ONLINE to play the grammar game

DISCUSSION POINT

6 Read the poem. Do you agree with it? What do you think are the most important benefits of exploration?

"We shall not cease from exploration
And the end of all our exploring
Will be to arrive where we started
And know the place for the first time."
—T.S. Eliot, *Four Quartets*, selected from *Oxford Essential Quotations*, 5th ed., edited by Susan Ratcliffe

GO ONLINE and listen to a podcast. Then add your comments to the discussion board.

ZOOM IN

7 What about you?

Task 1 Talk about a discovery that interests you.
Task 2 Find a photo of a place you would like to explore. Tell your group about it.
Task 3 Write a list of pros and cons of exploring the place you talked about.

8 Complete the table.

	I did this well	I need more practice
Task 1		
Task 2		
Task 3		

Unit 4

VOCABULARY

1 Put the words in order to make sentences. Add a capital letter and period.

___ a you need to / following that, / the main characters / decide on
___ b a story / is to think of / the first stage
___ c and comment / finally, / before / ask a friend to read it / you share it with the world
___ d start writing / then / you can / the first draft
___ e once / read it and / you have finished / improve it / the first draft,
___ f is to / the last step / cutting out any unnecessary parts / rewrite the story,
___ g think of / during this stage, / will feel about the story / how the reader

2 Number the sentences in Exercise 1 in order to make instructions. What are the instructions for? Have you ever done this?

3 Complete the text about the production of a very famous movie with the correct verbs.

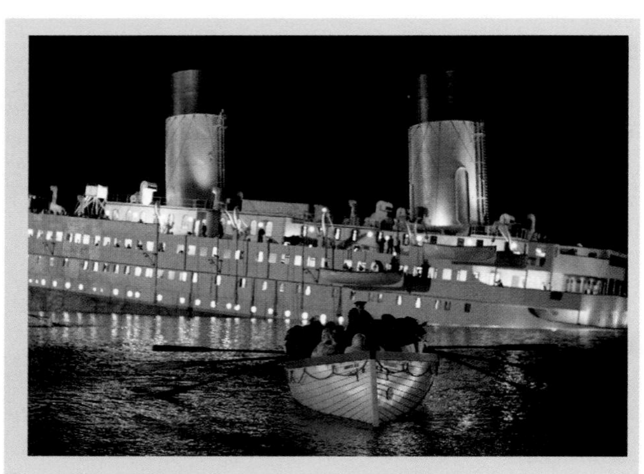

The movie *Titanic* was expensive to [1] **solve / revise / film**; it actually cost more than building the original ship. The results, however, were amazing, both on-screen and in the bank. The movie was written and [2] **produced / solved / promoted** by James Cameron, and he [3] **created / edited / selected** the main actors, Kate Winslet and Leonardo DiCaprio, very carefully. One difficulty was to have so many actors in the right costumes. Deborah Scott [4] **filmed / promoted / designed** the clothes, and she had to [5] **solve / revise / select** many problems to do this. Interestingly, during the stage when the movie was [6] **filmed / promoted / edited**, Cameron revised the ending to avoid it being too happy. A 3D version was [7] **developed / solved / selected** later to promote the film to 21st-century audiences.

GO ONLINE to play the vocabulary game.

GRAMMAR

4 Correct the grammar errors in the passive sentences with modals.

1 Plans must always be make before starting work.
2 The correct process must followed to get the correct result.
3 It could said that the result is more important than the process.
4 Writing can always improved by editing.
5 A traditional meal should be making according to the proper recipe.

5 Choose the correct preposition. Then complete the sentence so it is true for you.

1 I am never surprised *with / by / in* ________________.
2 I am pretty bad *by / at / about* ________________.
3 I am very interested *with / at / in* ________________.
4 I am really good *about / in / at* ________________.
5 I am most pleased *about / at / in* ________________.

GO ONLINE to play the grammar game.

DISCUSSION POINT

6  Read the quote. What kinds of things do artists produce? Why does an artist produce art? Why do people buy art? Share your ideas with the class.

"An artist is someone who produces things that people don't need to have but that he—for some reason—thinks it would be a good idea to give them."
—Andy Warhol, selected from *Oxford Essential Quotations*, 5th ed., edited by Susan Ratcliffe

GO ONLINE and listen to a podcast. Then add your comments to the discussion board.

ZOOM IN

7 What about you?

Task 1 Talk about one thing you want to learn to make.
Task 2 Write about two things you have made. Compare and contrast the experience of making them.
Task 3 Find an interesting diagram. Share it with the class.

8 Complete the table.

	I did this well	I need more practice
Task 1		
Task 2		
Task 3		

Unit 5

VOCABULARY

1 Match the nouns to the phrasal verbs. Then add one more noun for each verb.

1	look forward to ___	a	a vacation / _________
2	look ___ up	b	a problem / _________
3	look into ___	c	a word / _________
4	look up to ___	d	a house / _________
5	look around ___	e	a magazine / _________
6	look up from ___	f	a colleague / _________
7	look through ___	g	a computer / _________

2 Complete the questions with the correct words.

1 Do governments *prepare* / *destroy* / *forecast* enough for natural disasters?
2 Can we *react* / *destroy* / *protect* ourselves from all natural disasters?
3 How can a natural disaster *react* / *forecast* / *affect* people who were not where it happened?
4 Will we be able to *forecast* / *react* / *destroy* all natural disasters one day?
5 How do we usually *protect* / *prepare* / *react* when we see natural disasters on the news?

GO ONLINE to play the vocabulary game.

GRAMMAR

3 Match the advice to the problem.

1 A: There is a very bad storm coming. ___
2 A: We're going to get a new sofa. ___
3 A: I am really late with a project for work. ___
4 A: My child said something awful to the teacher. ___

a B: You'd better talk to your boss about it.
b B: He ought to say sorry immediately.
c B: You should check that the windows are closed.
d B: You shouldn't get a white one if you have children.

4 Complete the rules for when the fire alarm goes off in an office. Use each verb only once.

don't have to	must	can't	have to

You [1] _______________ leave the building immediately.
You [2] _______________ use the stairs and not the elevator.
You [3] _______________ spend time turning off computers.
You [4] _______________ return if it is the end of the workday.

5 Make the sentences stronger or weaker by changing the intensifier and the adjective. Use the adjectives and intensifiers in the box to help.

afraid	freezing	small	exhausted
important	awful	hardly	absolutely
fairly	a little	really	extremely

1 The last movie I saw was fairly bad.
2 I'm absolutely terrified of one type of animal.
3 It was extremely cold last winter.
4 The work I do is absolutely essential.
5 When I get home from work, I'm often really tired.
6 The place where I live is absolutely tiny.

GO ONLINE to play the grammar game.

DISCUSSION POINT

6 Read the quote. What have humans done over history to survive? What different ways do individual people have of surviving modern life? Would the modern-day person survive living 500 years ago, or have we changed too much?

"If we assume that mankind has a right to survive, then we must find an alternative to war and destruction."
—Martin Luther King, selected from *Oxford Dictionary of Political Quotations*, 4th ed., edited by Antony Jay

GO ONLINE and listen to a podcast. Then add your comments to the discussion board.

ZOOM IN

7 What about you?

Task 1 Talk about some really important advice somebody has given you.
Task 2 Write instructions for what to do in an everyday disaster.
Task 3 Find a photo of a natural disaster. Tell your group about it.

8 Complete the table.

	I did this well	I need more practice
Task 1		
Task 2		
Task 3		

Unit 6

VOCABULARY

1 Write at least five sentences about your clothes and fashion sense using the words in the box.

collar	heel	leg	pants	sleeve
top	casual	classic	formal	loose
stylish	tight	trendy	unfashionable	

2 Rewrite the sentences with the word or phrase for emphasis in parentheses in the best place.

1 Diets that promise fast weight loss never work. (clearly)

____

2 Most people believe anything a famous person says. (honestly)

____

3 Most people have at least one pair of jeans. (in fact)

____

4 Most people have terrible fashion sense. (to tell you the truth)

____

5 People should check work emails at home. (not even)

____

GO ONLINE to play the vocabulary game.

GRAMMAR

3 Complete the text with the present perfect or simple past of the verbs in parentheses.

Work places [1] __________ (improve) a lot in recent years. In the past, most work [2] __________ (happen) within the four walls of the office from 9 to 5. The landline telephone [3] __________ (be) the only way to connect with the outside world. Then the Internet and mobile technology [4] __________ (arrive), and since then, we [5] __________ (not look) back. In the modern workplace, many people carry work cell phones, and many of us [6] __________ (have) video conferences with people around the country or even the world. The downside is that since this change happened, many of us [7] __________ also __________ (start) taking our work home with us.

4 Add *do*, *does*, or *did* to the sentences to emphasize or contrast. Change the main verbs if necessary.

1 The modern workplace looks very different from the old one.

____

2 Workplaces didn't have mobile technology, but they used landline phones.

____

3 The Internet changed everything at work.

____

4 Lots of people have work cell phones nowadays.

____

5 We didn't use to work at home in the evening, but we work at home now.

____

5 Complete the sentences, so they are true for you.

1 I used to ____________________, but now ____________________.

2 I never used to ____________________, but now ____________________.

3 I'm getting used to ____________________.

4 I'm used to ____________________ because ____________________.

GO ONLINE to play the grammar game.

DISCUSSION POINT

6 Read the quote. How does something become fashionable or unfashionable? How many people need to like or do something for it to become a trend?

"Fashion is made to become unfashionable."
—Coco Chanel, selected from *Oxford Essential Quotations*, 5th ed., edited by Susan Ratcliffe

GO ONLINE and listen to a podcast. Then add your comments to the discussion board.

ZOOM IN

7 What about you?

Task 1 Talk about something you used to do but no longer do.

Task 2 Watch a video about a trend and write notes. Discuss the ideas with a group.

Task 3 Find a photo of one of your favorite fashion trends. Share it with your class.

8 Complete the table.

	I did this well	I need more practice
Task 1		
Task 2		
Task 3		

Unit 7

VOCABULARY

1 Choose the correct quantifier for each sentence.

1 There are *several* / *none of* / *not much* different places to sit.
2 I have *a little* / *a several of* / *a few* books on a shelf.
3 There is *a number of* / *most* / *not much* light in the room.
4 *Most of* / *A little of* / *Not much* the clothes are on the floor.
5 *A little* / *None of* / *A few* the things are in the right place.

2 Complete these sentences with your ideas.

1 In today's world you need an education to ________________________.
2 A good age to start to specialize in a subject is ________________________.
3 Good research skills are ________________________.
4 Good results are not as important as ________________________.
5 You need to attend college to ________________________.

GO ONLINE to play the vocabulary game

GRAMMAR

3 Complete the sentences with the verbs in parentheses in the present perfect continuous and either *for* or *since*.

1 I ________________ (travel) around South America ________ six months.
2 They ________________ (clean up) the house ________ 11 o'clock.
3 She ________________ (attend) class ________ three weeks.
4 We ________________ (wait) to speak to you ________ an hour.
5 He ________________ (study) philosophy ________ January.

4 Complete B's replies using the present perfect continuous and the words in parentheses.

1 A: You look tired. (work hard / 10:30)
B: Yes, I *'ve been working hard since 10:30.*
2 A: Why aren't you hungry? (eat / all day)
B: Because I ________________________.
3 A: Wow! The house looks clean. (clean / for hours)
B: It should. We ________________________.
4 A: Have you finished the first book already? (read / the second one / yesterday)
B: Yes, I ________________________.
5 A: Your clothes are all wet! (wash the car)
B: I know. We ________________________.

5 Choose the best form to complete the questions.

1 Have you *stayed* / *been staying* in a hotel on your own before?
2 What have you *been doing* / *done* since I last saw you?
3 Which countries have you *been visiting* / *visited* this year?
4 Have you *been working* / *worked* hard recently?
5 Have you *made* / *been making* plans for your next vacation yet?

GO ONLINE to play the grammar game

DISCUSSION POINT

6 Read the quote. What can we tell about people from their surroundings? Do we become different people when we change our surroundings?

"If a cluttered desk is a sign of a cluttered mind, then what are we to think of an empty desk?"
—Anonymous, selected from *Oxford Essential Quotations*, 5th ed., edited by Susan Ratcliffe

GO ONLINE and listen to a podcast. Then add your comments to the discussion board.

ZOOM IN

7 What about you?

Task 1 Talk about things you have been doing to change or improve your surroundings.
Task 2 Buy a postcard of some interesting surroundings, write it, and send it to a friend.
Task 3 Find a photo of a beautiful environment you would like to visit. Tell your group about it.

8 Complete the table.

	I did this well	I need more practice
Task 1		
Task 2		
Task 3		

Unit 8

VOCABULARY

1 Complete the phrases with the correct word. Use each word only once.

handheld	reality	application	download
upload	access	browsing	

1 _________ information online
2 use a phone _________
3 use a _________ device
4 _________ and _________ files
5 use virtual _________
6 spend time _________ the Internet

2 Complete the future time expressions with one word each.

1 _________ three days, I will…
2 _________ time next week, I will be…
3 _________ 2030, I will…
4 _________ Saturday, I might…
5 Thirty years _________ now,…
6 The day _________ tomorrow,…

3 Finish the sentences in Exercise 3. Compare your predictions with a partner.

GO ONLINE to play the vocabulary game

GRAMMAR

4 Read the statements, and complete the follow-up questions.

	Statement	Follow-up question
1	"I won't be home at noon on Monday."	"Where will you be then?"
2	"I won't be working here this time next year."	"Where _____________?"
3	"I'm not seeing my family tomorrow."	"When _____________?"
4	"I might not do my English homework today."	"When _____________?"
5	"I'm not going to go to the movies after class."	"What _____________?"
6	"I won't be living in the same home in ten years."	"Where _____________?"
7	"Our English test isn't next week."	"When _____________?"

5 Complete the conditional sentences with the correct form of the verbs in parentheses.

1 If I have problems uploading the files, I _______________ (call) you.
2 If I _______________ (have) a driverless car, my life would be so much more relaxed.
3 Many people will lose their jobs if companies _______________ (start) using more technology.
4 I _______________ (not choose) to learn in a virtual reality classroom if my college offered me one.

6 Finish these sentences with your ideas. Compare your sentences with a partner.

1 If I had a personal robot, _______________________________.
2 If drivers don't use GPS, _______________________________.
3 If my phone battery runs out, _______________________________.
4 If computers didn't exist, _______________________________.

GO ONLINE to play the grammar game

DISCUSSION POINT

7  Read the quote. Why do people usually have strong feelings about technology being good or bad? What other areas of life make people feel that way?

"Technology happens. It's not good, it's not bad."
—Andrew Grove, selected from *Oxford Essential Quotations*, 5th ed., edited by Susan Ratcliffe

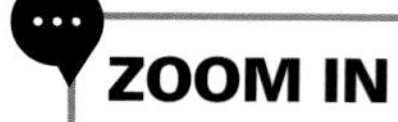

GO ONLINE and listen to a podcast. Then add your comments to the discussion board.

ZOOM IN

8 What about you?

Task 1 Talk about three major changes you think will happen in the world in the next 50 years.
Task 2 Write three predictions about what will happen tomorrow, and then see if you are right.
Task 3 Find a photo of something that won't be the same in five years. Tell your group about it.

9 Complete the table.

	I did this well	I need more practice
Task 1		
Task 2		
Task 3		

Unit 9

VOCABULARY

1 Complete the sentences with the words in the box.

script	plot	theme
scene	performance	

1 The _________ of the main character was good, but the others were quite weak.
2 I thought the opening _________ was amazing with all that action.
3 I couldn't really follow the _________; it was so complicated and had too many characters.
4 The book was very long, and the story got a little boring, but the overall _________ was interesting.
5 You could tell that some of the actors hadn't studied the _________ enough.

2 Add a suffix to each word to make an adjective. (Sometimes more than one is possible.)

-ful	-al	-ive	-able	-less

1 power_________
2 tradition_________
3 comfort_________
4 act_________
5 hope_________
6 use_________
7 creat(e)_________
8 success_________
9 enjoy_________
10 cultur(e)_________

GO ONLINE to play the vocabulary game.

GRAMMAR

3 Add the relative clause in parentheses to the best place in the sentence. Then decide if the clause is defining or non-defining. If it is a non-defining clause, add commas.

1 The movie was also the longest one. (that I liked best)
____
2 None of the actors has won an award before. (who are all American)
____
3 I love going to movie theaters. (that have big comfortable seats)
____
4 The worst review was about the restaurant service. (that I saw online)
____
5 The best review I read was about the food. (which I thought was delicious)
____

4 Complete these sentences so they are true for you.

1 I'm a person who ____.
2 I live in a place where ____.
3 I buy shoes that ____.
4 I prefer days when ____.
5 I have been to a restaurant where ____.

5 Add tag questions to the statements. Then ask your partner the questions.

1 You've been to a bookstore this week, _______________?
2 You hadn't read a story in English before starting this course, _______________?
3 You read online reviews, _______________?
4 You don't go to restaurants much, _______________?
5 You're going to the movies this weekend, _______________?

GO ONLINE to play the grammar game.

DISCUSSION POINT

6 Read the quote. What are your views about giving criticism? What is the point of doing this? Should we always listen to others' criticism?

"People ask you for criticism but they only want praise."
—W. Somerset Maugham, selected from *Oxford Essential Quotations*, 5th ed., edited by Susan Ratcliffe

GO ONLINE and listen to a podcast. Then add your comments to the discussion board.

ZOOM IN

7 What about you?

Task 1 Talk about a very bad movie you have seen.
Task 2 Write a review of a store you have visited.
Task 3 Find a photo of five-star place you have visited. Tell your group about it.

8 Complete the table.

	I did this well	I need more practice
Task 1		
Task 2		
Task 3		

Unit 10

VOCABULARY

1 Complete the sentences with the words in the box.

atmosphere	prove	mysterious	puzzled

1 Every year, people disappear in _________ circumstances.
2 He was_________ to discover that the house was empty.
3 It is difficult to _________ how animals see the world.
4 There was a strange _________ in the house; it was very quiet and dark.

2 Complete the sentences with the phrases with *on*.

on purpose	on display	on account of	on time

1 The bones are _______________ in a museum.
2 _______________ my fear of guns, I couldn't be a detective.
3 I think someone broke my phone _______________, and I am very angry.
4 You have to be _______________ for the surprise event. It starts at 9 p.m.

3 Complete the sentences, so they could be true for you.

1 On account of the darkness, I *went for a walk* / *stayed in my room.*
2 I have *never* / *often* tried to scare someone on purpose.
3 I am *always* / *usually* on time for appointments.
4 I *enjoy* / *don't enjoy* having things I make on display.

GO ONLINE to play the vocabulary game

GRAMMAR

4 Complete the text with a modal verb from the box.

might be	could be	must be	can't be

The place in the photo [1] _______________ in Africa or it [2] _______________ in South America—it looks hot. It [3] _______________ in Europe because there are wild animals. No, actually, it [4] _______________ Africa—I can see a giraffe!

5 Complete the sentences with the best verb. Use *could, couldn't, can,* or *was / were able to.*

1 When I was young, I _______________ sing very well, but I _______________ now.
2 _______________ you _______________ speak to him before he went home?
3 They _______________ understand the problem that everyone else was having.
4 Scientists _______________ explain as much in the past as they _______________ now.

6 Complete the mystery story with past modals.

> There was a strange noise outside last night. I think it [1] _________ been children playing, it [2] _________ been someone singing, or it [3] _________ been a party. My friend says I am wrong. She says it [4] _________ been a cat fight because her cat has a cut on its leg.

GO ONLINE to play the grammar game

DISCUSSION POINT

7 Read the quote. What are your views about the unknown? Why are some people frightened of it? Why are other people excited about it?

"The mind loves the unknown. It loves images whose meaning is unknown, since the meaning of the mind itself is unknown."
—Rene Magritte, selected from *Oxford Essential Quotations*, 5th ed., edited by Susan Ratcliffe

GO ONLINE and listen to a podcast. Then add your comments to the discussion board.

ZOOM IN

8 What about you?

Task 1 Talk about the plot of a mystery movie or book (without giving a spoiler!).
Task 2 Write a nice and friendly anonymous postcard to a friend.
Task 3 Find a photo of a mystery location. Ask your group to speculate about where it is.

9 Complete the table.

	I did this well	I need more practice
Task 1		
Task 2		
Task 3		

Unit 11

VOCABULARY

1 Choose the correct words to complete the sentences.

1 It is easy to *calm* / *adapt* / *cope* someone down when they are angry.
2 Most people *cope* / *regret* / *get wrong* with regrets over bad decisions.
3 We should *adapt* / *cope* / *get over* the bad choices we made in life by forgetting about them.
4 The biggest thing people *calm* / *deal with* / *regret* is choosing not to do something rather than doing something.
5 When you *calm* / *deal* / *regret* with a bad situation in your life, it makes you stronger.

2 Use the prefixes to make new verbs. (You can use different prefixes with some of the verbs.)

mis	re	over

1 ________build
2 ________place
3 ________behave
4 ________use
5 ________write
6 ________do
7 ________inform
8 ________load

GO ONLINE to play the vocabulary game.

GRAMMAR

3 Choose the correct time linkers to complete the sentences.

1 You will have gone home *by the time* / *until* they arrive.
2 I always listen to music *during* / *when* I study.
3 They called me *while* / *as soon as* they heard the news.
4 You should turn your phone off *during* / *by the time* the movie.
5 She won't finish *until* / *as soon as* at least six o'clock.

4 Put the verbs in the correct form to complete the third conditional sentences.

1 If I ________________ (not eat) the fish, I ________________ (not be) sick.
2 If my family ________________ (not move) to America, we ________________ (spend) our childhood together.
3 She ________________ (not become) an actor if she ________________ (not have) acting lessons.
4 If you ________________ (not lose) your passport, we ________________ (be) on vacation in Greece.

5 Rewrite the *if* clauses in the sentences from Exercise 6 as a regret using *should have* or *shouldn't have*.

6 Finish the sentences using *might have*, *could have*, or *would have*, so they are true for you.

1 If my teachers had been different, I
____.
2 If I had been brought up in a different place, I
____.
3 If I hadn't met my best friend, I
____.
4 If hadn't learned English, I
____.
5 If my family hadn't lived where they do, I
____.

GO ONLINE to play the grammar game.

DISCUSSION POINT

7 Read the quote. What are your views about wishing for things? How does it help us in life? Are there any drawbacks to wishing for things?

"It would not be better if things happened to men just as they wish."
—Heraclitus, selected from *Oxford Essential Quotations*, 5th ed., edited by Susan Ratcliffe

GO ONLINE and listen to a podcast. Then add your comments to the discussion board.

ZOOM IN

8 What about you?

Task 1 Talk about three things you don't regret doing. What would have happened if you hadn't done them?

Task 2 Write three wishes: one for the class, one for your country, and one for the world.

Task 3 Find a photo of a place you would have visited if you hadn't decided to go somewhere else. Tell a partner why you decided not to go there.

9 Complete the table.

	I did this well	I need more practice
Task 1		
Task 2		
Task 3		

Unit 12

VOCABULARY

1 Complete the expressions with *as*, *by*, *in*, and *to*.

1. Old people are wiser, according __________ my grandfather.
2. __________ Greek people say, don't send owls to Athens.
3. __________ reported by several experts, people need to spend less time on screens.
4. __________ our teacher's own words, we should stop worrying about things we can't control.
5. As reported __________ *City News*, the economy is improving.

2 Complete the sentences with the words in the box.

take	figure	give	make	get	notice

1. We don't have an answer for everything, but one day we will __________ **it out**.
2. I think we should __________ **an alternative approach** to education.
3. One solution for the problem of inequality might be to have higher taxes: we should __________ **it a try**.
4. We will never have an answer to everything: we just need to __________ **on with** life.
5. You will __________ **an improvement** in your life if you sleep more and eat more healthily.
6. If you have a lot of money, you should __________ **use of** it to improve the world.

GO ONLINE to play the vocabulary game.

GRAMMAR

3 Rewrite the direct sentences to make reported statements.

1. "I don't believe you."
   He told me ______________________________.
2. "He is a bad professor."
   She said ______________________________.
3. "Some people live in places with no clean water."
   They said ______________________________.
4. "I really like my new office."
   She said ______________________________.
5. "He didn't go to the meeting yesterday."
   They told me ______________________________.

4 Put the reported statements in order. Then write the original statement in direct speech.

1. old / for the job / me / I / was / too / told / they / that
2. had been / almost new / he / the cars / said
3. that / had left / the day before / a lot of / we told him / people
4. that / she / for two hours / said / had been / waiting / people / for her
5. him / said / he / had / they / stopped / asking

5 Change the reported questions into the original questions.

1. He asked me what great places I had lived in.
2. He asked me where I was going to live in the future.
3. She wanted to know how often I learned something new.
4. They wanted to know whether I had enjoyed solving problems in the past.
5. She asked me if my grandparents were wise people.

GO ONLINE to play the grammar game.

DISCUSSION POINT

6 Read the quote. Which would you choose: wisdom, wealth, or power? Why?

"We thought, because we had power, we had wisdom."
—Stephen Vincent Benét, selected from *Oxford Essential Quotations*, 5th ed., edited by Susan Ratcliffe

GO ONLINE and listen to a podcast. Then add your comments to the discussion board.

ZOOM IN

7 What about you?

Task 1 Talk about a quote that you really connect with.

Task 2 Write three important things that friends, family, or teachers have said that you have learned from.

Task 3 Take a photo of a "life hack" you use. Explain it to the class.

8 Complete the table.

	I did this well	I need more practice
Task 1		
Task 2		
Task 3		

Grammar focus

Unit 1

Simple present, present continuous, and present perfect

USE

We use the simple present to talk about facts.

*The sun **sets** in the west.*

*I **live** in Paris.*

We also use the simple present to talk about things that happen regularly or repeatedly.

*We **play** tennis every Tuesday.*

We use the present continuous to talk about things happening now or around now.

*What **are** you **looking** at?*

*Dave's **teaching** me to play the guitar.*

We also use the present continuous to talk about trends and things that are changing.

*Prices **are rising** all the time.*

*The Earth's temperature **is increasing**.*

We use the present perfect to talk about experiences up to now.

*I**'ve lived** here all my life.*

*I**'ve** never **met** a movie star.*

We also use the present perfect to talk about things that have already or just happened.

*Max **has** already **left**.*

*I'm not hungry. I**'ve** just **eaten**.*

State verbs

USE

Most verbs express actions, and we can use them in simple tenses…

*I **use** the Internet all the time.*

… and in continuous tenses.

*I**'m using** the Internet at the moment.*

Some verbs usually express states, such as thoughts, feelings, possessions, and things we experience. We usually use these verbs in simple tenses, even if we mean "just now."

*Do you **believe** me?* (NOT ~~*Are you believing me?*~~)

How we think: ***agree**, **believe**, **forget**, **imagine**, **know**, **prefer**, **realize**, **recognize**, **remember**, **think**, **understand***

*Do you **believe** me?*

*I don't **agree**.*

*I **think** it's a great idea!*

What we feel: ***appear**, **dislike**, **feel**, **hate**, **like**, **look**, **love**, **need**, **seem**, **sound**, **want***

*How do you **feel** about the news.*

*He didn't **sound** upset.*

*She **seems** nervous.*

What we possess: ***belong**, **have**, **own***

*Do you **have** any money on you?*

*My family **owns** the café in town.*

*It doesn't **belong** to me.*

What we experience: ***be**, **hear**, **look**, **see**, **smell**, **taste***

*Can you **hear** the phone?*

*The soup **tastes** delicious.*

*The flowers **smell** really nice.*

Some state verbs are used in both simple and continuous tenses with different meanings.

*I **have** a headache.* (ilness)

*I'm **having** lunch.* (action)

*I **think** it's a great idea.* (opinion)

*I'm **thinking** of getting a new phone.* (consider)

Each and *every*

USE

We can use *every* + singular noun or to talk about all the people or things in a group.

***Every person** in the photo is smiling!*

We use *each* + singular noun to talk about every individual person or thing in a group.

***Each child** is different and has different needs.*

We can also use *each* + *of the* + plural noun or pronoun with the same meaning. Use a singular verb.

***Each of the** places looks wonderful.*

We can also use *every* + *one of* + plural noun or pronoun with the same meaning as *each*.

***Every one of them** is smiling!*

GO ONLINE for the complete grammar reference.

Unit 2

Narrative tenses—simple past, past continuous, and past perfect

USE

When we describe events or tell a story in the past, we use the narrative tenses: simple past, past continuous, and past perfect.

We use the simple past to describe the main events in the story.

*It **was** a warm summer evening when Jack **left** work.*

We form negatives and questions with ***did*** and the infinitive without *to*.

*We **didn't recognize** the stranger who was standing outside the house.*

*What **did** he **want** with us?*

We use the past continuous for background events or longer actions which are interrupted by shorter actions. We use the simple past for the shorter actions.

*He **was walking** along the road when suddenly he heard a loud noise.*

We use the past perfect to talk about an action or event that happened before something else in the past.

*Suddenly, he heard a loud noise. A large stone **had fallen** from the sky.*

We also use the past perfect to look back to the past before the events of the story.

*He**'d never seen** a meteorite before!*

All, both, either, neither

BOTH

We use ***both*** + plural noun to talk about two people or things. We can use ***both*** without a following noun when it is obvious what we are talking about.

***Both** photos show forms of travel.*

*Photo A is similar to photo B because they **both** show people who are smiling and happy.*

We can also use ***both*** + ***(of) the*** + plural noun or pronoun with the same meaning.

***Both of the** photos show forms of travel.*

EITHER AND *NEITHER*

We use ***either*** + singular noun to talk about one of two people, things, or groups.

*You can describe **either** photo.*

We use ***neither*** + singular noun to talk about none of a group of two people, things, or groups.

***Neither** form of transport is very fast.*

We can also use ***either/neither*** + ***of the/these/those/them*** + plural noun with the same meaning. Use a singular verb.

*You can describe **either of the** photos.*

***Neither of these** forms of transport is very fast.* (NOT ~~*Neither of these forms of transport are very fast.*~~)

If ***neither*** is the object of the sentence, not the subject, use ***not…either*** instead.

*I **don't** recognize **either** of these places.*

ALL

We use ***all*** with a plural noun to talk about all the people or things in a group.

Use ***all*** + ***(of) the/them*** to talk about a particular group of people or things.

***All the children** are playing.*

***All of them** look happy.*

Use ***all*** + noun, without ***(of) the*** to talk about people or things in general.

***All children** enjoy playing games.*

Was / were going to

USE

We use ***was/were going to*** + infinitive to talk about intentions in the past. The action may or may not happen.

*I **was going to do** some homework, but I'm too tired.*

We use ***was/were going to*** + infinitive + ***but*** to give reasons why an action does/did not happen.

*We **were going to go** to Canada, **but** it's too expensive.*

We can use ***was/were going to…*** when we refuse an invitation and give a reason.

"Do you want to come to the movies?"

*"No, I **was going to call** Dad. Have a nice time!"*

We can use ***was/were going to…*** followed by a question when we offer something.

*I **was going to make** some coffee. Would you like some?*

We also use ***was/were going to…*** to talk about predictions in the past.

*I thought we **were going to be** late, but we weren't.*

For past predictions with ***would***, see here.

GO ONLINE for the complete grammar reference.

Unit 3

Verbs + *to* infinitive or *-ing* form

-ING FORM OR *TO* INFINITIVE?

Some verbs can take either the *-ing* form or the to infinitive, with little or no change in the meaning: ***attempt***, ***begin***, ***can't stand***, ***continue***, ***hate***, ***like***, ***love***, ***prefer***, and ***start***.

*I **started playing** the guitar when I was ten.*

*I **started to play** the guitar when I was ten.*

We don't usually use two *-ing* forms next to each other.

*I'm **starting to feel** better.* (NOT ~~*I'm starting feeling better.*~~)

Some verbs can take either the *-ing* form or the *to* infinitive, but with a difference in the meaning or use: ***stop***, ***forget***, ***remember***.

*I've **stopped buying** CDs. (I no longer buy CDs.)*

*I **stopped** on the way **to buy** you a gift. (I stopped (at a store). I bought a gift.)*

*Grandma **remembers dancing** when she was a girl. (She remembers an activity that she did regularly in the past.)*

*Grandma **remembered to send** me a card. (She remembered to do an action.)*

Verbs + *-ing* form and verbs + *to* infinitive

-ING FORM

We use the *-ing* form after the following verbs: ***admit***, ***avoid***, ***consider***, ***deny***, ***finish***, ***imagine***, ***practice***, ***recommend***, ***stop***, and ***suggest***.

*Dave **recommended seeing** the latest* Bond *movie.*

We use the *-ing* form after verbs that express likes and dislikes: ***can't stand***, ***enjoy***, ***feel like***, ***hate***, ***like***, ***love***, ***(don't/doesn't) mind***, and ***prefer***.

*I really **enjoy going** to the theater.*

We can also use the *-ing* form after the prepositions ***about***, ***at***, ***before***, ***in***, ***of***, ***on***, ***to***, and ***without***.

*Dad insisted **on paying** for the meal.*

TO INFINITIVE

We use the *to* infinitive after the following verbs: ***afford***, ***agree***, ***aim***, ***appear***, ***arrange***, ***choose***, ***decide***, ***demand***, ***expect***, ***fail***, ***forget***, ***hope***, ***manage***, ***need***, ***offer***, ***plan***, ***seem***, and ***want***.

*Emma **offered to give** me a lift to work.*

To form the negative, we put ***not*** between the two verbs.

*I **promise not to tell** anyone.*

So and *such*

FORM

	so/such	(article)	adjective	(noun)
It's	*so*		exciting!	
I'm			excited!	
It's	*such*	a	beautiful	day!
			wonderful	weather!
		a		nuisance!

USE

We use ***so*** and ***such*** to say that people or things are very happy, exicting, beautiful, terrible, etc.

We use ***so*** + adjective, without a noun.

*She's **so kind**.* (NOT ~~*She's a so kind person.*~~)

*The tennis match was **so exciting**!*

We use ***such*** + adjective + noun.

*Maya is **such a kind** person. She helps everyone.*

*It's **such a beautiful** day. I think I'll go to the beach.*

We can also use ***such*** + noun (without an adjective) when the noun is something that is always beautiful, exciting, terrible, etc.

*"The train was three hours late." "Oh, that's **such a nuisance**!"*

GO ONLINE for the complete grammar reference.

Unit 4

Present passive

FORM

We form the passive with *be* + past participle.

		be	past participle	
present	Our pizza	*is*	*baked*	in a special oven.
	The objects	*are*	*displayed*	in a museum.

USE

We use the active form when we focus on the person or thing that does the action.

*Shah Jahan **commissioned** the Taj Mahal in 1631.*

We use the passive form when we focus on what happens to someone or something. The person who does the action is less important.

*The Taj Mahal **is considered** one of the wonders of the world.*

We use *by* + noun if we want to say who or what did the action.

*It **is visited by** about 7 million people every year.*

We often use the passive form to continue talking about the same thing or person.

*Shale gas is an important source of energy in the United States. It **is extracted** by a process of "fracking."*

Past passive

FORM

We form the passive with *be* + past participle.

		be	past participle	
past	Stonehenge	*was*	*built*	5,000 years ago.
	All the documents	*were*	*destroyed*	in a fire.

USE

We use the active form when we focus on the person or thing that does the action.

*Shah Jahan **commissioned** the Taj Mahal in 1631.*

We use the passive form when we focus on what happens to someone or something. The person who does the action is less important.

*The main buildings **were completed** in 1643.*

We use *by* + noun if we want to say who or what did the action.

*They **were built** by workers from nearby towns.*

We often use the passive form to continue talking about the same thing or person.

*Kickstarter is a crowd-funding platform. It **was launched** in 2009.*

Present passive with modal verbs

FORM

We form the present passive with modal verbs with:

Subject + modal verb + *be* + past participle.

Subject	modal verb	*be*	past participle	
Calculators	*can*	*be*	*used*	on the exam.
Valuables	*should*	*be*	*left*	in the hotel safe.
Loud music	*shouldn't*	*be*	*played*	after 11 p.m.

USE

We can use the passive with modal verbs, such as *can, could, might, should, must*, etc.

We use the passive when we focus on what happens to something or someone. The person or thing that does the action is less important or not known.

*Microchips **can be manufactured** quite cheaply.*

*Triathlons **should not be attempted** without a lot of training.*

Adjectives with prepositions

FORM

Some adjectives are used with particular prepositions.

	adjective	preposition	
She's	good terrible	*at*	math.
Sam was	shocked surprised	*at/by*	their behavior.
I'm	fed up bored	*with*	my job.
They were	pleased worried	*about*	the result.

USE

We use prepositions after adjectives to talk about feelings, abilities, etc.

*She's **good at** languages.*

*We're **fed up with** the constant delays.*

We can use an *-ing* form after some prepositions.

*I'm **interested in** hearing all about your vacation.*

*He isn't **happy about** people smoking in his car.*

GO ONLINE for the complete grammar reference.

Unit 5

Advice and warning with *should*, *ought to*, *had better*

FORM

We use *should*, *ought to*, and *had better* with an infinitive without *to*. The form of each of these expressions is the same for every subject. We don't use *oughtn't to*.

Subject + *should/shouldn't* + infinitive without *to*.
Subject + *ought to* + infinitive.
Subject + *had better* + infinitive without *to*.

*I **should get** the flu vaccination.*
*You **ought to apologize** to him.*
*They **had better clean up** the mess.*
*You **shouldn't worry** so much.*
*We **had better not be** late.*

We usually use *should/shouldn't* in questions and answers.

***Should* + subject + infinitive without *to*?**
Question word + *should* + subject + infinitive without *to*?

***Should** I **call** the police?*
*What **should** we **do**?*

We use short answers with questions that begin with *should*.

*"**Should** I **call** the police?"*
*"Yes, you **should**."/"No, you **shouldn't**."*

USE

We use *should*, *ought to*, and *had better* to give and ask for advice. *Ought to* is more formal than *should*, and *had better* is a stronger expression.

*You **should** always **wear** a helmet when you ride a bike.*
*We **ought to get** more sleep before the journey.*
***He'd better not wear** that horrible old jacket to the theater!*

We don't use *ought to* or *had better* in questions. We use *should* instead, or start the sentence with *Do you think…*?

***Should** I **show** them my poems?*
*Do you think I **ought to show** them my poems?*

Obligation with *must* and *have to*

PRESENT

We use *must* or *have to* to say that something is necessary. We often use *must* to talk about the feelings and wishes of the speaker.

*We **must improve** conditions in the zoo.*

We usually use *have to* to talk about rules or obligations that come from someone or somewhere else.

*The government **has to announce** the date for the next elections.*

We use *can't* to say it is necessary NOT to do something.

*You **can't be** late for school.*

We use *don't have to* to say that something isn't necessary.

*You **don't have to eat** with us if it doesn't suit you.*

We usually ask questions with *have to*.

*"Do I **have to apply** online?" "No, you **don't**."*

PAST

Must doesn't have a past tense form. We use *had to* to say something was necessary in the past.

*They **had to land** at a different airport because of the strike at Heathrow.* (NOT ~~*They did must to land…*~~)

We use *didn't have to* to say something wasn't necessary in the past.

*We **didn't have to wear** a uniform when I was in school.* (NOT ~~*We didn't must to wear…*~~)

Intensifiers

USE

We can use an adverb before an adjective to say "to what extent" or "how much." The adverb makes the adjective stronger or weaker.

to a very low degree: *hardly*
to a low degree: *slightly*, *a bit*, *a little*
to some degree: *fairly*
to a high degree: *extremely*, *really*, *quite*
to the highest degree (with ungradable adjectives only): *absolutely*, *completely*

*The book is **slightly damaged**. I can offer you a discount.*
*Car racing is **extremely dangerous**. (It is one of the most dangerous activities.)*

The adverbs *slightly*, *a bit*, and *a little* usually describe bad qualities.

*The book's **a bit boring**.* (NOT ~~*The book's a bit exciting.*~~)

However, we can also use *slightly*, *a bit*, and *somewhat* before comparative adjectives, including adjectives that describe good qualities.

*The table is **a bit higher** than the desk.*

Some adjectives are "ungradable." They express qualities that cannot exist in different degrees. They often express perfection or its opposite.

*That's a **brilliant** idea! I can't think of a better one.*

With ungradable adjectives, we cannot use adverbs like *very*, *extremely*, *fairly*, or *really*. But we can use *absolutely*.

*That's an **absolutely brilliant** idea!* (NOT ~~*That's an extremely brilliant idea.*~~)

We can only use *absolutely* with ungradable adjectives. We cannot use it with other adjectives.

*That book's **interesting**.* (NOT ~~*That book's absolutely interesting.*~~)

GO ONLINE for the complete grammar reference.

Unit 6

Time expressions with the present perfect and simple past

USE

We can think of time periods as being unfinished (e.g., *this week, since 2013*) or finished (e.g., *yesterday, in 2014*).

We usually use the present perfect to talk about unfinished time periods.

*I've sent a lot of emails **today**.*

***Have** you **already eaten**?*

We usually use the simple past to talk about finished time periods.

*I **got** my first computer **when I was eight**.*

***Did** you **see** Cathy **last week**?*

Some time expressions can refer to either unfinished or finished time.

***Have** you **seen** Sarah **this morning**? (It is still this morning.)*

***Did** you **see** Sarah **this morning**? (The morning is finished—it is now afternoon or evening.)*

Used to and *be/get used to*

FORM

We use *used to* with an infinitive.

used to				
	subject (+ auxiliary)	used to/ use to	infinitive	
+	I	*used to*	*like*	listening to stories.
-	I *didn't*	*use to*	*like*	classical music.
?	*Did* you	*use to*	*play*	sports in school?

We use *be used to* with an *-ing* form.

be used to				
	subject + *be*	used to	-ing form	
+	I*'m*	*used to*	*bicycling*	to school.
-	I*'m not*	*used to*	*speaking*	in public.
?	*Are* you	*used to*	*getting up*	early?

USE

Used to and *be used to* are different expressions with different meanings.

USED TO

We use *used to* with an infinitive to talk about regular actions that we did in the past but don't do now, or about situations that were true in the past but are not true now.

*We **used to live** in Minneapolis. (but now we don't)*

*There **used to be** an office park here. (but now there isn't)*

Note that there is no final '*d*' in negatives and questions.

*I **didn't use to drink** tea.* (NOT ~~*I didn't used to drink tea.*~~)

***Did** you **use to play** sports at school?* (NOT ~~*Did you used to play sports at school?*~~)

BE/GET USED TO

We use *be used to* with an *-ing* form to talk about activities that we do regularly and find easy or familiar.

*We**'re used to working** hard.*

We use *get used to* to talk about activities that we started doing recently. We often use it in the present continuous tense, and it means that the activity is becoming easier or more familiar.

*We're **getting used to speaking** over the Internet.*

We can also use *be/get used to* with a noun.

*I'**m used to** hard work.*

*I'm still **getting used to** my new phone.*

We can also use *be/get used to* in other tenses to talk about activities or situations that were familiar in the past, have become familiar now, or will become familiar in the future.

*I found the work tiring at first, but I soon **got used to** it.*

Do for emphasis

FORM

	do/does/did	verb	
I	do	like	your new shoes.
We	did	enjoy	the party.
	Do	help yourself	to a drink.
	Do	take	a seat.

USE

We use *do, does,* or *did* before a simple present or simple past verb for emphasis.

*"Have you seen Emma?" "Yes. I **do like** her new hairstyle."*

*"Meetings with Tom always take a long time." "He **does talk** a lot."*

We can use *do, does,* or *did* to show a contrast.

*That job wasn't easy, but he **did finish** it on time.*

We can use *do* before an imperative especially for offers.

***Do help yourself** to some food.*

GO ONLINE for the complete grammar reference.

Unit 7

Present perfect continuous

FORM

We can use the present perfect continuous with *for* and a period of time.

We can use the present perfect continuous with *since* and a date, day, time, or event.

Positive and Negative

I ***'ve been working*** at the bank *for* two years./*since* 2013.

She ***hasn't been working*** here (*for*) long.

We can form present perfect continuous questions with *How long…?* or…*long?*

*"**How long have** you **been working** at the bank?"*

*"**For** six months./**Since** June."*

*"**Have** you **been waiting** here **long**?"*

"No, not long./About ten minutes."

USE

We use the present perfect continuous to talk about an activity or situation that started in the past and continues now or has only just stopped.

*She's **been working** here since January (= and she still works here).*

*I need a break. I've **been studying** all day (= and I have just stopped).*

We often use the present perfect continuous to ask or answer the question *How long…?* We can reply with *for* + the period of time…

*"**How long have** you **been waiting** here?" "**For** half an hour."*

…or we can reply with *since* + the time when the activity started.

*"**How long has** Jenna **been working** at the bank?" "**Since** May."*

We often use the present perfect continuous to give reasons for a present situation.

*Max knows everyone at the bank. He's **been working** there **for** ages.*

"Why are you so annoyed?"

*"**I've been waiting** here **for** 50 minutes!"*

Present perfect and present perfect continuous

USE

We use the present perfect continuous (*have/has* + *been* + *-ing* form) for actions that started in the past and continue now. It often asks the question *How long …?*

*It's **been snowing** all morning!*

*Scientists **have been investigating** climate change.*

*How long **have** you **been waiting** here?*

We use the present perfect (*have/has* + past participle) for actions that started and finished in the past, with a result now. We don't know, or it does not matter, exactly when the action happened.

*It's **stopped** raining. Shall we go out now?*

***Have** you **seen** the weather forecast?*

There is sometimes little difference between the present perfect and continuous. The choice is often about how we see the action.

*The weather's **been improving**. (We see this as something in process.)*

*The weather's **improved**. (We see this as a finished state.)*

Too and *enough* with the *to* infinitive

FORM

After *too* + adjective, we can use a to infinitive.

	too + **adjective**	***to* infinitive**	
He's	too young	to stop	working.
It's	too expensive	to eat	at that restaurant.

	(*not*) + **adjective** + *enough*	***to* infinitive**
He's	not old enough	to work
The sea	wasn't warm enough	to swim in.

USE

We often use a *to* infinitive after *too* + adjective to explain or give a reason for something.

*She's **too young to vote**.*

We can also use *(not) … enough* with a *to* infinitive.

*He's **not old enough to get** a driver's license yet.*

GO ONLINE for the complete grammar reference.

Unit 8

Talking about the future

USE

There are several different ways of talking about the future. In different situations, we use the present continuous, *be going to*, *will*, *might*, and the simple present.

PRESENT CONTINUOUS

We use the present continuous tense for fixed plans, when we know the time or place. We often use time expressions such as *tomorrow*, *tonight*, or *this evening/week/Friday*.

*She's **flying** from Sydney to Los Angeles.*

*Max **is traveling** to Africa tomorrow morning.*

BE GOING TO

We use *be going to* for plans and intentions, when we don't know or don't say the time or place. We can also use *be going to* for predictions, especially when there is some evidence for them.

*They're **going to visit** Rodeo Drive if there's time.* (plan/intention)

*It's **going to be** a busy week!* (prediction)

WILL AND *MIGHT*

We use *will* for decisions, and for predictions based on our personal feelings. We often use the expression *I think* + *will*.

*I think I'll **take** them to the exhibition.* (decision)

*She'll **probably have** a lot of luggage.* (prediction)

We can use *might* (not *will*) for predictions when we are not certain about them.

*She'll **be** tired after the long flight.* (I am certain.)

*She **might want** to stay longer in San Diego.* (I am not certain.)

SIMPLE PRESENT

We use the simple present for the future when we talk about schedules, e.g., flights or trips by public transport, or somebody's personal schedule.

*The flight **arrives** at 6 a.m.*

*She **has** exams the week before she **leaves**.*

Zero, first, and second conditional

FORM

We form conditional sentences with *if* clause + result clause.

The zero conditional uses the simple present in the *if* clause and the simple present or an imperative in the result clause.

*If there **is** a good health system, people **live** longer.*

The first conditional uses the simple present in the *if* clause and *will/might* + infinitive without *to* in the result clause.

*If you **eat** a balanced diet, you'**ll feel** healthier.*

The second conditional uses the simple past in the *if* clause and *would* + infinitive without *to* in the result clause.

*If you **got** more exercise, you'**d feel** healthier.*

USE

The first conditional and the zero conditional are sometimes called real conditionals. We use them to talk about things that are real or possible.

To talk about a possible situation in the present and the usual result, we use the zero conditional.

*If people **are** active, they **have** better health.* (Some people are active and they have better health.)

To talk about a possible situation in the future and its likely result, we use the first conditional.

*If you **exercise** regularly, you'**ll live** longer.* (It is possible that you will exercise regularly and then you will live longer.)

The second conditional is called an unreal conditional. We use it to talk about things that are unreal or imaginary.

*If children **didn't** spend so much time indoors, they'**d get** more exercise.* (But children do spend a lot of time indoors so they don't get much exercise.)

Will and the future continuous

USE

We can use *will* + infinitive without *to* or the future continuous tense (*will* + *be* + *-ing* form) to make predictions. We use them in slightly different ways.

WILL

We use *will* + infinitive without *to* to make predictions about future events.

*Murray **will win** the tennis match.*

We can also use *will* + infinitive without to to make decisions.

*I think I'll **have** coffee.*

FUTURE CONTINUOUS

We use the future continuous to make predictions about future situations. We often use a time expression to say when.

*This time next year, I'**ll be living** in France.*

We also use the future continuous to make predictions about future events that we expect to be happening at a specific time.

*This time tomorrow, I'**ll be flying** to Rio.*

We can also use the future continuous to make predictions about the present—that is, guesses about things that are happening now.

*Kate's in Rome this week. She'**ll be enjoying** the sunshine!*

We don't use the future continuous tense with state verbs like *know*. We use *will* + infinitive without *to* instead.

*Kate **will know** some new people by now.* (NOT ~~Kate will be knowing some new people by now.~~)

GO ONLINE for the complete grammar reference.

Unit 9

Defining relative clauses

FORM

A defining relative clause can refer to the subject of the sentence…

*Someone **who avoids** new technology is called a technophobe.*

… or defining relative clause can refer to the object of the sentence.

*A technophobe is someone **who avoids** new technology.*

USE

Defining relative clauses tell us which person or thing we're talking about. We can't understand what the sentence is talking about without this information.

We use the relative pronoun*who* to talk about people.

*Do you know anybody **who speaks Russian**?*

We use the relative pronouns *which* or *that* to talk about things.

*A car **which is over three years old** must have a government certificate.*

We use the relative pronoun *whose* to talk about things or people that belong to someone.

*Isn't that the woman **whose purse you found**?*

We can leave out the relative pronoun if it is the object of the verb.

*The first car **(that)** I bought was a Mini.*

We cannot leave out the relative pronoun if it is the subject of the verb.

*Is that the politician **who** visited your school?* (NOT ~~*Is that the politician visited your school?*~~)

We can also use the relative adverbs *where* and *when* in defining relative clauses.

*Is this the hotel **where we stayed last year**?*

We use *which* or *that*, not *where*, to talk about a place that is the subject of the defining relative clause.

*The museum **which** I visit most often is The Louvre.* (NOT ~~*The museum where I visit most often is The Louvre.*~~)

Non-defining relative clauses

FORM

A non-defining relative clause can give extra information about the subject of a sentence…

*Otto, **who died** in 1891, invented the gas engine.*

… or it can give extra information about the object of a sentence.

*I'm researching Alexander Fleming, **who discovered** penicillin.*

USE

We use a non-defining relative clause to give extra information about a person or thing. Non-defining relative clauses do not tell us which person or thing we are talking about – we already know this – so the sentence also makes sense without the extra information.

*Nicolaus Otto, **who died in 1891**, was the inventor of the gas engine.*

Nicolaus Otto was the inventor of the gas engine.

We use the relative pronoun *who* to give extra information about a person.

*Malala Yousafzai, **who was born in Pakistan**, was awarded the Nobel Peace Prize in 2014.*

We use the relative pronoun *which* to give extra information about a thing.

*Fleming discovered penicillin, **which is used to treat diseases**.*

We use the relative pronoun *whose* to give extra information about possessions and family relationships.

*Bell, **whose son also became an inventor**, produced the first telephone.*

We use commas around a non-defining relative clause, or we use a comma before the non-defining relative clause if it is at the end of the sentence.

*The Mini, **which was first made in 1959**, is one of the world's most popular small cars.*

The non-defining relative clause must go after the noun that it refers to.

*The inventor of the gas engine was Nicolaus Otto, **who died in 1891**.* (NOT ~~*Nicolaus Otto was the inventor of the gas engine, who died in 1891.*~~)

Tag questions

USE

We use tag questions to check information or to ask someone if they agree with us. We use a positive tag question after a negative statement, and a negative tag question after a positive statement.

*You've **read** the book, **haven't you**?*

*They **don't work** together now, **do they**?*

Statements with *be* in the simple past have tag questions with *was/were.*

*It **was** fun, **wasn't it**?*

We also use tag questions with *was/were* in the past continuous.

*The team **was** playing well, **wasn't it**?*

We use tag questions with *did* in the simple past with other verbs.

*We **enjoyed** the swimming, **didn't we**?*

We can reply to a tag question with a short answer.

"She's been in lots of movies, hasn't she?" ***"Yes, she has."***

GO ONLINE for the complete grammar reference.

Unit 10

Could, might, and *may*: Possibility and deductions

FORM

We use an infinitive without *to* after *could/might/may*. The form of each of these modal verbs is the same for every subject.

Subject + *could/might/may* + infinitive without *to.*

USE

We use ***could***, ***may***, and ***might*** to talk about possibility in the present and future and to make deductions. Their meaning is basically the same, though ***might*** and ***could*** can suggest more uncertainty than ***may***.

*This **could/might/may be** Ed's phone – he's got one like this. (about the present)*

*In the future, there **could/might/may be** many cities with populations over ten million. (about the future)*

We can use ***may not*** and ***might not*** when we are uncertain if something is true – but not ***couldn't***. We use ***couldn't*** or ***can't*** when we are certain that something is not true.

*This **might/may not be** Kate's house – I think hers has a green door.*

*This **couldn't/can't be** Kate's house – I'm sure hers has a green door.*

Deductions about the past

FORM

We use ***must***, ***can't***, ***couldn't***. ***could***, ***might***, or ***may*** with ***have*** and a past participle.

Subject + *must//can't/couldn't/could/might/may* + *have* + past participle.

In ordinary language, we usually use the short forms ***can't*** and ***couldn't*** (rather than ***cannot*** and ***could not***).

*He **can't have seen** your message yet.*

To form direct questions, we change the order of ***could/might*** and the subject.

Could/Might + subject + ***have*** + past participle?

***Could** you **have left** your keys at home?*

USE

We use ***must have*** to make deductions about the past when we are very sure that something is true. We use ***can't have*** when we are very sure that something isn't true. ***Couldn't have*** has the same meaning as ***can't have***.

*Someone **must have broken into** our hotel room, but they **can't / couldn't have taken** anything valuable because everything is locked in the hotel safe.*

When we are unsure about what has happened, we can speculate using ***could have***, ***might have***, ***may have***, and ***might (not) have***.

*They **could/might/may have taken** this photo in the UK – the traffic is on the left.*

Note that ***can't have*** and ***must have*** express opposite ideas. ***Can have*** is not used in this way.

*She **can't have been** telling the truth.* (NOT ~~*She mustn't have been telling the truth.*~~)

Ability and possibility: Present, past, and future

FORM

We use the form ***can/could*** + infinitive without *to*.

*I **can speak** Polish.*

*I **couldn't cook** very well until I had children.*

We can also use ***be able to*** + infinitive. Only ***be*** changes (***am***, ***are***, ***is***, ***was***, ***were***).

*I **was able to book** a table for us in that new Italian restaurant.*

When we are talking about the future, we use ***will be able to*** + infinitive.

*In the future we **will be able to talk** to robots.*

USE

We use ***can*** and ***be able to*** to talk about abilities and possibilities. ***Can*** is more common when we are talking about abilities in the present, and with verbs such as ***see***, ***hear***, ***smell***, etc.

***Can** you **ski**?*

We can use ***couldn't*** but NOT ***could*** to talk about particular possibilities in the past. We use ***was/were able to*** instead of ***could***.

*When I was at school, I **couldn't speak** German very well, but now I can.*

We can, however, use ***could*** and ***couldn't*** to talk about what people in general could do in the past.

*In the 1880s, you **couldn't fly** to other countries, but you **could travel** by train.*

Be able to can also be used in the present and past. It often sounds more formal than ***can/can't*** and ***couldn't***.

*The protesters **were not able to** speak to the President.*

We use ***be able to*** when we are talking about abilities and possibilities in the future.

*I **will be able to speak** English better after the course.* (NOT ~~*I will can speak English better ...*~~)

But when we have decided about something in the future, we usually use ***can***.

*I'm free tomorrow so I **can** do the test then.*

GO ONLINE for the complete grammar reference.

Unit 11

Should have: Retrospection and regrets

FORM

We use *should* with *have* and a past participle. The form of *should* is the same for every subject.

Subject + *should (not)* + *have* + past participle.

I should ***have waited*** before sending the email.

We often use the short forms *shouldn't* and *should've* when speaking and in informal writing.

*You really **should've contacted** me sooner about the problem.*

To form *yes/no* questions with *should have*, we put the subject between *should* and *have*.

Should + subject + *have* + past participle?

We can also form questions with question words.

What/When/Where/Who (object)/*Why/How* + *should* + subject + *have* + past participle?

Who (subject) + *should* + *have* + past participle?

*What **should** we **have done**?*

USE

We use *should have* and *shouldn't have* to criticize things we or other people did or didn't do in the past and to say what would have been the correct or better thing to have done.

*You **should've studied** Japanese instead of Portuguese.*

*"**Should** I **have taken** that job?"*

*"Yes, you **should (have)**."/"No, you **shouldn't (have)**."*

*Who **should** we **have told** about the change of arrangements for the meeting?*

Time linkers

USE

We use time linkers to show how one event connects to another event.

AS SOON AS AND *WHILE*

*I called Mom **as soon as** (immediately after) I arrived.*

*I saw my teacher **while** (at the same time as) I was waiting at the station.*

MEANWHILE AND *BY THE TIME (THAT)*

We use *meanwhile* (not *while*) when we use two sentences to talk about two things that happen at the same time.

*I drove to the airport. **Meanwhile** (at the same time), Sarah drove to my house. We missed each other!*

We use *by the time (that)* when one action is completed before the main action happens.

***By the time** (before) we got back again, Sarah had left!*

DURING AND *UNTIL*

We use *during* when something happens at a point within a period of time.

*I fell asleep **during** the movie.*

We use *until* when something happens up to a particular point in time.

*I was awake **until** 4 a.m.*

Third conditional

FORM

We form the third conditional with:

***if* clause + result clause**

We form the *if* clause with:

***If* + past perfect**

We form the result clause with:

***would/wouldn't have* + past participle**

	***if* clause**	**result clause**
	***If* + past perfect**	***would/wouldn't have* + past participle**
+	***If*** I ***had studied*** more,	I***'d have passed*** the exam.
-	***If*** I ***had studied*** more,	I ***wouldn't have failed*** the exam.
?	***If*** you ***had passed*** the exam,	***would*** you ***have gone*** to college?

USE

We use the third conditional to talk about unreal situations in the past. We use it to talk about situations or events that are the opposite of what actually happened.

***If** we **had left** on time, we **would have missed** Jack. (We didn't leave on time. We saw Jack.)*

***If** you **had locked** the car, no one **would have stolen** it. (You didn't lock the car, so it was stolen.)*

We can also use the modal verbs *could* or *might* instead of *would*.

*If the police had arrived earlier, they **might** have caught the burglar.*

*If we'd arrived on time, we **could** have sat at the front.*

In spoken English and informal writing, we usually contract *had* and *would* to *'d*, especially after pronouns. We sometimes also contract *have* to *'ve*.

*If I**'d** seen anything, I**'d** have told you.*

*OR: If I**'d** seen anything, I would**'ve** told you.*

GO ONLINE for the complete grammar reference.

Unit 12

Reported speech

FORM

Direct speech	Reported speech
"It's a great idea."	He said that it ***was*** a great idea
"I really ***like*** this new ad."	She said she really ***liked*** the new ad.
"What do you ***do*** in the evenings?"	She asked what I ***did*** in the evenings.

USE

We use reported speech to talk about what someone said. We often use the reporting verbs ***say*** and ***tell***.

We can use ***ask*** to report questions.

Tell must have a personal object.

*She told **me** ... I told **them** ... He told **us** ...*

Say does not have a personal object.

He said ... (NOT ~~*He said me ...*~~)

We use ***say*** and ***tell*** with or without ***that***.

*He **said it was** a great idea.*

*OR He **said that it was** a great idea.*

We can use ***ask*** with or without a personal object. We always use a question word with ***ask***.

*She **asked what** I did in the evenings.*

When we use reported speech, the tense usually moves back one tense. This helps to show that the words were spoken in the past.

is → was,do → did, did/have done → had done, will → would

"We*'re* hoping the weather *will* improve." → They said they ***were*** hoping the weather ***would*** improve.

The pronoun can also change (e.g., from ***I*** to ***he*** or ***she***, or from ***we*** to ***they***.

"*I* really like the new ad." → She said ***she*** really liked the new ad.

Words which talk about time and place may also sometimes change when the reporter's "here and now" is different from the original speaker's.

*"The movie was released **last summer**."*	*He said the movie had been released **the previous summer**.*
*"I saw him here **yesterday**."*	*He said that he'd seen him there **the day before**.*

Reported questions

FORM

We report *Wh-* questions with a question word (***when, where, what, etc.***).

Direct question:"When ***are*** they going?"

Reported question: She asked ***when they were going***.

We report *yes/no* questions with ***if/whether***.

Direct question: ***Did*** you ***understand***?

Reported question: She asked us ***if we'd*** understood.

USE

We use reported questions to say what someone asked. We usually use the reporting verb ***asked***. We can use ***asked*** with or without a personal object.

*He asked **me what** ... OR He asked **what** ...*

We can use ***wanted to know*** instead of ***asked***. We don't use a personal object with ***wanted to know***.

*He **wanted to know what** I was doing.*

We use a question word (not ***that***) with ***ask/want to know***.

*She **asked me what** I did in the evenings.* (NOT ~~*She asked that I did in the evenings.*~~)

To report *yes/no* questions we use ***if*** or ***whether***.

*He **wanted to know if** I'd seen Sue.*

When we use reported questions, the tense usually moves back one tense. This helps to show that the words were spoken in the past.

is → was,do → did, did/have done → had done, will → would

"What *do* you *do* in the evenings?" → He asked what I ***did*** in the evenings.

"Do you *understand*?" → She asked if we ***understood***.

Reported questions have the same word order as positive sentences. We do not invert the subject and auxiliary verb, and we do not use the auxiliary verb ***do***.

The pronoun can also change (e.g., from ***I*** to ***he*** or ***she***, or from ***we*** to ***they***.

"What are *you* doing?" → She asked me what ***I*** was doing?

Words which talk about time and place may also sometimes change when the reporter's "here and now" is different from the original speaker's.

Direct speech: "What did you do ***yesterday***?"

Reported speech: He asked me what I'd done ***the day before/on Saturday***.

 **GO ONLINE for the complete grammar reference.**